Indian Society

Ram Kumar Verma

SRISHTI BOOK DISTRIBUTORS
NEW DELHI (INDIA)

ISBN : 978-81-89948-87-0

Published by:
SRISHTI BOOK DISTRIBUTORS
4378/4-B-202, 2nd Floor,
J.M.D. House, Ansari Road,
Daryaganj, New Delhi-110002
E-mail : srishtibookdistributors@yahoo.co.in
Ph. : 011-23284904

***Edition* : 2012**

Rs. 1050/-

Typeset by :
Shubh-Deep Laser Printer
Delhi-110046

Printed at
Shivani Art Press
Delhi-110032

PREFACE

India is a huge country with people belonging to different cultural background making the people distinct from one another. The early Indian society was governed by 'Dharmashastra', the works of great sages helped to lead a harmonious life. According to *Manu Smriti*, early Indian society was divided into Aryans and Non-Aryans. The Aryans were further divided into four groups, includes the *Brahmins*, *Kshatriyas*, *Vaishayas* and Sudras.

Our Indian society is very ancient, it begins with the Indus valley civilization. The people of India are largely the product of successive invasions from immemorial times who had swept into the country. The existence of various types of people in our country created a spirit of tolerance among the people. We have developed a secular outlook from the ancient period.

In much of India, especially in the north, a marriage establishes a structural opposition between the kin groups of the bride and groom—bride-givers and bride-takers. Within this relationship, bride-givers are considered inferior to bride-takers and are forever expected to give gifts to the bride-takers. The one-way flow of gifts begins at engagement and continues for a generation or two. The most dramatic aspect of this asymmetrical relationship is the sytem of dowry.

Gandhi's idea to develop the Indian society was based on his understanding of the society and hence based on the village system. Talking about the importance of village, he wrote in 1936, in *Harijan* "I would say if the village perishes, India will perish too. It will be no more India. His one mission in the world will get lost."

He was aware of the realities of the village life and knew the plight of half starved masses of India. He often acknowledged the same in his vivid descriptions of Indian villages. He wrote, instead of having graceful hamlets dotting the lands, we have dung-heaps.

While compiling research material for this book, we surf many concerned websites, blogs for ensuring the authenticity of the matter and for checking facts and figures. All the resources have been acknowledged in bibliography section of this book. We are sincerely indebted to all these resources and librarians who provided books of various authors on this subject topic.

—Ram Kumar Verma

CONTENTS

1

INTRODUCTION TO INDIAN SOCIETY

The Indian society has been rooted to the *Manu Smriti* carried forward to the next generation in the four *varna* of class and caste hierarchy as social structure and social segregation since antiquity, but bound by a strong commonality in culture as religion, customs, rituals under a powerful authority. The disintegration process began with cross cultural interact with invasions in history or change in the authority from the Islamic period till the British rule. The diversity in society was regional but bound by legislative and cultural 'restraints'. The modern era saw the politicization of the society in its 'bowl of punch culture' as expediency along with the impact of globalization in multicultural setup with trace elements of the past .

More than a billion people live in India. Of every six people in the world, one is an Indian. Contemporary Indian society is heir to one of the world's great, enduring and eclectic civilizations. It permeates the entire Indian subcontinent, and its influence is manifest throughout Asia. In contemporary Indian society there are old ways that retain their vibrancy, their credibility and influence, and prevail. But, there are new ways as well: in a lively and well-established parliamentary democracy, a stable quasi-federal republic, programs of social and economic reform, modern agriculture and industry, science and technology, literature and art. In the meetings of old and new ways there are synergies no less than contradictions. Over the past decade or so, India has become an important player in the global economy. An increasingly assertive, nuclear- and missile-armed Indian Union is a major power today in Asia, the Indian Ocean and the world.

So, India is changing. Of course, it has always been changing: only the pace of change has varied from time to time, group to group and locality to locality. This insight of Hindu and Buddhist antiquity is apposite: change is the condition of everything that lives. Change is the condition of social continuity.

Our Indian history is very ancient, it begins with the Indus valley civilization. The people of India are largely the product of successive invasions from immemorial times who had swept into the country. The existence of various types of people in our country created a spirit of tolerance among the people. We have developed a secular outlook from the ancient period.

The term culture is expressed through language, literature, art, religion, architecture, philosophy, social customs and tradition. Indian culture co-existed for centuries under all our invaders from the 'Harappan civilization' to the modern days. Due to the foreign contacts and intermingling with the pre-existing cultures,our Indian culture instead of loosing its identity has only benefited. By absorbing the good features of other cultures we have indeed enriched our Indian culture.

Evolution of Indian Society

India is a huge country with people belonging to different cultural background making the people distinct from one another. The early Indian society was governed by 'Dharmasastra', the works of great sages helped to lead a harmonious life. According to *Manu Smriti*, early Indian society was divided into Aryans and Non-Aryans. The Aryans were further divided into four groups, includes the *Brahmanas*, *Kshatriyas*, *Vaishayas* and Sudras.

The brahmins occupied highest place in the society. Their duty was to teach vedic literature and to perform various sacrifices. They should maintain a high standard of morality and should lead a very simple life. The *Kshatriya's* main duty was to defend the country. The *Vaishyas* were required to attend to agriculture, trade,and commerce. The *Sudras* formed the majority of the society and their duty was to serve the other communities.As time passed each one of these subdivisions became a 'caste' itself and became very rigid.

The early society gave much importance to 'Varnasrama Dharma'.The life of an individual was divided into four stages known as 'Asramas'. They are *Bramacharia* or a student, *Grihasta* or a married householder, *Vanaprastha* a forest hermit and *Sanyasin* an ascetic who renounced the world. Women were not given a place of honour, they were not allowed to study Vedas. The early Indian society gradually lost its glory due to many kinds of abuses and superstitious beliefs in it. The Brahmins for their own benefit encouraged the superstitions. It was at this juncture, Buddhism and Jainism appeared in India.

Buddha and Mahavira preached in the language of common people. They opposed castesim, animal sacrifice and other superstitious rituals. They raised their voices against the evils and showed a new path to the people. They taught equality, universal peace, non-violence and kindness to all living things. They greatly reformed the society through their moral rules and new order of life.

Influence of Islam on Indian Society

During the early medieval period the conquests of 'Arabs' and 'Turks' resulted in the introduction of a new religion called 'Islam' in India. The society was divided into two communities namely the 'Hindus' and the 'Muslims'. Many Hindus converted themselves into Islam. The impact of Islam on Indian society led to the 'Bhakthi Movement'.

The saints who preached 'Bhakthi' taught 'tolerance' and 'devotion' to God. They proclaimed that there is only supreme God and absolute devotion to God is a means of 'Salvation'. They stressed the equality of all human beings and declared that it was only through 'Bhakthi' that man could experience God. They emphasized friendly relations between the two communities. Indian art, architecture and music also received new dimensions due to Islamic contacts. Hindi and urdu literature flourished.

The pioneers of Bhakthi cult were Ramanandha, Kabir, Guru Nanak, Chaitanya, Tulsidas and Surdas. They tried to harmonize Islam and Hinduism. The Bhakthi movement started in south India during 7th and 8th centuries by Alwars' and 'Nayanmars'. They sang devotional songs. The great saints like 'Aathi Sangarar', 'Ramanujam' and 'Madhwa' tried to bring about a revival of the old Hindu beliefs Bhakthi culture that was a movement of social integration. It united the Hindu and Muslim sentiments. People followed the preaching of their saints and abandoned superstitious beliefs and followed oneness of God.

Impact of British Rule on Indian Society

The most important impact of the British rule in India was the westernization of the Indian society. The western education awakened a spirit of reform among the various classes of Indian society. It modifies the ideas and customs of the educated Indians. It created a feeling of brotherhood among the Indians and enabled the people to think India as their motherland and united them. Knowledge of English helped to bring about development in every field. English education helped Indians learn nationalism and liberalism from the west. This period saw the birth of modern Indians who became more self-reliant and self-confident. Critical outlooks of past and new aspirations for the future developed. This new spirit made Indians to question the authority, reason and judgment over the blind faith and superstitious beliefs.

Thus there was growth and development in our culture. Our Indian society is a combination of cultures. This synthesis has made India a unique Mosaic of Cultures as described by our fivst Prime Minister Jawaharlal Nehru.

Unity in Diversity

According to this philosophy, the danger of fragmentation for a highly diverse society is so acute that it is forced to develop a heightened sense of tolerance of internal differences to survive. In other words, it is the threat of our country breaking apart that keeps us united.

While there is some truth in this idea, it neither captures the full picture, nor explains the mechanism by which such unity might actually be fostered. Consider that aggregation of 1.2 billion individual particles again, many of them rural and illiterate, all of them subject to intense pressure from their own particular needs and prejudices.

Surely the most immediate and compelling motivation that drives them is self-interest.

And yet, a model of independent entrepreneurship does not apply either. Rugged individualism in the American sense is not the order of the day. People belong to well-defined communities—clan, village, sect, biradari—and it is membership in these that turns out to be of primary significance. Rather than 1.2 billion separate particles, the Indian model can be thought of as organized into a much smaller number of groups. The sense of belonging within each such group is extremely strong—the individual's social sustenance (not to mention very identity) is often entirely dependent on it. As a result, self-interest is no longer always the dominant motivator, rather, it might be subsumed into the interests of the group.

At each stage, the primary role diversity plays is not necessarily to give birth to new conglomerations, but to provide the pressure that keeps them stable, no matter how they originated. An advantage of the model is that it helps explain why such an elaborate hierarchical structure of subcastes and castes continues to endure in India. It should be noted that significant overlap can exist between various groups and conglomerations - for instance, while an individual's primary identification might be with a professional, familial, or caste-based group, he might also feel a sense of allegiance to larger conglomerations structured around factors like language or religion.

While individuals or their immediate low-level groups have very limited power, rising through the hierarchy, we eventually reach conglomerations large enough to have political clout (for example, the group of all Dalits, of all Muslims, of Gujaratis, of Punjabis, etc.). How does "Unity in Diversity" apply at this level?

The answer is that groups, like individuals, also tend to act in their own self-interest, rather than out of nobility or altruism. If the membership of these large groups was economically stultified, and there were clear advantages to secession, then we would see vigorous campaigns for it played out all over the nation. But the fact is that people's lives in India have been improving - slowly, it is true, but steadily - as most indicators (poverty, rate of literacy, the UN's human development index) from the past three decades show. In addition, the boom of the last several years has infused sections of the population with a new optimism about the future, even if it might not yet be in their grasp. There does not seem to be a glaring economic imperative, either now or in the recent past, for a group to give up on India and strike out on its own.

When such secessionist ideas do arise, however, diversity plays an important role in damping them out. Recall how the top-level conglomerations arose in our model - through the combination of "building block" groups at lower levels. As we ascend this hierarchy of groups from the smallest to the largest, we can expect an increasing amount of variation in background, class, culture, religion. The fact that most individuals end up belonging to several different conglomerations contributes to this variation. The groups at the top, the ones large enough to effect political change, are the least homogeneous - consequently, they will generally have constituents with divergent aims and interests. Uniting all these constituents behind any action, particularly one geared towards radical change, is very difficult. A good example is the secession drive for Khalistan - the fact that the population of Punjab was so divided in terms of religion, class and economic well-being was an important factor in gutting the movement.

One vital element not mentioned yet in this picture is democracy. This is the crucial release valve which stabilizes the entire model. Disgruntled groups who feel they have been shortchanged know they have the opportunity to express their ire at the polls - they do not have to break away. It could be argued, therefore, that democracy is what really keeps the country intact - by enfranchising all individuals and groups, and providing them with a time-tested method of effecting change.

But suppose we delve a little deeper and ask why this form of government has worked so well in India. What gives Indian democracy its robustness, its longevity? As Edward Luce argues in his recent book, *In Spite of the Gods*, it is once again the diversity of the population that works behind the scenes to ensure democracy endures. The country, quite simply, is much too diverse for other forms of government to take root. "Far from endangering democracy, India's pluralism makes democracy essential," Luce writes. So even if we accept that democracy is one of the most important factors in fostering unity, we can still trace its continuing survival back to our old friend, diversity.

Sixty four ago, on the eve of Indian Independence, Nehru made his famous "Tryst with Destiny" speech. "A new star arises, the star of freedom in the East," he declared, but it was actually millions of tiny stars that arose that evening; that, at the stroke of midnight, were launched into the sky and set free. The usual Newtonian rules of gravitation did not apply to these stars - instead, what kept them from flying apart on their own independent trajectories was a much more complex force field. A field which drew them together by pulling them apart, a field which depended on their very diversity to ensure unity.

In the first decade of this new millennium, it is important to remind ourselves of what continues to keeps India aloft - the millions of attractions and repulsions taking place between its multiplying stars, between the clusters and constellations they form, between its galaxies both massive and small. The Finnish model will never apply - the romanticized ideal of all these components united in rosy, frictionless harmony. Rather, what's critical is to safeguard the rights, enfranchisement and continuing inclusion of each component, for the purely selfish reason of continued stability. Only then will India be assured of moving as one as it continues its cosmic voyage towards new trysts with destiny.

Diversity in Geographical Features

The physical features of a country influence to a great extent the life and history of its people. India has diverse geographical features. India is separated from rest of Asia by the Himalayas, with its western and eastern ranges. Mountains of the north, the northern fertile plain, the Thar desert, the Deccan plateau, western and eastern Ghats from part of its physical features. The vast dimensions of India, the varied climatic conditions across the various regions of India resulted in racial and linguistic differences. Yet there is a common bond among the people.

Geographical conditions play an important part in responding to human activities. Cherrapunji in Meghalaya receives highest rain fall and the dry Thar desert in Rajasthan receives only scanty rainfall. The Himalayan mountain ranges are snow clad peaks while the southern parts of India records highest average temperature. Animal and plant life also varies according to the climatic conditions. The soil is too variable it is fertile at the northern plains and saline dry soil is found at Rajasthan. This also brought about diversity in the life of the people.

Diversity in Population

Indian population is 16% of the world's population. The huge population is made up of different ethnic groups, following different religions, speaking different languages, observing different customs and traditions. It is marvelous diversity of people in India, which has made it both museum and a laboratory for the study of man. Hence, India is called as 'ethnological Museum'.

Diversity in Languages, Customs and Traditions

In India, people speak about 845 languages and has 545 dialects. At present, 22 official languages are recognized by the Indian government. The people of north India speak the Indo-Aryan group of languages and the Dravidian languages are spoken primarily in southern India. Hindi is the national language and English the concurrent language. People differ in race, figure, and mode of dress, food, customs, and habits from region to region.

Diversity in Religion

India is the birthplace of many religions. Hinduism, Buddhism, Jainism, and Sikhism have their origin in India. Vedic religion is an ancient religion of our country. In the first century B.C, St.Thomas an Apostle of Lard Christ first brought Christianity to India. The Persians brought

'Zoroastrianism'. Muslim conquest of India brought Islam into India. Religious tolerance is found in our country from the past till today. People are free to profess, practice, and propagate any religion of their choice. Different festivals are celebrated in India. Diwali, Muharram, Bakrid, Mahaveer Jayanthi, Guru Nanak Jayanthi, Christmas, Onam, Pongal, Dusshera etc.are celebrated with religious fervor and gaiety in India.

Diversity in Literature

The Vedas are the earliest literary works of our country.The Vedic hymns were composed in Sanskrit. Prakrit and Sanskrit were spoken throughout our country.The Vedic literature are the *Brahmanas*, *Aranyakas* and *Upanishads*. The *Ramayana* and *Mahabharatha* are the two epics of India. 'Thirukural' byThiruvalluvar is the greatest literary work in Tamil. The Bagavath geetha is the holy book of Hinduism. The hymns of Alwars and Nayanmars are compiled under the name of Naalayira Thivya Prabandham and Devaram.

Diversity in Art and Architecture

Different styles of art and architecture are found in India.The north Indian temples have towers like structure over the shrines and the Sikara bulges in the middle and ends almost in a point. The south Indian Sikara looks like a pyramid made up of successive storeys, each smaller than the one beneath it. Hindustani and carnatic music are the classical music of north India and South India respectively.Famous dance forms of North India are Manipuri, Kathak and Bhangra whereas in the south Bharathanatiyam, Kathakali and Kuchipudi are the famous dances. The pilgrim centers are found all over India. Amarnath, Badrinath, Kedarnath, Kasi, Rameshwaram, nagappatinam, Nagoor, Velankanni etc.are the religious centers visited by people all over India.The universities of Naalantha, Taxila, Kanchi and Vickramashila were the ancient centres of learning.

Magnificient palaces,Chaityas,Viharas and Stupas were built by the kings like Ashoka and chandra gupta Maurya.The inscriptions on the Rumindi pillar remain perfect even today. The Ghandhara and Madhura art flourished during the Kushan period. The paintings at Ajantha and Ellora caves are examples of Gupta's art. Rajput built large marble temples, forts, palaces in Rajasthan. The Chalukyas, Rastrakudas, Hoysalas, Pallavas, Cholas, Cheras, and Pandyas were also patrons of architecture.

The Pallavas of Kanchipuram laid the foundation of the Dravidiyan art. The Temples and sculptures of Pallavas at Mahabalipuram, the

Pragatheeswarar temple at Tanjore, Godess Sri Meenakshi Amman Temple at Madurai,Sri Ramanatha swamy temple at Rameshwaram and the Thirumalai nayak palace at Maduraiare the best examples of south Indian or Dravidian Art.

The medieval art of Sultanates and Moguls were Qutub Minar, the jama Masjid, the Gol Gumbaz, Fatepur Sikri, the tombs of imperial Mughals, the Taj mahal etc. are fine examples of the Indo-Islamic architecture. It developed due to the fusion of Hindu and Islamic cultures. During the British rule many buildings were built in western styles in big cities.

During the British rule the whole country was brought under one rule.Sardar Vallabhai patel integrated all the princely states into one political unit soon after Independence.

Though India is diverse in religion, culture, language, distinct from one another there is an underlying unity among our people, which is unique and not found in any part of the world.

Diversity in Indian Society

India is a country of diversity without any element of doubt about it. Much have been talked and discussed about multi-cultural, multi ethnic and multi-language issues and the very popular 'Unity in Diversity'. However, seldom the issue of multi-history has been brought to notice. When we discuss India as a country or rather the North and South India as singular entities, we have to keep in mind all the distinguishing factors, thereby highlight the immense hold that the uniting factors possess. Culture can be seen as a product of history if we add on the socio-cognitive progress of it. It implies that all the factors that 'divide' North and South of India are basically a product of historical dissimilarities along with the self-evident geographical differences.

It is often argued that the people of the north and south belong to different ethnic groups. As it is claimed, South Indians are a product of African genes and the Northerners definitely Aryan. However, The Indian Council for Historical research, in its 2006 report shows that all Indians belong to the African genetic pool and not the Asian or European Aryan groups as it is claimed. The report also states that it was 60000 years before Christ when the human race started to spread from Africa and through the sea route they entered India. If we take it to be true, it leads to a rather intriguing question-if the people are of the same origin, why is it so that they are so different in nature?

While discussing this debate, we have to keep in mind that differences are always relative; it varies on the parameters that we take into account.

We will start with mythology and then come to some historical facts to establish the differences. The 'Bindhya Parbat' has always been a divide between the North and South as evident in myths. We hear the story of Agastya who had to cross the huge mountation to go to south. We also hear how difficult it was for Ram and his royal troop to go to south in their journey. People also link the mythological 'Ram-Ravana war' as symbolic of an evergoing north-south conflict. Now this is not history, (However, with the Ram Sethu controversy and the attempts to prove the *Ramayana* as a historical piece going on, we would not be surprised if someday it actually turns out to be history!) but myths are literature nevertheless and literature always portrays the contemporary socio cultural milieu.

So we can see the North-South divide as an ongoing process from time unspecified. Historically also, the South was hardly related to the kingdoms of the North. Except from 273 BC to 232 BC when King Ashoka of the Maurya dynasty ruled over all parts of Indian sub-continent, the South never succumbed to any other unifying kingdom. The central Asian and European rulers ruled over the whole North coming from the North West (except for the North East) but could not penetrate the South. The Vijaynagara and other empires always denied the Mughals any chance of ruling over South India. After the Mughal rule was over and the British tried to 'form' a geographically huge colony, the north and south merged as a single entity. But the divisions remained. By increasing awareness about literature, the British installed (rather unintentionally) a sense of patriotism to the Indian minds and developed a common enemy in themselves. The British divided the South into the Madras Presidency that covered most of the place and a few other small parts as they did in North. It led to the freedom moment in 1947 when nobody demanded a different country for the Southerners.

Now we also have to look at the cultural aspect of the divide. Culture, the huge phenomenon that it is, includes a lot of things-right from language and dance forms to the ideas about beauty and nature. We will look at some of the aspects and try to derive more information about it. Indian languages are very interesting research subjects. It is commonly mistaken that since Sanskrit and Tamil are closest to each other, they belong to the same language group. But it is not so. According to linguistics all the south Indian languages Tamil, Telugu, Malayalam, Tulu, Kannada, & Brahui (spoken in Balochistan, Pakistan) and few handful of lesser known languages fall under 'dravidian' language group. They are separate language group and very different from the Indo-European/Indo-Iranian/Indo-Aryan language groups. Sanskrit, Persian etc., falls under Indo-Iranian sub-group and along with Latin etc falls under the very broad Indo-European language group. Borrowing vocabulary from each other is a natural phenomenon and it has nothing to do with differences or similarities. But in this context, we can refer to to the Tamil Nadu riots of early 1960s . When Hindi was declared the official national language, it led to a huge outroar expanding all over South India. The impact was of such a great measure that after 1969 no national political party has been able to come to power in the state.

Now, culture reflects in habitual behaviour of people. We can easily recognise the difference of North and South in their dress code, food habits and mostly in their language. But this does not mean they are separate from each other. They are not, yet the differences are there.

Now, it is clear that despite the 'North South divide', India still has lots of unifying parameters to keep it bound together. Cultural values that come out of historical or rather historiographical facts definitely do leave some serious room for distinguishing measures. Yet barring some odd incidents like creating a Telegu speaking state or creating bridges and destroying mosques, the whole of India has stood together. If we leave out certain parameters, there is hardly any room to separate the North from the South. As we mentioned earlier, the comparison is hugely relative. Even though the differences are culturally distinct, culture alone can nullify all these issues and the 'Unity in Diversity' sentiments will never be hurt. With cricket and movies already playing a cupid between the two places, we can safely say that the North -South divide is not historical or cultural anymore, it is simply geographical. And we cannot help it!

Unity in Indian Society

India is so fascinating and fantastic, with all its variety of colours, dresses, languages, dialects, religions, faiths, faces, races, customs, rites and cults. All these present a feast of colours of a panoramic scene painted on a huge, single piece of canvass, as it were. Notwithstanding all these apparent and endless diversities, India has always been one integrated whole as a nation—from Kashmir to Kanyakumari and from Dibrugarh to Dwarka.

India is a land of great variety and its unique and ancient civilisation has been a great unifying factor. The vast number of diverse faiths, cults, beliefs, sects, religions, languages, manners, and lifestyles, etc. may confound a stranger, but in essence they represent the different aspects of one nation as do the petals of a lotus flower in bloom. These give you the same fascinating sweet fragrance, whether you take these petals severally and separately or collectively. This spirit of unity in diversity is very well enshrined in our Constitution, which says that it is the primary duty of every Indian citizen "to promote harmony and the spirit of common brotherhood amongst all the people of India, transcending religious, linguistic and regional or sectional diversities."

Tolerance and respect for all religions and faiths has been the hallmark of Indian civilisation. The religious life of India makes a complex but a wonderful pattern.

Besides Hinduism, Christianity, Islam, Buddhism, Jainism, Sikhism have large following. Muslims in India form the largest religious minority and make India one of the largest Islamic nations. In fact, after Indonesia, India has the largest Muslim population in the world. The Christian Church in south India is much older than the coming of Islam in India.

Fundamentally, India is secular as a nation and yet profoundly spiritual and religious. The Indian Constitution guarantees all its citizens freedom of faith and worship. One can follow and preach any faith, religion and sect as long as it does not interfere in the religious freedom and rights of others. All are equal before law, without any discrimination of faith, cult, caste, creed, sex or language. India has always believed in freedom of thought, expression and faith. The people of this ancient nation have always been at liberty to pursue cultural, religious and spiritual goals of their own selection and choice. They have varied views and opinions on religion, political systems, economic order, and social problems, etc.

India is geographically, culturally and politically one united and strong and yet allows differences of thought, approach, religion and faith. It is this tolerance which has been a benchmark of Indian culture and thought since times immemorial. India has an immense capacity and power to imbibe and absorb all good alien influences. If it didn't have this tolerance and power to assimilate foreign cultural influences, thought and philosophy would have been now extinct, as has been in the case of many ancient civilisations of the world. There has been useful interaction between the cultures of India and that of the other countries for the last several millennia. In the process, the Indian mind has assimilated much of the thoughts and conceptions of the cultures of other nations. Thus, India's contribution to world culture and civilisation has been immense. It has been the cradle of such great religions as Hinduism, Sikhism, Buddhism and Jainism.

But it is really regrettable that in recent years, particularly after 1947, so many ugly forces have raised their heads in the form of casteism, communalism, regionalism, and terrorism, etc. They pose a great threat and challenge to the unity, integrity, stability and progress of the country. These undesirable forces of evil, let loose by certain vested foreign powers, are hell bent on exploiting our spirit of tolerance, secularism, variety and diversity of faiths, religions, and languages, etc. But these nefarious designs of our enemies will never succeed. We are well aware of our responsibilities and duties as worthy citizens of this great ancient land and ready to fight tooth and nail to defeat these disruptive forces challenging our age-old solidarity and integrity. We shall definitely overcome, sooner rather than later, these fanatics, bigots and extremists trying to create communal tensions, religious intolerance and regional hatred at the instances of some hostile nations.

We should identify such narrow, parochial, selfish and communal mischief makers and eliminate them forever. Nobody can be allowed to encourage separatism, division, disharmony and disintegration. Some political parties are also to blame for it. They fight elections on the lines of caste, community, religion, region or language. They divide the people on communal basis, to use them as their vote banks in elections. These parties should be derecognized and their policies condemned in no uncertain terms. Unfortunately, some of the Indian political leaders are following in the footsteps of the British rulers who always adopted the policy of 'divide and rule'.

In spite of all these odds that have surfaced in recent years, India is one and united politically, culturally, geographically and socially. Our way of life, thinking, literature, heritage, customs and traditions are basically the same. The institutions of family and marriage are the same, so are our social and religious customs throughout the length and breadth of the country. Similarly, there are many fairs and festivals, etc., observed and enjoyed by the people of all communities and castes in common. All these facts and factors underline our cultural and emotional unity and integrity.

The unity of Indian society and culture surges ahead and blossoms like a flower in spite of several diversities. This indeed is strange enough a factor which often eludes the plausible answer. Indians are highly emotional and they exhibit their emotional unity at moments of national crises. Indians have been bound up socio-culturally and emotionally for at least 2,500 years, i.e. from the time of Indus Valley Civilisation. Indian has always attracted peoples from outside and many of them have settled down in this subcontinent. It can be said that the lap of mother India is cosy soothing and comfortable. The flow of outsiders to India continues till today at least from two neighbouring countries, one in the east and the other in the West.

The national government of India and t benevolent people of India have never repulsed anyone who is genuinely interested settling down in the country. In the world, all countries are not equally hospitable a sympathetic towards refugees who are embroiled in some kind of predicament. It is fact the later immigrants to India have found cooperation and all kinds of assistance from the host population of India. There has not been reports of strong conflicts a feuds between the guest population and host population. Therefore it can be concluded that India and her denizens are catholic, magnanimous and benevolent towards people who are in distress.

Indian history is a mute witness to the influx of outsiders who came into the subcontinent either to conquer territories and people or to plunder wealth or to settle down as citizens. History tells us that people of many nationalities came to India subcontinent with imperial designs; some of whom settled down as citizens and some others departed from India. The Indian national movement was directed against the British colonial government.

The British had come initially as traders, but later on the assumed the role of rulers and ruled India for 150 years. One thing need be mentioned here that India was not territorially one country before the British occupation of India Undoubtedly the British made a very positive contribution by unifying disparate tiny kingdoms and monarchies of India. India had probably achieved near-complete territorial integration during the rule of imperial Mauryas. Mauryan rule from the time of Chandragupta to Samudra Gupta and Ashoka exhibited the glory of territorial unity in India. But this territorial unity and integrity did not last long. The subsequent Hindu rules were not-worthy of integrating the disparate territories politically although Indian society demonstrated some sort of socio-cultural integration.

During the time of Mauryas India society was by and large co-terminus with Hindu India. The ethno-religious trend Indian society took a different turn with the advent of Muslims, Mughals and Christian. At different points of time, it is not out of place to draw the attention of our readers the fact, that the great visionaries, like Lord Buddha and Lord Mahavir have expressed their dissatisfaction with the Brahmanical form of Hinduism and rigid norms of caste society which was prevalent during that time. They attempted to wipe out socio-cultural inequalities from Indian society through the social commandments which they had propounded. Indian society remained a proverbial elephant not yielding to reformist movements.

Social Reformers like Guru Nanak, Swami Dayanand Saraswati, Raja Rammohan Ray, E.V. Ramaswamy Nicker, Gujarati Saint Narasimha Mehta and many other reformists tried to remove inequality from Indian social structure and they succeeded with limited achievement. However, their struggle and endeavour are not gone in vain. Their sole aim was to integrate Indian society on the basis of equality of status. Some say that despite discriminations and differentiations in social hierarchy, the Indian society functioned cohesively. Some social scientists may not accept this argument because Indian society till today is not based on complete Socio-cultural equality. Age-old and anachronistic socio-cultural practices continue to divide the Indian society impairing its vitality.

Factors that Effects Unity in Indian Society

India was not politically united before Independence except for short spells, the natural geographical boundaries, a common history, social values and systems, linguistic relations and religious harmony were the factors, which unified India strongly. Hinduism has always been the religion of its majority community.

India exhibits a fascinating picture of unity in diversity. There is co-existence of varied belief, patterns and thoughts due to racial intermixing and cultural mingling. More than anywhere else in the world, it holds a multitude of thoughts, processes them and practices them. This is the reason for its being one of the oldest, continuous and uninterrupted living culture in the whole world.

The factors, which keep its unity and continuity intact are:

Indian philosophy, Vedic literature and its value system

Indian philosophy, contains a vast reservoir of knowledge. It is found in *Vedas*, *Upanishads*, *Sutras* and *Smritis*. Basham says that Vedic literature contains "an ocean of knowledge in a jar."

The Vedic literature is a magnificent example of scientific division and orderly arrangement of rules, in a few words, in different branches of human knowledge, covering almost all the aspects of life, be it phonetics, arts, literature, medicine, polity, metrics, law, philosophy, astrology or astronomy.

Indian philosophy and its value system still commands the respect and attention of an average Indian. The priestly schools had devised a most remarkable and effective system of transferring knowledge to succeeding generations in the form of hymns, restricting it only to those, possessing brilliant feats of memory and capability to keep extreme sanctity.

Doctrines of Varna, Dharma *and* Karma

The foundation pillars of the Indian civilization are the principles of *Varna*, *Dharma* and *Karma*, which give to the people, a purpose to live for and ideals to be achieved.

1. Doctrine of *Varna* gives the Indian society a stable, sustainable social structure, which distributes and organizes performance of various functions. It has made it possible for the people to lead a quality of life and ensured the continuity despite numerous foreign invasions, migrations and assimilation of various groups.
2. The doctrine of *Dharma* defines the duties and vocations for different sections of society, ensures social harmony and prevents rivalries and jealousies.
3. Doctrine of *Karma* makes the inequalities, prevalent in the society, tolerable to an average Indian.

Together these principles laid the foundation stones of Indian social structure and contributed to its growth. It has organised inter-relationship of various groups of society It has given to the people a distinct character. It has defined their roles by distributing various functions and manage the performance to improve quality of life.

In the past, these principles had wisely directed all the activities—social, political, intellectual or economic—into proper life functions and controlled its malfunctioning or disfunctioning. It had made it possible for people to reach a high level of intelligence having specialisation in different areas. It contributed to all round growth of cultural heritage and encouraged self-discipline, consciousness, self control and self-direction. Decentralised self-regulated systems were the mode in social, political and economic life in ancient India.

It had prepared an atmosphere for co-existence of different groups be it ruler or ruled/rich or poor. It had provided unity of culture throughout India and served to give Indian society coherence, stability and continuity.

'Sanatan Dharma' of Hinduism takes care of the basic physical, mental and spiritual needs of the human beings at different stages of life. It nurtures the basic instincts of human beings over nature, after a deep study of natural instincts, inherent attributes and natural behavioral pattern.

Spirit of Tolerance

The spirit of tolerance and firm belief in the principle, 'Live and let live' has always been the part of Indian ethos. Indians believe in *Vasudhaiva Kutumbakam* which means. The whole world is one family. Truth, Ahimsa, peace and non-aggression are the hallmark of Indian culture. Tolerance is most evident in the field of religion.

Validity to all religions - Hindu faith in an all pervading omnipresent god, multiplicity of god and goddesses as representing some portion of the infinite aspect of the Supreme Being, inspired it to accommodate people of all faiths.

Hinduism concedes validity to all the religions and does not lay down strictures against any faith or reject any religion or its god as false. That is why, all the twelve major religions of the world are present and flourishing in India without any hindrance.

Path of assimilation - Hindu religion neither repulses any trend vehemently, nor allows others to sweep its established culture off its roots. It has adopted the path of assimilation. It does not force others to convert. It does not impose its beliefs, practices and customs on others. In the past, it has assimilated numerous social groups willing to join it.

Extent of Tolerance - Tolerance is not confined to religion alone. It is seen everywhere in the Indian way of life. The people endure injustice and unfairness until they are pushed right to the wall.

Fusion of Different Cultures

C. Rajgopalachari said, "If there is honesty in India today, any hospitality, any charity.... any aversion to evil, any love to be good, it is due to whatever remains of the old faith and the old culture".

As India passed through various phases in the past, each and every group left its influence on its culture, which came down to the present generation in an unbroken chain of succession, with some modifications and adaptations. All the sects present in India, whether foreign or indigenous, have been influenced greatly by Hindu thinking, practices and systems. Different religious communities also influenced Indian culture.

Following factors have contributed in enriching the composite culture of India : -

1. The growth, influence and refinement of values of different religions generated within the land of India.
2. The interaction between value-system of indigenous religions of India and religions of diverse migrating or foreign communities like Islam, Christianity, Zorastarianism etc.

Vedic Hindu Culture

Vedic Hindu Culture is one of the oldest living cultures in the world. It mainly originated and flourished in northern parts of India and later on spread throughout India. The word 'Vedic' is derived from the word 'Vid' meaning 'Knowledge' and signifies' 'knowledge par excellence'.

The Vedic culture came into being due to intermixing of the culture of Aryan with the culture of indigenous tribal people of India during second century BC to 650 AD. The origin of the Vedic culture cannot be traced in any single founder; neither can it be confined in one single authoritative text.

Its knowledge has been handed down from time immemorial, earlier by verbal transmission and later on, in written form by the ancestor to succeeding generations. It has not prescribed final absolutes. It is a constant search for more knowledge. Vedas are not supposed to be the end of quest for knowledge. It is a non-ending process.

The strength of Vedic culture is proved by the facts: -

1. Despite centuries of foreign rule, over 75% of Indian population remains Hindu.
2. Had it become obsolete, it would have given place to other religions and cultures.
3. It influenced almost all other religions found in India.

Buddhism and Jainism

Budhism and Jainism has influenced the thought, moral and life style of many Indians. Buddhism attracted equally the elite as well as the lower strata of Hindu society. Buddhism drew the attention of people towards the harsher effects of the caste system, sympathetic attitude towards lesser human beings and system of organised education. Major contribution of Jainism is the principle of non-violence.

Dravidian culture

After the sudden disappearance of Indus valley culture, of which the most characteristic feature was its town planning, Dravidian culture with its advanced social system, industry and trade made a mark in the South.

Islamic culture

After the tenth century, Islamic culture influenced the Indian culture substantially. Its influence could be seen in the rejection of elaborate rituals and caste pretensions. It preached a simple path of faith, devotion, brotherly love and fellowship. With the growing political strength of Muslims, the need for mutual understanding and communal harmony gave rise to Sufi tradition of Islam and Bhakti movement of Hindus. Both these emphasized the need for mutual appreciation, tolerance and goodwill. Like Buddhism, Islam also provided an alternative to people, wishing to opt out the caste system.

British Culture

Eighteenth century onwards, the British culture influenced the Indian culture substantially, especially that of elite and intellectuals. Access to modern education, Western literature and philosophy gave Indians the understanding of liberal and humanitarian ideas of the West.

Some of the contributions of the British to India are political and administrative unity, many democratic institutions like Parliament, bureaucracy and concepts like rule of law, unified nationality, a common currency, a common Judiciary. They gave a new economic structure based on industrialization. British-rule gave an impetus to social progress and brought many reforms.

The British influence on Indian minds was as discussed below:

1. Many reformers welcomed rationality and other good features of English culture. They advised people to interpret religion rationally and make efforts to eradicate social evils like Sati, child marriage, untouchablity etc. prevalent at that time.
2. Some people were so influenced by the alien culture, that they developed a complex about the primitiveness of Indian society.
3. Some reformists tried to revive their own rich ancient culture and prevent the masses from being swayed away by the glamour and materialism of Western culture. It gave the call for 'Back to Vedas'.

Multi-Generational Diversity in Indian Organizations

While existing literature in the Indian cultural context is diverse and fragmented, there is no single study which has focussed on generations in the Indian milieu. SHRM India is doing a research project focused on "Multi-generational Diversity in the workplace" in collaboration with Prof. Vasanthi Srinivasan from IIM-Bangalore. This study will fill a long standing gap in this research area.

The broad objectives of the study are:

1. How do we categorize generations in the Indian workforce context meaningfully?
2. How do multiple generations interact in the workplace?
3. Are there inter-generational gender differences in the workplace?

4. What are the mechanisms that organisations use to strengthen multi-generational collaboration?
5. What are the implications for Leadership and Human Resource Management in the new conceptualization of generations?

In this study we propose to conceptualize generations within the context of organizations. Multiple levels of reporting relationships in organizations make cohorts the distinctive natural basis of division. This natural division of authority and responsibility is built on the notion of chronological succession-the idea that each generation passes through a social system or a social role, succeeding one generation and preceding another. The unique location of a generation in a chronological order gives each cohort access to a set of skills, knowledge, experiences, and resources that can potentially be passed on to or exchanged with the succeeding generation. Such a chronological succession creates opportunities for learning, collaboration, knowledge transfer, building and shaping ideas and innovation to build vibrant organizations. At the same time, this can also result in inter-generational conflicts, communication breakdown, knowledge hoarding and opportunities for self-centered conduct which can promote highly individualistic behaviour.

However, in a highly diverse country like India, the variation within a generation is likely to be accentuated by factors like rural - urban background, caste, gender and other socio-cultural factors. This diversity is likely to negate the proposition that people who share common birth and growth stages in a similar time frame have comparable access and go through the same defining events that influence their values and approach to various aspects of life. We will postulate that given the geographical location and the demographics, intra-generational differences are likely to be as many as inter-generational differences.

In western studies, generations are defined based on birth years and cohorts, and then subject to study through examining the similarities and differences between various groups through the use of surveys and focus group discussions. However, in the Indian context, there is a need to take into consideration a host of other social, cultural and demographic factors that could play an important role in determining values and attitudes of different individuals so that they could be classified into groups based on common patterns. Given this background, a study of generations in India needs to be anchored in an "emic" (an insider's definition) perspective of what generations are within an organization. Hence, this study looks forward to inputs from a large number of people across various strata in organizations.

Once the definition of generations in the Indian context is landscaped, the variables to be studied in depth within organizations will be identified followed by an exploratory research. Subsequently, focus group discussions and interviews will be conducted in organizations to understand multi-generational diversity amongst assorted work groups. Based on the analysis, in depth case studies will be done in organizations which will provide practical insights to handle multiple generations from a culture perspective.

Themes in Indian Society

Hierarchy

India is a hierarchical society. Whether in north India or south India, Hindu or Muslim, urban or village, virtually all things, people, and social groups are ranked according to various essential qualities. Although India is a political democracy, notions of complete equality are seldom evident in daily life.

Societal hierarchy is evident in caste groups, amongst individuals, and in family and kinship groups. Castes are primarily associated with Hinduism, but caste-like groups also exist among Muslims, Indian, Christians, and other religious communities. Within most villages or towns, everyone knows the relative rankings of each locally represented caste, and behavior is constantly shaped by this knowledge.

Hierarchy plays an important role within families and kinship groupings also, where men outrank women of similar age, and senior relatives outrank junior relatives. Formal respect is accorded family members-for example, in northern India, a daughter-in-law shows deference to her husband, to all senior in-laws, and to all daughters of the household. Siblings, too, recognize age differences, with younger siblings addressing older siblings by respectful terms rather than by name.

Ritual Purity and Pollution

Many status differences in Indian society are expressed in terms of ritual purity and pollution, complex notions that vary greatly among different castes, religious groups, and regions. Generally, high status is associated with purity and low status with pollution. Some kinds of purity are inherent; for example, a member of a high-ranking Brahmin, or priestly, caste is born with more inherent purity than someone born into a low-ranking sweeper, or scavenger, caste. Other kinds of purity are more transitory, for example, a Brahmin who has just taken a bath is more ritually pure than a Brahmin who has not bathed for a day.

Purity is associated with ritual cleanliness like daily bathing in flowing water, dressing in freshly laundered clothes, eating only the foods appropriate for one's caste, and avoiding physical contact with people of significantly lower rank or with impure substances, such as the bodily wastes of another adult. Involvement with the products of death or violence is usually ritually polluting.

Social Interdependence

One of the great themes pervading Indian life is social interdependence. People are born into groups—families, clans, sub-castes, castes, and religious communities—and feel a deep sense of inseparability from these groups. People are deeply involved with others, and for many, the greatest fear is the possibility of being left alone, without social support. Psychologically, family members typically experience intense emotional interdependence. Economic activities, too, are deeply imbedded in a social nexus. Through a multitude of kinship ties, each person is linked with kin in villages and towns near and far. Almost everywhere a person goes, he can find a relative from whom he can expect moral and practical support.

In every activity, social ties can help a person and the absence of them can bring failure. Seldom do people carry out even the simplest tasks on their own. When a small child eats, his mother puts the food into his mouth with her own hand. When a girl brings water home from the well in pots on her head, someone helps her unload the pots. A student hopes that an influential relative or friend can facilitate his college admission. A young person anticipates that parents will arrange his or her marriage. Finally, a person facing death expects that relatives will conduct the proper funeral rites ensuring his own smooth journey to the next life and reaffirming social ties among mourners.

This sense of interdependence extends into the theological realm. From birth onward, a child learns that his "fate" has been "written" by divine forces and that his life is shaped by powerful deities with whom an ongoing relationship must be maintained.

2

STRATIFICATION IN INDIAN SOCIETY

Introduction

Stratification describes the way in which different groups of people are placed within society. The status of people is often determined by how society is stratified - the basis of which can include:

- Wealth and income
- Social class
- Ethnicity
- Gender
- Political status
- Religion (e.g. the caste system in India)

Stratification is a hierarchy of positions with regard to economic production which influences the social rewards to those in the positions. When we are growing up, we might hear our parents talk about others as being from the 'wrong side of the tracks,' or not being 'our kind.' We also begin to become aware of what kind of toys they have (or don't have), the way others dress, what kind of house they live in, what job their parents have, and due to this some are treated differently and have better opportunities than others. We see differences in elementary schools and high schools in our city. If our parents belong to the upper class, we have a good chance of graduating high school and entering higher education. The more education we have, the more active we will be in political life, the more traditional and conservative our religious affiliation, the more likely we will marry into a family with both economic and social capital, and the more likely we will eat better food, will be less exposed to unhygienic conditions, and be able to pay for good health care. Stratification and inequality are everywhere and impact us throughout our lives.

Stratification refers to the hierarchical arrangement of people in a society. This chapter focuses on economic stratification; meaning how people are differentiated based upon their wealth (and/or power). Sociology has a long history of studying stratification and teaching about various kinds of inequality, including economic inequality, racial/ethnic inequality, gender inequality, and other types of inequality. Inequality means people have unequal access to scarce and valued resources in society. These resources might be economic or political, such as health care, education, jobs, property and land ownership, housing, and ability to influence government policy.

Socioeconomic Status of Stratification

Building on the ideas of Max Weber, who saw three main dimensions of stratification (class, status, and party), contemporary sociologists often define stratification in terms of socioeconomic status (or SES). There are a variety of ways to measure SES, including educational attainment, income, wealth, and occupational prestige. These measures reflect three characteristics of individuals: power, property, and prestige. These three characteristics combine to indicate someone's social class or socioeconomic status.

Power

Power refers to someone's ability to get others to do his/her will, regardless of whether or not they want to. Legitimate power, power given to individuals willingly by others, is called authority. Illegitimate power, power taken by force or the threat of force, is called coercion.

Property

Property, as used in this context, refers to the sum total of one's possessions as well as their regular income. Property goes beyond income as a measure of social class as it reflects the accumulated wealth (e.g., homes, stocks, bonds, savings) in addition to one's earning potential.

Property is a better overall measure of social class than income as many individuals who are considered wealthy actually have very small incomes.

Prestige

Prestige refers to the reputation or esteem associated with one's position in society. Prestige used to be associated with one's family name, but for most people in developed countries, prestige is now generally tied to one's occupation. Occupations like physicians or lawyers tend to have more prestige associated with them than occupations like bartender or janitor. An individual's prestige is closely tied to their social class - the higher the prestige of an individual (through their occupation or maybe family name), the higher the social class.

These three indicators tend to go hand-in-hand or lead to each other, such as a Supreme Court justice who is usually wealthy, enjoys a great deal of prestige, and exercises significant power. In some cases, however, a person ranks differently on these indicators, such as funeral directors. Their prestige is fairly low, but most have higher incomes than college professors, who are among the most educated people in America and have high prestige.

Can we make a society in which people are equal?

Societies could be redesigned so that they are based on cooperation. Marxists argue that a central component of a more equitable and humane society would be based on the idea, "from each according to their ability, to each according to their need." In other words, each person should produce or work to the best of their ability according to their talents, and each person should receive the fruits of this labor according to their need, irrespective of what they have produced. Conflict theorists also believe that democracy or some sort of group decision making is more humane and more effective. Stratification systems that concentrate decision making and power in the hands of a few are destined to not serve the interests of most people at the bottom of the pyramid.

Analysing Stratification

There are three levels of analysing stratification:

1. Micro Level
2. Meso Level
3. Macro Level

Micro-level prestige and influence

Stratification occurs in small groups and face-to-face interaction. At the beginning of the chapter, we looked at how stratification begins when we are young. Clothing, expensive toys, a new bicycle, a fancy car, and what job our parents had were symbols that differentiated us and separated us in elementary schools and impacted which friends we played with and the interactions we had.

Throughout our lives, wealth, power, and prestige are given to individuals who have knowledge and access to important information and influential people in society. Gender and race influence our degrees of networks, as well as individual qualities of leadership, self confidence, and physical attractiveness.

Meso-level access to resources

Our positions and connections in organizations and institutions lie within the stratification system. This impacts how we experience life and how we interact with other individuals and groups. As mentioned earlier, parents, teachers, and friends show us our position in society and teach us to expect that same level. Education prepares each social class differently, with different skills and values taught to each class. The police, courts, and prisons reinforce the stratification system. Our position in the system reflects the type of health care we receive. All of these institutions support the stratification system by favoring the rich and powerful.

Macro-level factors influencing stratification

Our position in the international economic system in the world shapes our opportunities throughout our life and our access to important resources. Macro level factors such as policies implemented by the World Bank and International Monetary fund impact the job opportunities, prices of food, water, and electricity, and day-to-day life for citizens.

Major Forms of Stratification

Primitive communalism characterized by a high degree of sharing and minimal social inequality. Slavery involving great social inequality and the ownership of some persons by others. Caste in which an individual is permanently assigned to a status based on his or her parents' status. Estate in which peasants are required by law to work land owned by the noble class in exchange for food and protection from outside attacks.

Weber's three dimensions of stratification:

1. Class or a set of people with similar amounts of income and wealth.
2. Party or a set of people with similar amounts of power.
3. Status group or a set of people with similar social prestige or positive regard from members of a society.

Why Inequality Exists?

Natural inevitability which suggests that inequality exists because of natural differences in people's abilities and is a just system. Structural - functionalist which states that stratification is useful to society because it enhances stability and induces members of the society to work hard. Conflict which suggests that stratification occurs through conflict between different classes, with the upper classes using superior power to take a larger share of the social resources. Evolutionary which states that people will share enough resources to ensure the survival of the group until a surplus exists at which time power determines how the surplus is distributed. Symbolic Interactionist which calls attention to the importance of symbolic displays of wealth and power that influence one's definition of self and the importance of ideas in defining social situations.

In what regard is some stratification inevitable?

Inequality may emanate from natural differences in people's abilities. What are the functionalist and conflict theories as to the reasons for stratification? Structural-functionalists believe that societies tend to be stable and are held together through consensus.Stratifiction provides an important function to society by aiding this process because it lessens conflict and provides structure. Conflict theorists believe that society tends toward conflict and change and that stratification system coerce the lower classes in order to benefit the upper classes.

Social Stratification

Every complex society faces the difficult task of placing its members into roles that are necessary for the society to survive. These roles must be filled with as little conflict and confusion as possible. There must be people willing to perform jobs with little status and those that carry a great deal of prestige. In our community, there are people who are doctors, lawyers, and teachers. Others collect trash, direct traffic, and put out fires. Although, these roles do not all carry the same prestige, there is very little conflict involved in determining who will perform which one. In India, caste is one set of role cards and perhaps the most important one.

One's caste is ascribed; that is, children inherit the status and functions of their parents. At birth Indians are dealt their caste card. This is alien to what many people in the United States believe about the "good society." Our parents, relatives, teachers, and friends tell us in a thousand ways that what we make of our lives depends on our efforts, and many of us think all societies should play by the same rules, or at least strive to do so. But it is important to remember that there is no society where individual effort is the sole criterion for status.

While caste is a very important set of role cards, Indians, like Americans, also use class (economic) cards. Both caste and class operate at the same time. A person of very low caste such as a sweeper may get a good job that has nothing to do with sweeping and save some money. With this wealth the sweeper may build a fancy house and educate his children who then become doctors, lawyers, and government leaders. This type of role is usually achieved, although some people inherit their wealth.

There is also the possibility of achieving political power in India quite apart from class or caste status. A low caste person might be very good at winning elections and become a member of the central government. Jagjivan Ram, a member of one of the Dalit (ex- Untouchable) castes, has held many cabinet posts in his political career. This system of gaining status is based on power. Power is usually achieved status rather than a role that is dealt at birth. People in India participate in the caste game, the class game, and the power game.

In India, castes are ranked, and caste members in a specific geographical area can identify those castes that are above and below them. The ranking of castes is based on purity and pollution, often associated with functions of the human body. Roles associated with the head such as thinking, talking, teaching, and learning are considered pure. Activities associated with waste, feet, and skin are considered polluting. Consequently, Brahmins at the top of the purity scale were scholars who traditionally taught and presided at religious functions. Untouchables, at the bottom of the scale, cleared away human waste, collected garbage, cut hair, skinned animals, and washed clothes. Because their occupations mainly dealt with human, animal, and societal waste, society believed that contact with an Untouchable was highly polluting.

Preparing and sharing of food reveals how castes are ranked. Food cooked in oil and prepared by a Brahmin can be accepted and eaten by any caste below it. Food cooked in water can generally be accepted by one's own caste members or inferior castes. Leftover, uneaten food almost always is taken only by the very low castes. Food that can be eaten raw is the most freely distributed and can be accepted by any caste from any caste. In addition, prasad, blessed food that is left over from religious offerings, is given to anyone regardless of caste.

There is also a range of pure and impure foods. Vegetables and grains are purer than meat and eggs. Fish is the purest of the non-vegetarian foods, followed by chicken, goats, pork, and water buffalo; the most impure is beef. Sweet pastries, fried in deep fat, are among the most widely acceptable foods from any caste. By observing how food is prepared and with whom it is shared, one can begin to determine the ranking on a purity-pollution scale of the caste groups involved.

Social stratification refers to the existence of inequalities between groups on the basis of wealth, power, race, income, age, prestige or some other characteristic which are built into the fabric of society. Social stratification is not simply the existence of social inequalities it is a peculiar sort of social inequality. It refers to the presence of social groups which are hierarchically ranked. Those who belong to a particular group (or social stratum) have some awareness of their common interests and a common identity. They share a similar style of life and social habits, which distinguish them from members of other social groups above and below them in the hierarchy. Sociologists have distinguished three types of stratification: caste, estate and class. There is a certain amount of debate as to whether stratification is universal.

Hierarchy of Power

The Indian caste system is one example of social stratification. Hindu society in traditional India was divided into five main strata: four castes (varna) and an outcaste, the untouchables. They are ranked in a hierarchy of ritual cleanliness which derives from the lifestyles and occupations permitted to members of a particular caste. This hierarchy of prestige, grounded in notions of ritual purity, is mirrored by a hierarchy of power. The upper castes are the Brahmins (priesthood), followed by the *Khasatriyas* (secular and military rulers and landlords), the *Vaishyas* (entrepreneurial middle classes) and the *Shudras* (workers and slaves). The Harijans stand outside the hierarchy as outcastes or untouchables who perform only those degrading tasks which are considered unclean. So polluting is the presence of the untouchables that if their shadow falls across that of a Brahmin then it renders it unclean. Within the different castes themselves thousands of sub-divisions (jatis) exist and these determine occupation.

In modern society it is generally assumed that class is the basis of social stratification. The major classes in the West are: an upper class (the wealthy, employers and industrialists, plus top executivesâ€"those who directly own productive resources); a middle class (which includes most white-collar workers and professionals); and a working class (those in blue-collar and manual jobs). In some industrialized countries, such as

France and Japan, a fourth class peasants (people engaged in traditional types of agricultural production) has until recently been important. Some have argued that American society does not fit this class system of stratification: other attributes such as race and gender are often identified as important sources of social inequality.

The social stratification is a concept of class, involving the "classification of persons into groups based on shared socio-economic conditions ... a relational set of inequalities with economic, social, political and ideological dimensions."

In modern western societies, stratification is broadly organized into three main layers:

(1) Upper Class: The "upper class" is the group of people at the top of a social hierarchy. Members of an upper class may have great power over the allocation of resources and governmental policy in their area.

(2) Middle Class: The middle class is any class of people in the middle of a societal hierarchy. In Weberian socio-economic terms, the middle class is the broad group of people in contemporary society who fall socio-economically between the working classand upper class. The common measures of what constitutes middle class vary significantly between cultures. In urban India, for example, a family is considered middle class if it resides in an owner-occupied property.

(3)Lower Class: It is also known as working class or labouring class, this term used in the social sciences and in ordinary conversation to describe those employed in lower tier jobs (as measured by skill, education and lower incomes), often extending to those in unemployment or otherwise possessing below-average incomes. Working classes are mainly found in industrialized economiesand in urban areas of non-industrialized economies. Working class is defined and used in many different ways.

When used non-academically, it typically refers to a section of society dependent on physical labor, especially when compensated with an hourly wage. The term is usually contrasted with the upper class and middle class, in general terms of access to economic resources,education, cultural interests, and other goods and services. The cut-off between working class and middle class is more specifically where a population spends money primarily as a lifestyle rather than for sustenance (for example, on fashion versus merely nutrition and shelter). Problematically, relying on this method of distinction would rule out many of the people who are often identified as working class. Its usage can alternately be derogatory, or can express a sense of pride in those who self-identify as working class.

Each class may be further sub-divided into smaller classes (e.g. occupational). These categories are particular to state-based societies as distinguished from, for instance, feudal societies composed of nobility-to-peasant relations. Stratification may also be defined by kinship ties or castes. For Max Weber, social class pertaining broadly to material wealth is distinguished from status class which is based on such variables as honor, prestige and religious affiliation. Talcott Parsons argued that the forces of societal differentiation and the following pattern of institutionalized individualization would strongly diminish the role of class (as a major stratification factor) as social evolution went along. It is debatable whether the earliest hunter-gatherer groups may be defined as 'stratified', or if such differentials began with agriculture and broad acts of exchange between groups. One of the ongoing issues in determining social stratification arises from the point that status inequalities between individuals are common, so it becomes a quantitative issue to determine how much inequality qualifies as stratification.

Social Stratification in Indian Society

According to Wilbert More and Kingsley Davis, stratification system came to be evolved in all the societies due to the functional necessity. As they have pointed out main functional necessity of the system is "the requirement faced by any society of placing and motivating individuals in the social structure. Social inequality is thus an unconsciously evolved device by which societies ensure that the most important positions are conscientiously filled by the most qualified persons". As analyzed by H.M. Johnson certain things here can be noted about the "functional necessity' of class stratification system".

1. *Encourages hard work* : One of the main functions of class stratification is to induce people to work hard to live up to values. Those who best fulfill the values of a particular society are normally rewarded with greater prestige and social acceptance by others. It is known that occupations are ranked high if their functions are highly important and the required personal is very scarce. Hard work prolonged training and heavy burden of responsibility are associated with such occupational positions, people undertaking such works are rewarded with money, prestige, comforts etc. still we cannot say that all those positions which are regarded as important are adequately compensated for.

2. *Ensures circulation elites* : To some extent, class stratification helps to ensure what is often called "the circulation of the elite". When a high degree of prestige comforts and other rewards are offered for certain

positions, there will be some competition for them. This process of competition helps to ensure that the more efficient people are able to rise to the top, where their ability can best be used.

3. *Serves as an economic function* : The competitive aspect has a kind of economic function in that it helps to ensure the .rational use of available talent. It is also functionally necessary to offer differential rewards if the positions at the top are largely ascribed as it is in the case of caste system. Even in caste system, the people at the top can lose their prestige if they fail to maintain certain standards. Hence, differential rewards provide the incentives for the upper classes to work at maintaining their positions.

4. *Prevents waste of resources* : The stratification system prevents the waste of scarce resources. The men in the elite class actually possess scarce and socially valued abilities and qualities, whether these are inherited or acquired. Because of their possession of these qualities their enjoyment of some privileges such as extra comfort and immunity from doing mental work are functionally justified. It becomes functionally official for the society to make use of their talents without being wasted. For example, it would be a waste to pour the resources of society into the training of doctors and engineers and then making them to work as peons and attenders. When once certain individuals are chosen and are trained for certain difficult positions it should be dysfunctional to waste their 'time and energy one takes for which there is enough man power.

5. *Stabilizes and reinforces the attitude and skills* : Members of a class normally try to limit their relations to their class. More intimate relationship are mostly found between fellow class-mate members. Even this tendency has its own function. It tends to stabilize and reinforce the attitudes and skills that may be the basis of upper-class position. Those who have similar values and interests tend to associate comfortably with one another. Their frequent association itself confirms their common values and interests.

6. *Helps to pursue different professions or job* : The values, attitudes and qualities of different classes are different. This difference is also functional for society to some extent. Because society needs manual as well as non-manual workers. Many jobs are not attractive to highly trained or refined people for they are socialized to aspire for certain other jobs. Because of the early influence of family and socialization, the individuals imbibe in them certain values, attitudes and qualities relevant to the social class to which they belong. This will influence their selection of jobs.

7. *Social control* : Further, to the extent that 'lower class' cultural characteristics are essential to Society, the classes are of course, functional. In fact, a certain amount of mutual antagonism between social classes is also functional. To some extent, upper class and lower class groups cannot act as negative reference groups for each other. Thus, they act as means of social control also.

8. *Controlling effect on the 'Shady' World* : Mass stratification has another social control function, Even in the 'shady' world of gamblers and in the under world of lower criminals, black-marketeers, racketeers, smugglers etc. the legitimate classes structure has got respectability. They know that money is not a substitute for prestige but only a compensation for renouncing it. Hence, instead of continuing in a profitable shady career, such people want to gain respectability for their money and for their children. They try to enter legitimate fields and become philanthropists and patron of the arts. Thus the legitimate class structure continues to attract the shady classes and the under world. This attraction exerts a social control function.

3

INDIAN FAMILY STRUCTURE

In India, people learn the essential themes of cultural life within the bosom of a family. In most of the country, the basic units of society are the patrilineal family unit and wider kinship groupings. The most widely desired residential unit is the joint family, ideally consisting of three or four patrilineally related generations, all living under one roof, working, eating, worshiping, and cooperating together in mutually beneficial social and economic activities. Patrilineal joint families include men related through the male line, along with their wives and children. Most young women expect to live with their husband's relatives after marriage, but they retain important bonds with their natal families.

Despite the continuous and growing impact of urbanization, secularization, and westernization, the traditional joint household, both in ideal and in practice, remains the primary social force in the lives of most Indians. Loyalty to family is a deeply held ideal for almost everyone.

Large families tend to be flexible and well-suited to modern Indian life, especially for the 67 percent of Indians who are farmers or agricultural workers or work in related activities . As in most primarily agricultural societies, few individuals can hope to achieve economic security without being part of a cooperating group of kinsmen. The joint family is also common in cities, where kinship ties can be crucial to obtaining scarce jobs or financial assistance. Numerous prominent Indian families, such as the Tatas, Birlas, and Sarabhais, retain joint family arrangements even as they work together to control some of the country's largest financial empires.

In India, family forms the basic unit of society. An individual is ideally nurtured and taught within a typical Indian family, which often extends beyond the immediate to the joint family structure.

Globalization and western influence have failed to change the character of Indian family life even today.

Family life varies with regional diversity in India in terms of religion, culture, traditions, rituals and general life style. This is also dictated by caste and class in many cases.

Traditional roles in family structure are changing in urban areas but even modern and educated families imbibe the intrinsic values of family life in India.

Indians tend to give priority to the welfare of thc family unit as whole. Individuals are brought up in a group situation and taught to remain united and support each other for progress.

Many Indians still live in the joint family system where elders are valued and protected and youngsters nurtured and cherished.Children are ensured family support and taught to honor their responsibility towards the whole family from the beginning. Unfortunately, girl child is still given less preference.

Family ties are very important to Indians. Arranged marriages within the caste are still common all over the country. Men are required to support the family economically through out their life.

The traditional role of a woman is to look after the domestic chores like cooking, child-care and service to the elders. Working women in urban areas are also expected to fulfill their domestic responsibilities.

The joint family in its conventional form as a rigid institution has undergone many changes with rapid urbanization and growing forces of individualism in modern India.

Rapid urbanization has played an important role in the break down of the joint family system in India, but there are still many families who still swear by the institution. The joint family system gradually started disappearing mostly due to migration of people from towns and villages to cities in search of employment. Another important reason was the gradual increase of unproductive dependents on the family, leading to financial and other constraints. The net effect of all these is the division or partition of joint and ancestral properties.

It is amazing to see how often well-educated, independent professionals have to consult their parents before accepting a job offer or traveling abroad. At the core of Indian culture lies an innate respect for parents and other elders in the family, and usually no major decision is taken without consulting them. Parents often live with their married children, typically with a son. There is really no concept of a grown-up son or daughter 'moving out of the house' unless it is the result of circumstances like a job in a different city.

Family is essentially made of those people who look after, who play a crucial role in our upbringing and who teach us such lessons in life, which can never be learned through any textbook. We assimilate the basics of discipline and responsibilities from our family relationships. The various characters in the family, imbibe in us the true meaning of family. Let's try to see who are these characters and how they reveal to us the real meaning of family.

Building Strong Ties Within A Family

Family ties are very important in India. Earlier days the concept of joint families or many members of a family living under the same roof came into practice largely due to economic considerations. Later it became a social norm. Multiple families shared the same household, kitchen, bathrooms and even professions. In a joint family, businesses were a joint set up and families practiced the same trade for generations.

In India, people learn the essential themes of cultural life within the bosom of a family. In most of the country, the basic units of society are the patrilineal family unit and wider kinship groupings. The most widely desired residential unit is the joint family, ideally consisting of three or four patrilineally related generations, all living under one roof, working, eating, worshiping, and cooperating together in mutually beneficial social and economic activities. Patrilineal joint families include men related through the male line, along with their wives and children. Most young women expect to live with their husband's relatives after marriage, but they retain important bonds with their natal families.

The culture and society of a nation is very much affected by the way the families live in that country. Family life is important. People become what they become because of what the family life teaches them. A family unit is capable of teaching a person more than any other group of people in his life. There are certain steps which should be taken to ensure the stability of relations and stronger ties among the members of a family.

You should avoid all such practices which can create problems in your family life.

There is no doubt about the importance of family unit existence in this world. As the world is changing today at a very fast pace, it is important that you put some effort into building a family life for yourself and your family. You may need to put a lot of effort in at some stages. But the efforts you make will result in a family with stronger bondage with each other. This will in turn enrich your experience with your family. Living a life which is full of love and care is a dream for all of us. It is very important to everyone.

There is no doubt about it that the family unit is the most important unit from the point of view of demography. It is a very important social and cultural concept. The way family members behave with each other affects the way a culture or a society flourishes. All these factors lead us to the conclusion that family unit is a very important. We must keep on assessing ourselves as to whether we are able to provide our share of responsibility in making our family a happier one or not. We also should assess our family members and talk to them about making the family ties even stronger. We must create understanding between the members of the family. If the people belonging to a family understand each other, the ties of the family will automatically be stronger.

Spend time with Each Other

To build strong ties with in your family you need to spend time with each other. It may not be possible for every one to stay together at all the times. But there can be at least one time of the day when all of you can sit together to chat casually with each other., for example, many eastern families have dinner together so that every one can discuss whatever is going on in life with the other members of the family. This is important. In this way you are able to keep each other informed about what you are doping and what they plan to do.

You can build your relationship as a family and make it stronger by giving the other members of the family both the space to breathe as well as the closeness and trust to feel comfortable. Mutual trust and interdependence is a must to create the ideal family unit. Although you need to be together more often than not, it is very important that every member of the family is given due privacy and breathing space. This will result in a better atmosphere in the family. All the members of the family will love these ties as these ties will help them whenever they are in need but they will still have their own space. It is important that we respect each other's privacy. This is the only way we can bring all the family members closer to each other.

Similarly there are certain other practices which can help in building a stronger family unit. You need to give your family members a level of confidence as well as lots of unconditional love. These factors add life and zest to your family life. Family unit is a very important unit and it plays a very important role in shaping up your personality. This unit must be given all due importance.

Family Relationships

Family relationships are based on the strongest bond you could probably forge, they are equally sensitive. The bond of parents with children, of children with their siblings, among extended family, are all important family relationships that need to be nurtured with time and effort. It is this lack of time and effort that results in, sometimes minor and sometimes major, family relationship problems. The meaning of family gets altered, the strong bond weakens, and if not taken care of, withers away into nothingness. Here, we try and understand this sensitive bond and the problems it endures, and ways of strengthening family relationships.

Understanding Family Relationship Problems

Taking Family Relationships for Granted

"The great gift of family life is to be intimately acquainted with people you might never even introduce yourself to, had life not done it for you".

—Kendall Hailey

The biggest problem that affects family relationships is the fact that they are taken for granted. 'She is my mother, so she will cook for me', 'He is my father, so he will pay for me', 'He is my brother, so he will stick up for me', etc. are all thought processes that signify you are taking your bond for granted, and that your meaning of family is that only they should be there for you, irrespective of whether or not you are there for them. It also signifies a lack of respect and value for all that you are being given without being asked for anything in return. But remember, every relationship is one of give and take. Though parents' love is known to be unconditional and that is what you have been taught all your life, there is something that they expect out of you. It may not be materialistic, but just simple appreciation of the fact that they do so much for you. Similar is the case with your siblings.

Taking any relationship for granted, be it one with your family, one with your partner, or with a friend, is one of the biggest mistakes all of us make at some point in life. Every time such an instance occurs, your relationship will be affected, and weaken over time. So show your appreciation every once in a while, say it or express it with a gesture, but do it. It keeps the love alive and the relationship strong.

Not Being There for Each Other

The second biggest problem that family relationships have to endure is the lack of time for each other. You are probably so caught up with your work, your social life, or your self, that you have no time to bond with and understand the importance of family. This is in fact, a very serious problem, because there have been disastrous cases of children having the worst childhood, simply because their parents did not spend enough time with them. They grow up with bitter feelings in their hearts, and blame every negative instance, or attribute that they possess, to the fact that there was no one to teach them the difference between the right and the wrong. Some children have the maturity to understand the issue and deal with it, others don't. You definitely don't want to be one of those parents.

Also remember, that if you don't teach your little ones the value of spending time together as a family, as they grow up, they won't have enough time for you. That means when you are ready to listen to them, take care of them, and simply be there for them, they will probably have found another shoulder to cry on and another person to share their happiness with. This is probably when you will feel most regretful. Even spouses face the problem of lack of time for each other, and this results in serious relationship issues, such as emotional cheating, infidelity, and divorce. The fact that you promised to share your lives together, no matter what, is completely forgotten, and a bitter battle of words and emotions takes its place.

Not Communicating with Each Other

According to Letty Cottin Pogrebin

"When a family is free of abuse and oppression, it can be the place where we share our deepest secrets and stand the most exposed, a place where we learn to feel distinct without being "better," and sacrifice for others without losing ourselves".

Lack of communication is another problem amongst families. This may be due to the lack of time, or due to a particular fear of communicating with the family. For instance, kids are scared of their parents because of a fear that has been inculcated into them, which is why if they happen to do something wrong, they don't tell their parents, as they expect to be severely berated, labeled and blamed for their doing. Spouses don't communicate with each other for the same reason. Parents don't tell their children what they feel for the fear of causing bitterness in their hearts. Yes, family relationships are sensitive, but they are definitely stronger than your fears. You have only your family to back you up in tough times, and sometimes, even the tiniest amount of support from your little one can strengthen you enough to tackle the world.

Similarly, forging a bond with your kids so that they can easily come up and talk to you about any of their problems is important. This does not mean that you do not tell them when they are doing something wrong. There is a fine line between respect and fear that kids have for their parents. Command this respect, and leave no room for fear by opening up to them, and having them open up to you.

Not Saying 'I Love You' Enough

The phrase 'I Love You' has a lot of value, in spite of the fact that it is loosely used nowadays for any Tom, Dick and Harry. The difference is when you say it, you have to mean it. Internally in a family, saying 'I love you' to each other, and meaning it every time you say it, is very important. You probably don't realize it, but it strengthens not only your bonds, but also your own self. We're all humans, and all we want is a little love, and this expression of love from our family makes a whole world of a difference to the people we are. If not verbally, say it by means of a gesture, like cooking up a great family dinner, taking your kids to the new amusement park in town, giving in to their demands every once in a while, spending time with your spouse with a quiet dinner, or anything you think is an expression of your love for your family.

"Good family life is never an accident but always an achievement by those who share it".

—James H.S. Bossard

With all said and done, family relationships can strengthen you, but sometimes weaken you too. Sometimes, your loyalty to your family is so great, that you are unable to make certain decisions that you know would benefit yourself. Sacrifices are not always termed as a good idea, because it is a fact that you cannot make someone else happy unless you are happy yourself. In some cases, it is necessary to separate from the family that is weakening you, to find yourself, and then return to nurture and recreate family relationships.

However, just remember the very important bottom line here. Not every human being is blessed with a family, and those of you who are, carve out some important family time, put in your efforts to nurture your relationships with every family member, have some good old family fun, and you will find yourself blessed, strong, and capable of tackling any problem that life throws at you.

Strong Family Relationship Makes Healthy Society

A family in any society consists of an inherited group of people who are related with by birth or marriage. It is a relation between parents and children, relations between spouses or between grand parents and grandson. Good family relationships are vital for the development of child's personality. Developing healthy relation is in the hand of family members. Their habits, way of working, problem solving approach all together makes a home haven or hell. All of us want home to be a place where we can relax and be ourselves, and recover from the conflicts of the external world.

There are different types of family structure in Indian culture. In past, there were joint families because members were involved in home business or farming. They live together and jointly work in specialized area to generate income for family. There are many benefits for joint family. Children can get better environment. Many members are there to take care in case of any problem. There were less security problems.

Members enjoy their festival with full enthusiasm. Still there are happy joint families. But in modern times, nuclear families are developing. Sons or daughters have to leave parent's house for job and they have separate unit. They have to face many problems but somehow they manage because it is necessary for earning money. There is some freedom in nuclear family. Individual can take his own decision to make their future bright. They can ignore some orthodox belief.

Family relationships never lose colors. Though there may be some disagreement between family members. It is very imperative that everyone must remain trustworthy to all relatives and spend lots of time with them. It will augment relationship and can avoid major family conflicts. In order to solve family relationship problems, everyone need to go off his consciousness up a level and take a deeper look at his values, beliefs, and his characterization of terms like loyalty and family. Family member must share their problems and take major decision in discussion with each member of the family.

Families who have high moral values have prestigious status in society and they are the ideal for those people in society who are confused or did not learn good ethics in teenage. Living with unity and following ethics, families can contribute to eradicate societal problems. It is observed that in hi tech world, people do not have any relation with neighbor. All are too busy in their work. They don't have time to expand social relationship. So, there is a need to develop strong relationship by following family traditions which provides a good base for bringing the family closer together. We all must step forward to unite family members, respect elders to create an atmosphere of affection.

Concept of Family

The social sciences include many concepts that are basic to the understanding of the subject matter. Some of these concepts are defined differently and measured differently by social researchers, such as those concerning socioeconomic status. Others are defined and measured in a fairly consistent way across studies and over time. These latter concepts usually follow previous usages either because of research tradition or because of limitations in the collection of data, race perhaps being an example.

A key concept in the social sciences, and especially in demography and sociology, is that of the family. The family is generally regarded as a major social institution and a locus of much of a person's social activity. It is a social unit created by blood, marriage, or adoption, and can be described as nuclear (parents and children) or extended (encompassing other relatives).

It is generally assumed today that the modern family has undergone significant transformations in its structure. We are told that societal changes have contributed to a sharp reduction in the percentage of classical "typical" families, principally "nuclear" families. Replacing these, we are made to understand, are childless families, one-parent families, other family configurations, and quasi-family units based on non-marital cohabitation. This argument of the decline has been advanced for a number of decades, but little research has been conducted to test the premise. Bane (1976) disagreed with that conclusion and pointed out that family sizes were getting smaller and mobility was splitting up some families, but the family remained as a functional social institution.

The main contention of this study is that analysis of changing family patterns is distorted by the definition of the family that is generally used and the way relevant data are collected. In support of this contention, two different approaches will be used to gauge family status, and the two will be compared. First, the standard demographic approach to defining and measuring the family concept will be reviewed. Second, the genealogical view of the family will be examined. A comparison will then be made of the two perspectives and their consequences for understanding the nature of changes in the modern family.

Standard Demographic Approach

The family is generally recognized as an element of a broader kinship network that links ancestors and descendants of a person. Most published statistics on the family are based on census or household survey questions and responses.

Persons who might be considered part of a family but do not reside at the same residential address are not included in demographic data. They may be part of a family at another address or they may be living alone or in group quarters (housing for a substantial number of unrelated individuals). This is the case even if such persons live close by (maybe even next door) and/or visit or otherwise regularly communicate (by phone or mail) with their family of origin. Additionally, because of census and survey residence rules, college students living in a college community and some long-term workers at remote places are excluded from the family group even if their intention is to return to the family's residence after school or work is completed. In other words, the family definition is controlled by the household definition, where households describe current or potential housing markets.

In fact, some persons who meet the standard demographic definition of the family and are included may have little association with other family members in the same residence. For example, they may have different schedules of sleep, work, or other activities, and they may not communicate by phone or mail. Their inclusion in the family is pro forma and based only on the given family definition. These facts raise questions about the boundaries of the standard demographic definition of the family and its consequences for interpretations of how family structure might be changing over time.

Genealogical Approach

Genealogy is the study of family structural history, drawing basically on demographic data sources such as censuses, birth and death certificates, immigration records, and other administrative records. The aim of genealogical research is to construct a family tree of ancestors and dependents of a key person. The tree can be limited in its extension to cousins and other persons remotely related, but typically the attempt is to be inclusive of related kin. Some genealogists prefer the term "family history" to "genealogy" because the latter term implies a genetic connection that may not be real because of questionable paternity and because it would not apply to adoptive persons.

Many types of information can be included in family trees, but the pattern of relationships is not dependent on residential locations. Residence can be one item of information for each individual in the tree, along with such items as dates of birth and death, place of birth, occupation, and other personal markers. One can examine a family tree and extract a family structure using a variety of family definitions, based on how extensive one wishes to consider the family.

Family trees typically distinguish between living and dead members of the family, so that several family definitions can be applied to only living members. In this sense, the genealogical approach to looking at family structure provides for a broader range of family forms than is possible from the demographic approach. Thus, one can describe a couple and their offspring, living together or not; a multi-generation family, living together or not; as well as extended family groupings.

Genealogies have not been incorporated into family research very much. Smith (1987) indicates that obtaining any type of kin count or structure (and, by implication, residence-based families) "is often difficult or impossible .... Genealogical research, even when done with the aid of computers, is labour- intensive and requires extensive archival data." The use of genealogies in demographic research has been heavily oriented to estimating population size, as well as fertility and mortality of communities.

Because sets of family trees are often hard to come by, the broader kinship network that the family tree describes can be obtained by having survey respondents reconstruct the history of a family's changing structure by tracing the family's evolution from the marriage date of a couple to the point where only one member of the family group is still living.

The family is the basic unit of society. Families exist in all sizes and configurations and are essential to the health and survival of the individual members and to society as a whole. As the primary group for the individual, the family serves as a buffer between the needs of the individual and the demands and expectations of society. The role of the family is to meet the needs of society.

The family is a unity of interacting persons related by ties of marriage, birth or adoption, whose central purpose is to create and maintain a common culture which promotes the physical, mental, emotional and social development of each of its members.

In today's society, Friedman defines the family as composed of two or more people who are emotionally involved with each other and live in close geographical proximity.

The family provides a set of functions important to the needs of the individual members and to society as a whole. The family provides the individual with the necessary environment for development and interactions; it also provides new and socialized members for society.

Family Structure

Traditional Family

It is composed of a father, a mother and their children. These people, married and living together in one house make up the nuclear family. Relatives, such as aunts, uncles, cousins and grandparents, who may or may not live with the nuclear family are part of the extended family. This family group usually live in close geographic proximity to members of the extended family, who provided a sense of stability and belonging.

Single Parent Families

Single parents may be never married, separated, divorced or widowed. Most often, the single parent is divorced or widowed, but increasing numbers of never married men and women are choosing to become parents.

Alternate Family Structure

Cohabiting Families

It includes those individuals who choose to live together for a variety of reasons: relationships, financial need and changing values. Although the single person is not living with others, he or she is a part of a family of origin, usually has a social network with significant others. Majority of single adults living alone are found in to age groups: the young adult who has achieved independence and enters the work force and the elderly person, left alone through death of a spouse.

Concept of Family Settlement

Family settlement is an instrument to achieve a larger purpose i.e. peace and harmony in the family. The object of an arrangement is to protect the family from long drawn out litigation and to bring goodwill in the family. The parties must held settlement which is in the interest of the family and which avoid disputes between the members of the family.

Family settlement should be a *bonafide* one so as to resolve family dispute, it must be fair and equitable division or allotment of properties between the various members of the family, it must be voluntary and not induced by fraud, coercion or influence, it needs to be signed by all the co-sharers.

Family settlement or arrangement is an instrument effecting distribution of family assets, wherein a family organizes within itself the shares of properties to which each party therein is entitled.

It is a complete settlement, providing how assets are to be valued, how they are to be divided, how a scheme for dividing some of the specified companies has to be prepared and who has to do this work. Some 'give and take' is necessary for the purpose of arriving at a settlement, a partition by metes and bounds may not always be possible.

Such settlements have to be viewed a little differently from ordinary contracts and their internal mechanism for working out the settlement should not be lightly disturbed.

In the catena of judgment, the open court as well as the subordinate court heavily rely upon family settlements entered between the parties and favour the settlements. Every family settlement is not necessary to be registered under S.17 of the Indian Registration Act. The Oral settlement agreed upon can be reduced into writing herein shall supersede any and all prior settlements/agreements between the parties.

Family settlements help in resolving any dispute at a preliminary stage and saving both time and cost of long pending litigations in the court of law. These disputes also hampers the goodwill of the company in the market.

Such kind of disputes related to public sector enterprises directly effects the general public at large. These disputes should be avoided keeping in mind the interest of general public.

Importance of Family

Family is inseparable part of our daily life. It helps us in improving our overall personality. It also helps us in shaping our life. It teaches us the value of love, care,, affection, self-confidence and truthfulness and provides us tools and suggestions which are essential to get success in life.

Family is a place where you can be yourself. It is a place where you're admitted for what you are, thus there are no terms and conditions.

This is where you're completely tension free and everyone is there to help you. Family supports you when you are surrounded by troubles. It helps you endure through tough times and bring joy and pleasure into life.

Decency is extremely important in the communication of everyday life. It helps us make strong bond with others and make us come across as a very intelligent, likable and gentle person. Everyone loves to be in a group of such person. Family helps bring politeness into our life which is essential to lead a happy life.

One of the most imperative aims of our life is to put up a successful and highly rewarding profession. Our families help us in creating a strong future. It gives us important suggestion about different career potential. It not only guides us in selecting the best but also financially helps us to cover the expenditures related to education and other daily needs. Thus it helps us in building a good future.

The importance of family is undoubtedly realized when one went to vacation or celebrate an occasion without family members. It will be extremely hard to holiday or to celebrate an occasion without being surrounded by family members. At that time possibly we realize that how important they are to us. At that time, we came to know about the significance of our families.

Today, most people do not realize the importance of family. They choose to spend most of their time with their friends. But when they're surrounded by problems, it was their family that helped them in thrashing down their problems. At the time, when even our best friends snub to help us, it was our family that came to help us. So, it is very important for each and every individual to give significance to their families above anything else and enjoy spending time with family members; please note that Quality time not Quantity time.

A family is a miniature replica of the society in itself. Its importance lies in the fact, that it cements a nation or a society together by providing it a past, a present and a future.

A family unit is the unit which builds up a person's personality. How you behave and what you become in life is very much dependent on your family life. Psychologists believe that a child learns the most from his or her family life. The way your family members deal with you has a life long effect on your personality. Keeping in view all these facts the importance of your family life cannot be denied. Family unit happens to be the most important part of your life till you grow up.

The children are usually closer to their parents and their siblings as compared to any other person in the world. As the children grow up they find good friends, spouses, their own kids and colleagues to share their lives with. Although time brings this change but the importance of family remains there. The children who have a sound family background and who belong to a family with strong family ties are almost always happier. Thus one cannot deny the importance of family life.

Role in Personality Development

The life with your family is very important it plays a major role in your development into the person you become. The goals you set for yourself in your life are very much dependent on the life you have with your family. Those children who belong to the families which have a rich education background tend to learn more. They are interested in learning more and thus it is easy for their parents to get them educated.

Similarly, for example, children who belong to a family from which a few of the people are in the field of professional sports, the kids tend to have an interest in sports and they also plan to go into the same field. The sons and daughters of stars from the film industries usually plan to follow the suit of their parents. Thus, it is the effect of your family life which guides you to decide what profession you want to do as an adult.

Family life is also important in the sense that it gives you your basic strength as a person. The people who have a smooth and well settled family life are generally less scared of life. Those who are a part of a broken family are generally less confident. These people always expect the worst in life. This is a general state of mind which results in building up of a negative personality. Family life is also important to people as it is the part of our life which has more effect on us compared to any other part of our life. The way a mother treats her kids is actually the deciding factor of what those kids will be like as human beings when they grow up.

As important as family life is, it is a big problem in the world of today where the family units are breaking up more often and the divorce rates have grown very high. The higher divorce rates result in more broken families that in turn lead to a lot more number of children who suffer through this insecurity in their early ages and as a result they are not that stable. These people tend to have a variety of fears and insecurity.

They do not have the courage to face their life. As family life plays a very important role in shaping you as a person, lack of security in your family life makes you a bit unstable as a person.

In today's world a big social problem is that the family unit is not being considered as important by the people as it used to be. In many parts of the world the time period for which people live together as a family is shrinking. The family life adds a sense of responsibility in your personality which lacks in those people who have not had a very nice family life.

Functions of the Family

With the changing of time various external and internal forces have acted upon family and brought a great change both in the structure and functions of family. The changes particularly in the functions of family have reduced the importance of family considerably and also have drawn a line between traditional family and modern family. *The changes which have occurred in the functions of family in modern times are examined below*:

Changes in the primary functions: Modern Family in most of the societies fails to exercise its traditional control in regulating sexual behavior. With the development of science and more particularly genetic engineering test tubes babies are born as a result bringing changes in the traditional reproduction function of family. The childcare functions of the family have been shifted to certain external agencies like hospital, maternity homes, nurseries, kindergartens etc.

The modern family fails to give traditional protection for the aged, diseased, mentally retarded, physically handicapped etc. The modern family is gaining increased attention in socialization of it's newly members. It is giving more attention to the all round development of child personality. Modern youngsters prefer to establish their own house for independent living.

Changes in the Secondary functions: Now-a-days, family is no longer self-sufficient. It is more a consumer unit than a producing center. Whatever functions the family was performing as an economic unit have been shifted to market economy. Many external agencies are performing the economic functions, which the family used to perform in the past.

The religious functions of the family have also undergone a great change. The religious practices have lost their traditional importance. More secular attitude and outlook is spreading day by day. This secular outlook has considerably reduced the importance of religious function family.

The recreational functions of the family have been shared by the external agencies like movies, hotels, parks clubs, youth organisations and other centers of recreation. These recreation centers are highly commercialised. Thus, the recreational function which was considered as one of the thread of cohesion has lost its significance.

In spite of the above changes that have occurred in the functions of family in modern time, the family is still persisting as one of the most important social institutions. This is because the traditional functions of family have been modified than lost.

Family Life in Today's World

A healthy family unit is very important for every human being. Our family members are those persons to whom we are related by blood. People of one family usually share the place they live in; they share their surnames. A major chunk of time of their lives is shared with each other as well. Family unit is very important to people as it is the basic tool that shapes you as a person.

Your personality development is very much dependent upon it. If a person has seen a secure family life with lots of love and affection, he or she will be more aggressive and positively driven towards life. Your family is the group of people you can trust the most. These are the people who add meaning to your life. A person can survive through very tough times if he or she has a supportive family. All these factors and many more make your family life important to you. Psychologically, those people are stronger and better equipped to face the ups and downs of life who have a nice family with strong ties with each other.

The family unit is the most important social unit in most of the countries of the world. Every culture promotes the importance of family. These people who share their lives with us are important to us. These people, our family members, add meaning to our lives. Family is considered to be the most important unit from the point of view of demography. Every country tries to promote the concept of a strong family unit as this is a major social strength of human beings. From the historic past, the family unit has been considered the most important part of anyone's life.

Today's world is a changed world. It is no more like the world we had just five decades back. It is much more innovative. The technology is much more advanced now. People, as well as the ways of life, have changed. The improvement in the field of science has worked wonders in more than one dimension of human life.

As a result, the pace of life is now much faster. This fast pace has hit the family unit directly. In many countries the average number of years a family used to spend together before the partial disintegration is shrinking. In most countries now, people leave their parents' home earlier than they did in the past.

In today's world the importance of the family unit has increased as much as the unit has been damaged by the faster pace of life. People living in different countries now understand it much better that there are a lot of benefits and good things attached to a sound family unit existence in the society. The family unit structure in a country makes the people more responsible. As every one is related to every one else in a home, they help each other in doing everything together. The love people feel for their family members helps them ignore their shortcomings. This is the origin of peace and harmony. When you start caring about others more than you care about yourself, peace is bound to be there.

Importance of Family Life

Although people understand the importance of family life today, the major issue is that the number of family units which are happy with each other is decreasing all around the globe. This problem is not related to any particular nation or people from any one culture. The whole world is going through this problem these days. People are suffering from different psychological disorders of high intensity because they do not get the much required love, attention and affection which comes so easily with the stable family unit. If we want to reduce such problems from our world today, we need to understand the practical importance of the family unit. We need the family ties today more than ever.

A family unit is undoubtedly the most important unit in human social life. Our family members are the people to whom we are related due to our blood ties. The people who belong to one family share the place in which they live, as well as surnames and the experience of their lives. Family units are important they play a very prominent role in building the personality of a person. Everyone experiences family life. For some this experience is very good and it brings positism to their lives, while others suffer just because the family unit to which they belong is not the one which can give them much-needed love and affection. What you become in your life and how you behave is very much dependent upon your family life. Thus we can easily say that family life is very important to everyone.

Children from broken families suffer a lot. They are not that confident when they move on and face the world. They often expect that the world will not treat them in a fair manner. This psychological complexity develops due to the lack of the care and protection that only a healthy family unit can provide.

In the world of today, we can say that family life is even more important. As the number of broken families is on a rise, so is the rate of crime in our societies. The kids who suffer in their childhood because their families lack in some aspect may not be able to become very good human beings. Thus we have to fight against the trend due to which the family ties are dissolving fast and blood relations are losing their meaning to people.

Although, all the different cultures and countries promote family life, there are very peculiar differences in the way people behave in their families in different parts of the world. Broadly speaking, we can divide the world in two parts. One part is the highly developed part of the world where some say the family unit is losing its grip over the society. The other part of the world is the part in which people are still trying to retain the roots. They are still related to their family and the family bondage is as sacred to them today as it was many years back. These two extremes exist very clearly in the world.

Cracks in Family Units

In recent years, trends in family life have changed a bit all around the globe. All cultures promote the family life and all of these cultures appreciate close relationships between the members of a family. But in the recent past it has been apparent that family life is not that important to many people now. This is very important overall. If you look at the demographic figures of any country, the most important figure which is considered to be the most relevant indicator of peace and harmony existing in a society is the existence of family units.

The family unit is the most important group of people in anyone's life, especially when you are a kid. People learn a lot from the family environment, and the ties which exist between the members of a family are responsible in building a person. The way, he or she, will behave as an adult is very much a result of the family life experience. It is a big social problem that now our family unit is not very important to people. The importance in the society is still there; it is even more than yesterday. But to some individuals family is not as important as it used to be. Almost all the cultures and societies are experiencing these cracks in the family unit. We need to understand how damaging these cracks can be to our culture.

The disadvantages of not having the strong ties with your family members can only be understood by taking a look at the advantages which strong family ties give to a society and to a culture. In different parts of the world, the way families live is different. In the more developed regions of the world it is no longer the typical and traditional family. It is a bit different than that now. People are responsible for each other, but to a much lesser extent. This results in a lack of sense of responsibilities, and those individuals can damage our society.

The cracks in a family unit can affect the culture and society. It has been observed that crime rate is higher in the countries where people do not consider their families to be very important to them. In such cultures people usually start working for themselves as soon as they can. This is a good thing at one end, as due to this the country achieves economic stability. On the other hand this practice is dangerous as people become too independent and there remains no meaning in the concept of family ties.

This is the time we should question ourselves what the effects are of loosened family ties to our society and culture. When you look into this matter in detail you observe that people may have earned a bit more space for themselves by being independent and by being able to earn more, but there is generally a lack of satisfaction in the world of today. As you start believing in not doing things for others and doing everything for yourself, you start losing the zest for life.

The cracks in family units may develop due to the lack of understanding between the family members. It is not healthy. You must talk to each other; you must discuss and decide what should be done. The goal for all the family members should be to bring your family even closer.

Survival Plan for Family

You must ensure that as a parent even if you are no longer there and you are not able to support your children and spouse due to your death, there must be arrangements so that your family is in the position to live without you. The survival of your family in your absence must be planned by you.

There are two major aspects which you should consider in this regard. First one of those is how your family will survive financially without you. If you are the only bread winner for your family, how will your kids and your spouse survive with out you? You need to plan for such situations.

You must invest in such things which can pay back in time for your kids when they will need money to go to college or to set up some venture. You must consider this factor that your family members will need money to survive if something happens to you and you are no longer there. Or, if you are simply not able to earn something to support them. You must have a plan keeping the worst in your mind.

The other important thing which must be considered is the emotional aspect. If you are no longer there, how will your kids react? If you are a father to them they will need you for more than one reason. Fathers are a protection for their kids from the outside world. If you are a mother your kids need you today and they will need you even after half a century. It cannot be easy for the kids to lose their mother or their father. This will disturb them very much. It can be very difficult for your kids to survive without you.

You must be very open to them in this regard. You must prepare them for the worst. Although you do not need to scare them or make them think that you are planning to die, you must make them realistic enough to think that even if the people whom you love very dearly are no more there, life goes on. The people who die, or leave, are no longer there. But those who are living have to keep living, and that they should do so happily. Make your kids understand this fact.

Although, all cultures promote family life, the pace of life is becoming faster with each passing day and the world is changing with every passing minute, the family unit is becoming even more important. We understand the importance of family in a better way because now the percentage of broken families is on a rise.We can now see very clearly and understand the damages brought to society by the lack of the existence of family units in our cultures.

Still as the world is becoming more and more materialistic, it is difficult for people to continue spending their lives in the traditional ways. This is creating a lot of problems for everyone. The peace and harmony a nation experiences due to the presence of strong family ties are no longer there. Everyone has his or her responsibility towards his or her family and you need to have a plan in place if your no longer there to support your family. You need to give it a lot of importance.

The family unit is a community of persons where moral values are taught and the spiritual and cultural heritage of society are passed on.

The family is also essential in ensuring people are strong in their commitments, and promote both social responsibility and solidarity.

Given its vital importance the family has priority over society and the state. "Every social model that intends to serve the good of man must not overlook the centrality and social responsibility of the family."

Invoking the principle of subsidiarity the text affirms that public authorities must not take away from the family tasks that it can carry out by itself, or in association with other families.

Marriage and Family

The arranged marriage is another practice that illustrates the importance Indians place on the family. A majority of marriages in India are arranged by families and several people are involved in the decision-making process. As popular belief goes, a marriage tied with many knots will not come undone. This is in complete contrast to the American culture where only two people tie the knot and experience has indeed shown us that it can be undone more easily. The divorce rate in America is much higher than in India.

With regards to marriage, the family is founded on the free choice of spouses to unite themselves. The institution of marriage, while it is regulated by human institutions and laws, is, even more importantly, a partnership established by God and endowed with its own laws.

Marriage's divine character, and the natural right to marriage, places limits on what society can legitimately do in regulating marriage. The dignity and specific characteristics of marriage must be safeguarded. The fundamental characteristics of marriage are: totality, in which the spouses give themselves to each other mutually; unity, created by the union of the couple; indissolubility and fidelity, which a definitive mutual self-giving requires; and fruitfulness, to which marriage is open.

An important part of marriage is the transmission of life through the birth and nurturing of children. Nevertheless, procreation is not the only reason for marriage and that when a couple is unable to have children the value of communion between the spouses remains.

Love within Marriage

The role of love within marriage and the family is another theme dealt with in the text. The family is a place where communion is brought about, and thanks to love each person is recognized, accepted and respected.

Love is essential for human beings. But marital love is more than just emotions or sexual expression. It is a full and total gift, marked by unity and fidelity. Moreover, the nature of conjugal love requires the marital union to be stable. The introduction of civil divorce "has fueled a relativistic vision of the marriage bond" and can be termed "a plague on society."

For those couples who have divorced and remarried the Church does not abandon them. "She prays for them and encourages them in the difficulties that they encounter in the spiritual life, sustaining them in faith and hope." Nevertheless, they cannot receive the Eucharist until they obtain reconciliation through the sacrament of penance.

The text also rejects attempts to redefine marriage through the introduction of new concepts that see gender as dependent merely on social and cultural factors. "Physical, moral and spiritual difference and complementarities are oriented towards the goods of marriage and the flourishing of family life." It is therefore incongruous to demand that same-sex unions receive the status of marriage. At the same time, homosexuals to be fully respected in their human dignity, but also encouraged to exercise chastity.

Marriage is more than a simple agreement to live together but is a social instrument and the principal means for helping each person to grow in an integral manner.

Uppringing of Children

The family's function in bringing up children, "a completely original and irreplaceable role." The parents' love is placed at the service of their children and animates all educational activity. Parents have both a right and a duty to educate their children, which the state should respect. The text also insists that to carry out this function parents have a right to found educational institutions and that the state should provide economic support to these non-public schools.

The primary role of the parents in education is particularly the case when it comes to religious and moral formation. But it must also be respected in the area of sexual education. The importance of linking sexual education with an instruction in moral norms and the human values. Children's dignity must also be protected, first of all by protecting their right to be born within a real family.

Communication Problems in the Family

Problems do not erupt out of nothing. They most often are a result of ego clashes and sometimes of denial. Some of the most common factors that lead to communication problems in families are:

(1) Lack of Time for Each Other: Not so much of a shocker, is it? The lack of time for members of the family is invariably a reason that leads to communication problems in families. Makes sense if you really think about it. With the fast paced lives that we seem to be leading these days, it hardly comes as a surprise that the lack of time for each other is one of the key aspects leading to family problems. Parents hardly have the time for children, spouses too, don't have much time for each other, it's almost heart breaking to see family's lose their closeness due to reasons that would seem almost trivial.

(2) Lack of Patience: This is yet another largely contributing factor leading towards family communication problems. A lack of patience can be one of the biggest downfalls when it comes to the levels of closeness of most families too. A snappy parent, or even a snappy child can be quite a

hassle to handle under certain circumstances. The easiest way out in situations like that then is ignoring the person in question, because it is a much simpler escape route.

(3) Lack of Discipline: This is the worst problem in terms of communication problems with children. A badly behaved child could ruin the peace of a family, like a tornado waiting to happen. What's worse is, while parents may have some semblance of control when the child is little, this could go way out of hand when he/she gets older, thus leading to a constantly disharmonious atmosphere within the family.

Solving Family Communication Problems

If there are problems, there are solutions, that is a given. If worked on the right way, even these problems can be put to rest. The best solutions for family problems are as follows:

(1) *Be Patient*: If the lack of patience is one of the causes of communication problems, very evidently the solution is developing the virtue of patience. Hearing out what the children have to say on a certain matter, or even consulting the significant other in issues where their consent is required is one way to start.

(2) *Spend Time Together*: Not being in on each other's lives can vastly cause communication problems too. It is therefore essential to have quality family time with one another. Bear in mind though, while being in on the other person's life is a good thing, it shouldn't border on interference in any way. An overdose of time spent with each other too can lead to problems, so this must be worked on with a certain balance.

(3) *Stay Focused and Don't Assume*: This one goes more for the seniors of a family. It would be natural to see juvenile behavior being displayed by the younger members of a household, but it is up to the elders, be it parents or siblings, to control the atmosphere and keep it calm. A hot headed adult can make situations worse. Also, being presumptuous about the behavior and attitude of the younger ones can lead to problems, so rather than working on assumptions, talk things out. A comfortable environment will help allow truth from them too. This will act well in favor of the family.

Most of what was given above were some of the most common problems that most families are faced with. Working on them could help to a great extent. At the end of the day, it is important to maintain the best relations possible with your family, because if not for family, there is nobody else to act as a real support system to you.

Communication Barriers in Relationships

Communication is the process of transferring information from one person to the other through the medium of language and/or gestures. So then, communication is a two way process. But for a successful communication to take place, there have to be certain factors fulfilled. Without these factors, the communication process is incomplete and does not fulfill what it set out to be. It is, therefore, a good idea to be acquainted with the different barriers to communication in relationships.

Barriers, as in the factors that prevent a successful communication from taking place. In the following article, we will take you through the different communication barriers that cloud relationships and prevent them from being successful.

Barriers to Effective Communication

If you look at any communication process, you'll find that there are several factors that work towards completing it. What are the factors that work towards completing a communication process? These would include the sender, the receiver, the message, the medium and the feedback.

Technically, there could be problems in some or all of these factors which could lead to a failure in the completion of the communication process. It is on the basis of these that several barriers to effective communication in relationships come about.

Communication in Relation to the Sender and Receiver

Why is an entire section dedicated only to the people involved in the communication process? This is because, it has been found that it is usually the sender and the receiver who contribute to the barriers. What are the barriers to communication in relationships that can develop between the sender and receiver?

(1) Inability to Listen : One of the main barriers in the communication process is that of listening, or the lack of it. People have the habit of not listening to what is being said with an objective of understanding it. They also keep interrupting when the other person speaks or do not let him complete what is being said by starting out on a tangent about themselves. Similarly, their gestures could also suggest that they are not interested in what is being said.

(2) Criticism : The other factor that acts as a strong barrier in the communication process is that of criticizing the other person. Putting the other down by labeling them with names or making their work seem unimportant or inconsequential can affect the communication process in no vague ways.

(3) Preconceived Notions : Another important factor that can act as a major barrier is when people have preconceived notions about the other. This can prevent them being open and a closed attitude is always a barrier to proper communication.

Nuclear Family vs Joint Family

Family is probably the most important faction of the society and also the most powerful social institution. There are several definitions and from the viewpoint of sociology, 'a social unit or institution of member's living together' is understood to be an apt definition. The meaning of family is moreover a connotation than a definition. The importance of family is highly pronounced as it is a building block of the society and apart from being a social faction and institution, having a family is one of the most important necessities of every human being.

Civilizations such as Roman, Vedic, Babylonian and Greek, had highly sophisticated and evolved societies due to the powerful institution of families. Indeed if we look back in time and take a look at the society back then, we always find that the institution of family had been highly sophisticated and powerful back then. In today's world, there are two predominant classifications of families, one, a nuclear family and joint family. The debate nuclear family vs joint family has been summarized in the following paragraphs.

Nuclear Family

- In modern times, a nuclear family is simply defined to be a social unit with a mother, father and children and a pet being the key constituents.
- The nuclear family, as defined above, has certain subsets, such as live-in relations, dating individuals, individuals living alone, or living with their pets.
- Nuclear family is principally based upon the emotion of parental love and sibling bonding and hence the structural functionalism (mechanism of relationships) is quite simple, yet the psychology involved becomes quite complex.

Joint Family

- The institute of joint family, constitutes all first-blood relatives living under the same roof. This includes all first cousins and their respective hierarchical generations.

- There are some subsets to the joint family such as an extended family (second cousins under one roof), nuclear family living with grandparents of the youngest generation. Polygamy and polyandry which is practiced in some parts of the world is also a joint family.
- In case of a joint family, the primary emotion is a general affectional bond between two generations and within the members of the generations.

4

MARRIAGE SYSTEM IN INDIAN SOCIETY

It is said that marriages are made in heaven and celebrated on earth. The popular belief is true to many extent, because it is a special bond shared between two souls, who tie the wedding knot after promising to be companions for a lifetime. It is the physical, mental and spiritual unison of two souls. It brings significant stability and substance to human relationships, which is otherwise incomplete.

I Indian cotent marriage encompasses a number of meanings, apart from being a legalized way of uniting two people. It bears a lot of social significance. This is primarily because in India, marriage has been considered a way to bring the families of two individuals closer. Since the ancient times, marriages have been celebrated as ceremonious occasions, just like the religious festivals, wherein a number of rituals and customs are followed. A number of ceremonies are observed before, during and after wedding.

In India, there is no greater event in a family than a wedding, dramatically evoking every possible social obligation, kinship bond, traditional value, impassioned sentiment, and economic resource. In the arranging and conducting of weddings, the complex permutations of Indian social systems best display themselves.

Marriage is deemed essential for virtually everyone in India. For the individual, marriage is the great watershed in life, marking the transition to adulthood. Generally, this transition, like everything else in India, depends little upon individual volition but instead occurs as a result of the efforts of many people. Even as one is born into a particular family without the exercise of any personal choice, so is one given a spouse without any personal preference involved.

Arranging a marriage is a critical responsibility for parents and other relatives of both bride and groom. Marriage alliances entail some redistribution of wealth as well as building and restructuring social realignments, and, of course, result in the biological reproduction of families.

Some parents begin marriage arrangements on the birth of a child, but most wait until later. In the past, the age of marriage was quite young, and in a few small groups, especially in Rajasthan, children under the age of five are still united in marriage. In rural communities, prepuberty marriage for girls traditionally was the rule. In the late twentieth century, the age of marriage is rising in villages, almost to the levels that obtain in cities. Legislation mandating minimum marriage ages has been passed in various forms over the past decades, but such laws have little effect on actual marriage practices.

Marriage Practices in India

Essentially, India is divided into two large regions with regard to Hindu kinship and marriage practices, the north and the south. Additionally, various ethnic and tribal groups of the central, mountainous north, and eastern regions follow a variety of other practices. These variations have been extensively described and analyzed by anthropologists, especially Irawati Karve, David G. Mandelbaum, and Clarence Maloney.

Broadly, in the Indo-Aryan-speaking north, a family seeks marriage alliances with people to whom it is not already linked by ties of blood. Marriage arrangements often involve looking far afield. In the Dravidian-speaking south, a family seeks to strengthen existing kin ties through marriage, preferably with blood relatives. Kinship terminology reflects this basic pattern. In the north, every kinship term clearly indicates whether the person referred to is a blood relation or an affinal relation; all blood relatives are forbidden as marriage mates to a person or a person's children.

In the south, there is no clear-cut distinction between the family of birth and the family of marriage. Because marriage in the south commonly involves a continuing exchange of daughters among a few families, for the married couple all relatives are ultimately blood kin. Dravidian terminology stresses the principle of relative age: all relatives are arranged according to whether they are older or younger than each other without reference to generation.

On the Indo-Gangetic Plain, marriages are contracted outside the village, sometimes even outside of large groups of villages, with members of the same caste beyond any traceable consanguineal ties. In much of the area, daughters should not be given into villages where daughters of the family or even of the natal village have previously been given. In most of the region, brother-sister exchange marriages (marriages linking a brother and sister of one household with the sister and brother of another) are shunned. The entire emphasis is on casting the marriage net ever-wider, creating new alliances. The residents of a single village may have in-laws in hundreds of other villages.

In most of North India, the Hindu bride goes to live with strangers in a home she has never visited. There she is sequestered and veiled, an outsider who must learn to conform to new ways. Her natal family is often geographically distant, and her ties with her consanguineal kin undergo attenuation to varying degrees.

In central India, the basic North Indian pattern prevails, with some modifications. For example, in Madhya Pradesh, village exogamy is preferred, but marriages within a village are not uncommon. Marriages between caste-fellows in neighboring villages are frequent. Brother-sister exchange marriages are sometimes arranged, and daughters are often given in marriage to lineages where other daughters of their lineage or village have previously been wed.

In South India, in sharp contrast, marriages are preferred between cousins (especially cross-cousins, that is, the children of a brother and sister) and even between uncles and nieces (especially a man and his elder sister's daughter). The principle involved is that of return—the family that gives a daughter expects one in return, if not now, then in the next generation. The effect of such marriages is to bind people together in relatively small, tight-knit kin groups. A bride moves to her in-laws' home--the home of her grandmother or aunt—and is often comfortable among these familiar faces. Her husband may well be the cousin she has known all her life that she would marry.

Many South Indian marriages are contracted outside of such close kin groups when no suitable mates exist among close relatives, or when other options appear more advantageous. Some sophisticated South Indians, for example, consider cousin marriage and uncle-niece marriage outmoded.

Rules for the remarriage of widows differ from one group to another. Generally, lower-ranking groups allow widow remarriage, particularly if the woman is relatively young, but the highest-ranking castes discourage or forbid such remarriage. The most strict adherents to the nonremarriage of widows are Brahmans. Almost all groups allow widowers to remarry. Many groups encourage a widower to marry his deceased wife's younger sister but never her older sister.

Among Muslims of both the north and the south, marriage between cousins is encouraged, both cross-cousins (the children of a brother and sister) and parallel cousins (the children of two same-sex siblings). In the north, such cousins grow up calling each other "brother" and "sister", yet they may marry. Even when cousin marriage does not occur, spouses can often trace between them other kinship linkages.

Some tribal people of central India practice an interesting permutation of the southern pattern. Among the Murias of Bastar in southeastern Madhya Pradesh, as described by anthropologist Verrier Elwin, teenagers live together in a dormitory (ghotul), sharing life and love with one another for several blissful years. Ultimately, their parents arrange their marriages, usually with cross-cousins, and the delights of teenage romance are replaced with the serious responsibilities of adulthood. In his survey of some 2,000 marriages, Elwin found only seventy-seven cases of ghotul partners eloping together and very few cases of divorce. Among the Muria and Gond tribal groups, cross-cousin marriage is called "bringing back the milk," alluding to the gift of a girl in one generation being returned by the gift of a girl in the next.

Finding the perfect partner for one's child can be a challenging task. People use their social networks to locate potential brides and grooms of appropriate social and economic status. Increasingly, urban dwellers use classified matrimonial advertisements in newspapers. The advertisements usually announce religion, caste, and educational qualifications, stress female beauty and male (and in the contemporary era, sometimes female) earning capacity, and may hint at dowry size.

In rural areas, matches between strangers are usually arranged without the couple meeting each other. Rather, parents and other relatives come to an agreement on behalf of the couple. In cities, however, especially among the educated classes, photographs are exchanged, and sometimes the couple are allowed to meet under heavily chaperoned circumstances, such as going out for tea with a group of people or meeting in the parlor of the girl's home, with her relatives standing by.

Young professional men and their families may receive inquiries and photographs from representatives of several girls' families. They may send their relatives to meet the most promising candidates and then go on tour themselves to meet the young women and make a final choice. In the early 1990s, increasing numbers of marriages arranged in this way link brides and grooms from India with spouses of Indian parentage resident in Europe, North America, and the Middle East.

Almost all Indian children are raised with the expectation that their parents will arrange their marriages, but an increasing number of young people, especially among the college-educated, are finding their own spouses. So-called love marriages are deemed a slightly scandalous alternative to properly arranged marriages. Some young people convince their parents to "arrange" their marriages to people with whom they have fallen in love. This process has long been possible for Indians from the south and for Muslims who want to marry a particular cousin of the appropriate marriageable category.

In the upper classes, these semi-arranged love marriages increasingly occur between young people who are from castes of slightly different rank but who are educationally or professionally equal. If there are vast differences to overcome, such as is the case with love marriages between Hindus and Muslims or between Hindus of very different caste status, parents are usually much less agreeable, and serious family disruptions can result.

In much of India, especially in the north, a marriage establishes a structural opposition between the kin groups of the bride and groom--bride-givers and bride-takers. Within this relationship, bride-givers are considered inferior to bride-takers and are forever expected to give gifts to the bride-takers. The one-way flow of gifts begins at engagement and continues for a generation or two. The most dramatic aspect of this asymmetrical relationship is the giving of dowry.

Dowry : Burden or Prestige Tssue

In many communities throughout India, a dowry has traditionally been given by a bride's kin at the time of her marriage. In ancient times, the dowry was considered a woman's wealth—property due a beloved daughter who had no claim on her natal family's real estate—and typically included portable valuables such as jewelry and household goods that a bride could control throughout her life. However, over time, the larger proportion of the dowry has come to consist of goods and cash payments that go straight into the hands of the groom's family. In the late twentieth century, throughout much of India, dowry payments have escalated, and a groom's parents sometimes insist on compensation for their son's higher education and even for his future earnings, to which the bride will presumably have access. Some of the dowries demanded are quite oppressive, amounting to several years' salary in cash as well as items such as motorcycles, air conditioners, and fancy cars. Among some lower-status groups, large dowries are currently replacing traditional bride-price payments. Even among Muslims, previously not given to demanding large dowries, reports of exorbitant dowries are increasing.

The dowry is becoming an increasingly onerous burden for the bride's family. Anti-dowry laws exist but are largely ignored, and a bride's treatment in her marital home is often affected by the value of her dowry. Increasingly frequent are horrible incidents, particularly in urban areas, where a groom's family makes excessive demands on the bride's family--even after marriage--and when the demands are not met, murder the bride, typically by setting her clothes on fire in a cooking "accident." The groom is then free to remarry and collect another sumptuous dowry. The male and female in-laws implicated in these murders have seldom been punished.

Such dowry deaths have been the subject of numerous media reports in India and other countries and have mobilized feminist groups to action. In some of the worst areas, such as the National Capital Territory of Delhi, where hundreds of such deaths are reported annually and the numbers are increasing yearly, the law now requires that all suspicious deaths of new brides be investigated. Official government figures report 1,786 registered dowry deaths nationwide in 1987; there is also an estimate of some 5,000 dowry deaths in 1991. Women's groups sometimes picket the homes of the in-laws of burned brides. Some analysts have related the growth of this phenomenon to the growth of consumerism in Indian society.

Fears of impoverishing their parents have led some urban middle-class young women, married and unmarried, to commit suicide. However, through the giving of large dowries, the newly wealthy are often able to marry their treasured daughters up the status hierarchy so reified in Indian society.

After marriage arrangements are completed, a rich panoply of wedding rituals begins. Each religious group, region, and caste has a slightly different set of rites. Generally, all weddings involve as many kin and associates of the bride and groom as possible. The bride's family usually hosts most of the ceremonies and pays for all the arrangements for large numbers of guests for several days, including accommodation, feasting, decorations, and gifts for the groom's party. These arrangements are often extremely elaborate and expensive and are intended to enhance the status of the bride's family. The groom's party usually hires a band and brings fine gifts for the bride, such as jewelry and clothing, but these are typically far outweighed in value by the presents received from the bride's side.

After the bride and groom are united in sacred rites attended by colorful ceremony, the new bride may be carried away to her in-laws' home, or, if she is very young, she may remain with her parents until they deem her old enough to depart. A prepubescent bride usually stays in her natal home until puberty, after which a separate consummation ceremony is held to mark her departure for her conjugal home and married life. The poignancy of the bride's weeping departure for her new home is prominent in personal memory, folklore, literature, song, and drama throughout India.

Marriage as a Concept

The people entangle into wedlock with a lot of expectations but the questions are: where from the people derive these expectations and whether these expectations are fulfilled and, if not, what will be the problems, if so, how are the problems peep-in, what are the consequences if the problems are not tackled and what are the solutions for such problems? More than anything else what are the terms and factors for a happy married life? After all the whole aim in anybody's life is to have happiness throughout one's life. To have this happiness, the materialistic security, security of care and health are the primary factors and to avail these factors thro'out all the stages of life, a system in the interest of all its members is evolved by every society, and this system is called marriage.

In the beginning, man couldn't stand alone against animals and therefore he started living in a group; slowly such groups became sects. Even now, togetherness has become the basic concept of his way of living thereby emerged the concept of family society, culture and religions.

We can observe, off the record, that the religion, instead of guiding the people in implementing the principles of philosophy, slowly started misusing the concept of social environments to their selfish advantage; this point is to be properly understood on account of the unwarranted influence of religion into the married life, especially in the conjugal side of it, of innocents and ignorants.

Family and Society

Coming back, to out subject, in fact, we have to understand that the society for its survival has created the concept of family which is the base of society and, in turn, the family is consequence of marriage. Even though the materialistic and physical powers have generally corrupted a man to feel as if independent but whereas, in fact, he is dependent for emotional and sentimental support and care. In the case of woman, she is totally dependent, in many cases materialistically and, in most cases, for protection and care against the exploitation for sex, for the consequences of her sexual interactions and for her children; thus to balance the dependency of human being, the concept of care is utilised and the two sides of the coin, viz. Care, are affection and love which are the basic necessities for family and marriage. In fact, selfishless care with understanding for mutual satisfaction, satiation and happiness is the golden principle of marriage.

In everybody's life, the very important factors to be taken care are: character, security and health, of which security can be sub-divided into two categories: one is security of materialistic necessities, needs and comforts and second is love, whereas here love means caring and satisfying the other, in other words, caring to keep the other happy. Good character, conduct, and morality help every individual, society and humanity, in general, to have happiness and peace; as such building-up good character is given the most importance and prominence in social-values throughout the ages. It is obvious that everybody strives hard to have the security of materialistic needs for present and future for oneself and one's family.

But security of materialistic needs alone cannot give the happiness and peace; basically one should maintain good health to enjoy the materialistic needs and comforts and moreover one requires somebody to take care of his health either in the ordinary course or at least at the time of necessity. Apart from the materialistic needs and health, the most important third requirement, or expectation, in one's life is himself being taken care of and be kept happy by satisfying his both physiological and psychological needs; this particular type of care has got two sides: first being affection and the second being love. Here affection means caring and satisfying the necessary needs of the individual who is related to self and with whom self will not deal sexually, and the second being marital love where care is taken care of on mutual basis including satisfying the sexual needs.

The above-mentioned points indicate clearly that good character and health and security of materialistic needs and proper care are must in everybody's life throughout. Therefore, a necessity has arisen to evolve a system whereby the above mentioned basic concepts of life should automatically be taken care of by a system in everybody's life that too throughout life.

Now coming back to marriage, marriage is meant for security and responsibility; security here means the guarantee of love, or care, and materialistic needs for present and future, wherein the love is caring and satisfying each other's needs including sex, and responsibility here means the responsibility being parents to bring up their children of course with good character, and morality. Hence, by virtue of marriage two categories of people are created:

(1) husband and wife; and

(2) parents.

Now looking into the stages of one's life; in the early, or first, state of one's life, one's character, materialistic needs, love and health are taken care of by one's parents, the characters created by marriage; in the later stage of one's life the above-mentioned necessities will be taken care of on mutual basis in marriage; and in the last, or third, stage of life, these will be looked after on mutual basis by the marriage-partner and as well be their children the creations on account of marriage.

Hence, the basic factors for one's life viz. Character, security and health are automatically taken care of in everybody's life from childhood to old age, generation after generation, without any stoppage, or hurdle, and this system, called marriage, is working as an ideal one without any substitute, or alternative.

Moreover as the responsibility of bringing-up children is fixed in marriage, automatic balancing the population in accordance with the economic condition is taken care in the society on account of the system that is marriage. Therefore, the only ideal system which has been success thro'out centuries, and in every generation, without availability of an other alternative, or substitute, in which everyone gets involved is marriage.

Causes of Marriage

One of the numerous causes which sociologists have adduced for the rise of the marriage institution, only two deserve consideration at this stage of our inquisition.

(1) First, it has to be remembered that a review of the history of civilization shows that as men rose a level or two higher than their original barbarity, they ceased to lead each his own solitary life and began to live in groups. At the stage men gradually realised how marriage in a very great measure secured the internal unity of a group and it was precisely this realisation which made for the adoption of the marriage custom. Now we will see a rough idea of the different forms which marriage assumed one after another as a result of the changing conditions of advancing civilization. It was a common practice in those times for a mighty group

to invade smaller and weaker groups vanquish them and capture as many men as possible and carry them as slaves. With men came women too whom did the victors take unto wives. Marriage was thus based on this idea of women's servitude, and this form of marriage prevailed during the whole period of struggle and strife. But times slowly changed, the sword gradually ceased to the sole arbiter, smaller wandering groups evolved into big and stable societies, peace came to be loved, and law and order began to have a hold on people. This change brought a corresponding change in men's outlook on things and fellow beings, and women were no longer regarded as serfs. With this advent of a more generous attitude towards the weaker sex woman obtained the right of choosing her lover, and this gave rise to new forms of marriage like swamyamvara, gandhrva vivaha and love marriage.

(2) The next important stage in the history of the marriage custom was marked when marriage came to be swayed by religion and began to be regarded more as a religious than a social duty. Religion gradually assumed such an unquestioned authority that it took upon itself the right of defining the duties and obligations of the husband and the wife and laid various functions on the wedded couple; and at last its word was law as to the rituals which alone rendered marriage valid. Mr.V.Vaidya's (an accomplished deccani scholar) idea is that if we take the list of eight varieties of marriage described in the *shrutis*, viz., Brahma, daiva, arsha, prajapaatya, gandhrva, asura, rakshsa and paishacha and read it from the end backward we really shall have gone over the chronological order of the different phases through which the institution of marriage passed in India. Paishach kind of marriage is nothing but anarchy in sexual matters, the rakshasa marriage consists in carrying off the bride by force and based on the conception of woman's slavery, in the asura marriage the bride is purchase, and in the gandharva form the lovers choose each other and enter into wedlock. The remaining four kinds are an indication of the times when religion predominated and determined the whole process of marriage. In short these eight kinds are a record in brief of the various forms, which marriage took at different stages of civilization.

Aims of Hindu Marriage

The aims of Hindu marriage are said to be *dharma*, *praja* and *rati*. Though sex is one of the functions of marriage, it is given third place, indicating thereby that it is the least desirable aim of marriage. To stress the lower role of sex in marriage, the marriage of sudra is said to be for pleasure only. Hindu marriage is considered sacred rites accompanied by the sacred formulae. Similarly marriage is said to be essential for woman because that is only sacrament that can be performed for her. As marriage is said to be sacred it is irrevocable. The parties to the marriage cannot dissolve it at will. They are bound to each other until the death of either of them; and the wife is supposed to be bound to her husband even after his death.

This concept of marriage, that it is indissoluble, is a lofty one because it means that the husband and wife after marriage have to adjust their tastes and temper, their ideals and interests, instead of breaking with each other when they find that these differ. It thus involves sacrifices on the part of both husband and wife as each is called upon to overcome the incompatibility of the other. Hindu marriage, thus viewed, is not an ordinary affair wherein the weakness of flesh plays a dominant part. On the contrary, demands of personal gratification and pleasures are subordinated, and the individual is called upon to make marriage a success by means of compromises and adjustments.

In Hindu marriage, despite the fact that marriage was considered to be irrevocable, the two partners were not regarded as being equals in their obligations and privileges. The ideal of 'pativruta', i.e. being devoted to the husband alone, popularised by the puranic writers, not merely implied fidelity to the husband but make service to the husband the only duty of the wife and her main purpose of life. A wife's only concern in life was to see that all services needed by her husband were properly performed by her, the satisfaction of her husband being her sole of joy in life. On the death of the husband, the wife had either to live chastely, renouncing all the joys of life, to follow her husband by immolating herself with his body on the pyre. However, nowadays the modern woman is no longer prepared to accept a social code which recognizes the dominance of the male as binder on her. Conventional morality is receding into the background and emotional integrity has become the ideal of marriage. Further, the democratic ideal to which Indians are now committed by their constitution and which has been defined as political, social, religious equality, lends force to economic processes and the findings of psychological investigations. Social coercion and legal sanctions become less necessary when society accepts the principle that the sex life of responsible adults is their own concern. This principle provides for the satisfaction of the emotional requirements of the partners in marriage, a factor of which our social ideology has, in the past, taken no account. There is nothing sinister or dangerous in the concept of freedom in marriage. According to Ellis, who is quoted by Mahatma Gandhi, freedom cannot destroy but confirms marriage's stability and purifies its practice. In short, marriage continues to be sacrament; only it is raised to an ethical plane. We rather go back to Vedic ideal embodied in the saptapadi formula, 'i take thee to be my companion in life'.

Features of Marriage

Arranged-cum-love Marriages

Along with time, the Indian society has witnessed substantial changes in the social and marital set up. Though most of the parents still remain staunch about their kind of arrange marriage, a wave of change have been brought by few parents who whole heartedly welcome the choice of their kids in their family. Unlike west where every kind of marriage is a love marriage, Indian society on a verge of transformation has three different kinds of marriages- the arrange marriage, which is perfectly arranged by the family of the bride and the groom, the love marriage, solemnized by the choice of the life partners themselves and the third- love cum arrange marriage where the life partner is selected by the boy or girl himself/ herself but rest of the formalities of arranging it is done by their parents.

From the very beginning in the country it has almost been an understood fact that parents have to find a suitable bride and groom for their son and daughter and solemnize the entire marriage according to their wishes. As the custom of child marriage was very prevalent in the Indian society earlier and the child were married much before they were aware of the feeling of love and attraction, it is very clear that why parents were the one to find a perfect match for their kids. Though the trend of child marriage have gradually faded from the Indian society, the fashion of arrange marriage is still very much prevalent due to its deep rooted existence in our culture.

The strong wave of changes were introduced in the Indian society in 1970s when the education and literacy spread to the urban society of India and people started the realization of individuality. This realization made people more aware of their choices and necessities. The same rational though came to be applicable in regard of marriage where people stood against the staunch system of caste, creed or social status based marriage and asked for the freedom of choosing their life partner themselves. At that time this step was considered to be revolutionary and rebellious. However, with time people have understood the importance of marrying with the person of one's choice. As the realization of individuality have increased parents have also agreed to accept the choices of their kids shedding the old tradition of fixing and arranging marriage.

In the Urban society, People have widened their choices, when it comes to their life partner. Love cum arranged marriages has traversed the boundaries of a single community. Today, inter-caste and inter-religion marriages are a common sight in the country, which otherwise were considered strictly against the Indian culture. This brings out the fact that the outlook of people regarding marriages has been revolutionized due to the modernization of the Indian society. However, this acceptance is yet only limited to the urban and educated Indian society. Though this favorable change has paved the way for a revolutionary change in the rural society also, any substantial change is yet to be observed.

Arranged Marriages

he concept of arranged marriage may sound impractical to the Western world, but in India, it is a usual norm. No matter how westernized India may have become, arranged marriages are still viewed as the most preferred choice in the Indian families. This kind of marriage has its roots laid to the time, when the ritual of child marriage prevailed in the country. Child marriage was essentially performed, so as to restrict the children from marrying outside their community and social status. The practice was essentially a way of uniting and maintaining the difference between the rich upper class society and the poor lower class society. This practice of caste system gave rise to the concept of arranged marriages.

Earlier, an arranged marriage in India was seen as a way of promoting caste system or racism. It was just a tool for the upper caste people to protect their community and to maintain their social status. As such, they married their children to the person of the same caste or same social background. The practice eventually passed on to the lower caste as well, where it is used for the same purpose. The rituals and customs of arrange marriages in India vary depending on the caste and religion of the people. The system, though very old, still is one of the most prevalent practices performed and has today, become synonymous with the Indian society and culture. The only difference with the yesteryears is that it is less rigid than that practiced in the past.

While the above negative aspects can still be dealt with, one of the most crucial drawbacks of arranged marriage is that the boy and the girl do not know each other. Two unknown people get married without knowing and understanding each other, as according to the concept, it is not important to know your partner before marriage. As such, chances of not gelling well with the partner are very high. If either of them thinks absolutely contradictorily to what the other believes in, there would hardly be a mutual level of understanding between the two and life would be merely a compromise for the two. The only way an arranged marriage can succeed is through acceptance. One has to accept the other the way he/she is and look for striking a mutual level of understanding.

Present Scenario

Progressively, the concept of arranged marriage has changed considerably. Today, parents are concerned about the life of their child and take the consent of their kid, before deciding the marriage. Over the time, people have understood that marriages can only be successful when the parents do not force their children to marry someone he/she doesn't want to marry. Good arrange marriages happen when the parents support and help their children to find their life partners according to their desires and likings. Mutual consent and understanding are the only ways a marriage can sustain.

Present Scenario

People have realized that a successful marriage is not dependent on factors such as same caste and religion. It is on the other hand, built on the aspects of mutual understanding and compatibility. It is how well the two understand each other's need and feel for your partner. It is not necessary that you have to belong to the same community or caste to understand your spouse better. Today, there are ample of examples when two people from totally different background and lifestyle come together and spend their entire life happy with each other, thanks to education.

Education has broadened the periphery of thinking and helped people develop analytical powers. It has not only altered their perception about life, but also about social concerns such as marriage and relationship. Inter caste and inter religion marriages serves as a beacon light for social equality. In order to break the perils of caste-system, it has becomes incumbent that there should be inter-caste marriages. Marriage is mostly dependent on true love and feeling and once this is achieved, caste and religion all becomes secondary issues.

Marriages in Villages of India

With the changing social scenario, a change in the mindset of the people can be seen, but mostly among the city people. Though people in cities have learned the nuances of caste system and the positives of inter-caste marriage, the villages of India have still not welcomes the concept of inter-caste marriages. In villages of India, even today people are very rigid in matters of marriages. They prefer that their sons and daughters should marry in the same caste and community; else they disown their son/daughter. Though there have been numerous incidents of the wife attempting suicide or being murdered, this has still not evaded the theory of caste system. People in villages need to be taught about the menaces of caste system and initiatives should be taken to fight against it. After all, a marriage is all about coming together of two souls, irrespective of social background and class!!

Love Marriages

"Happy marriages begin when we marry the ones we love, and they blossom when we love the ones we marry."

—Tom Mullen.

Have you ever tried defining the relationship between love and marriage? If yes, then you would have realized that both are synonymous to each other. Love is a dream and marriage is just an extension of this dream to reality. When both dream and reality comes together, it is the best thing that can happen to a person. Love is the subtle emotional wave within us, which is perennial in this world of death and passing away. The feeling of love is inexplicable - we start feeling good about things, which we earlier overlooked. The company of the person we love can make the most mundane chores seem like an exciting job. So, love can be best defined, as a feeling of bliss and ecstasy.

In India, love marriages are becoming a popular trend these days. While traditionally arranged marriage was the only option girls and boys had, the scenario has changed considerably. Parents, today, have a broader perspective and are fully aware of the nuances of caste system, thanks toeducation. They have understood that it is mutual understanding and feeling of love that matters most in marriage and not the caste and status of the bride/groom.

Marrying the person you love is just like taking a step ahead in life and strengthening the already strong relationship, with commitment and efforts. However, love marriages are restrained to the city culture and are not a part of rural India, wherein arranged marriages are still viewed as the right thing.

Love vs Arranged Marriage

Whenever we talk of Indian wedding, we try to associate it with arranged marriages. Due to the social structure, the concept of arranged marriage is prevalent in the Indian wedding scenario, since ages. On the other hand, love marriages were considered as a taboo among many Indian people, who do not have a modern outlook of life. For them, two people should tie the wedding knot only with the consent of their parents and the blessings of their relatives.

Nonetheless, love marriages are prevalent in almost all the societies of India, given the fact that they are still considered inferior to the weddings arranged by many parents in the country. People supporting the concept of love marriage strongly believe that it is very important to know the partner before marrying him/her. On the other hand, people who believe in solemnizing the wedding with the permission of parents and relatives think that arranged marriages are long lasting. In this article, we have discussed love marriage *vis-à-vis* arranged marriage.

Pros & Cons of Love Marriage and Arranged Marriage

When it comes to love marriage, the two people tie the nuptial knot only after falling in love with each other and probably, after knowing each other for a long time. They get ample time to explore both the good and the bad things about each other, well before marriage. This helps them to develop a good comfort level after marriage, very effortlessly. On the other hand, if two people do not know much about each other, when their marriage is arranged by their parents, then they might take some more time to develop a level of comfort, understanding after marriage. Here, love marriage scores more than arranged marriage in this case.

It is said that compromise is a factor that decides whether the marriage would work out or not. In case of love marriage, people might expect more from their partner, largely because they have fallen in love before marriage. This leads to lesser compromises, as the person expects more from his/her partner. On the other hand, compromise and adjustments form the foundation of arranged marriage, largely because the married couple does not have any preconceived notions or expectations from one another. The compromise factor might work wonders in case of most of the arranged marriages, while in love marriages, that might prove to be yet another cause for altercation. Due to this factor, people consider arranged marriage as long lasting and better than love marriage.

In case of arranged marriage, the married couple could resort to their parents or acquaintance at the time of financial crises or other problems. In addition, if the marriage proves to be a failure, they have a number of people around them to put seek support or to put the blame on. Their parents would come forward to solve the problems between the couple, if they have married with the elder's consent. This is the reason why arranged marriages are considered secure for the people in India.

On the other hand, the couples who have solemnized love marriage would have to tackle all their crises on their own, because they might have been separated from their family. Resentment drives the parents and the relatives to remain dormant in case the married couple wants any financial or moral support - a common sight seen in love marriages in India. Due to this factor, many people do not want to marry without their parent's consent, because they would be ultimately cut off from the family ties.

Wedding Trends in India

Concept of Arranged and Love Marriage

The custom of arranged marriages has been a part of Indian culture since the fourth century. The practice was begun primarily to maintain and pass on the family traditions from one generation to the other. It is still prevalent in both rural and urban parts of India, former being more inclined towards the system. In fact, arranged marriages are in majority, because not all people have accepted the concept of love marriage. However, with the changing time, people in India have accepted the concept of love marriage, which is otherwise considered against the Indian culture. People in the rural India are now more liberal, when it comes to love marriages. Therefore, both arranged and love marriage find equal importance in the wedding scenario of India.

Inter-Caste and Inter-Religion Marriage

Until some time back, marrying a person belonging to some other caste or religions was strictly not permitted by the families. With the modernization of the Indian society and social awareness of the people, inter-caste and inter-religion marriages have become a common sight. This is primarily due to the acceptance of the concept of love marriage.

Nonetheless, people with an orthodox or conservative outlook of life are still firm about marrying within the same caste, community and religion. Contrary to this thought, people in the present time do believe in solemnizing weddings of two different individuals belonging to different family background and culture. The recent trend in Indian marriages is the acceptance of the concept of homosexual marriage.

Wedding Attire

The wedding attire has also seen a drastic change, over the passing years. Initially, the bride and the groom used to wear traditional dress, of their respective religions, regions or community. Today, although they still wear their traditional dress during the important wedding ceremonies, they resort to the outfit that is different from the traditional ones for other rituals.

With the changing fashion trend, the way of getting dressed for a wedding has also been changing. People, especially in the elite class, are now hiring fashion designers to choose the wedding attire for the bride and the groom. Inspired by the high-profile weddings of business tycoons and Bollywood stars, people now want to look like a celebrity, on their 'important day'. Hence, the attire chosen for the wedding ceremony is often a reflection of the hot trend.

Planning

People's perception of planning the wedding has also changed over the passing years. Few years back, wedding and engagement were the sole responsibility of the bride's family. People within the family took efforts in decorating the venues chosen for conducting different ceremonies. Moreover, the wedding expenses were also borne by the bride's parents. Today, although the bride's parents still finance for the wedding ceremony, (except the reception party, which is thrown by the groom's family), people are now resorting to professionals to make arrangements for their weddings, right from the menu to the decorations. They hire wedding planners for the purpose. This is especially prevalent in the urban upper-middle class of India, where they want their wedding to be a trendsetter and the talk of the town for a long time.

Hindu Marriage

Under Vedic Hindu traditions marriage is viewed as one of the sacraments, which is a lifelong commitment of one wife and one husband. In India marriage has been looked upon as having been made in heaven and considered as a "divine knot sanctified by fire". Hindu families are patrilocal.

The Hindu wedding ceremony may vary in minor details from region to region and different priests may adopt some variations. A Hindu marriage joins two individuals for life, so that they can pursue *dharma* (duty), *artha* (possessions), *kama* (physical desires), and *moksa* (ultimate spiritual release) together. It also joins two families together. The colours are normally red and gold.

Wedding marks the coming together of two individuals. It is a bond not only between two individuals but also between two souls. Indian marriages are clad with rituals and customs. It is an elaborate concept in every Indian community. Nowadays, Hindu weddings are celebrated on a large scale. Family and friends get together to celebrate the occasion. The marriage ceremony includes various pre wedding and wedding functions.

Most of these functions take place mostly at the bride's place and some at the groom's place. The main wedding ceremony usually takes place at the bride's home. On the main day of the function a mandap is erected and the interior is beautifully decorated with flowers, colorful personal adornment, and decorative items. Mostly the wedding is held on a garden, courtyard of the bride's house, a blocked-off street or square. It is an elaborate affair.

After the marriage rituals the guests are served with lavish dinner. Indian wedding is all about fun and feast. According to Indian custom, the bride and groom are showered with gifts and attention. Their family and friends treat them royally. In Hindu wedding rituals are performed in front of the Hindu deities and joining the bride and groom in an eternal bond of love and commitment.

Types of Marriage

Eight different types of Marriages have been documented in the ancient Indian scripture *Manu Smrti* III.20-34. These eight types of marriages are:

1. *Brahma Vivaha*: In Brahma marriage once the boy completes his Brahmacharya Ashram, he is eligible to get married. His parents then approach the parents or guardian of a girl belonging to a good family and same Varna and ask them for the hand of their daughter for their son. The father of the girl also carefully chooses the groom who is well versed in *Vedas* and of a noble character. This is how a Brahma marriage was arranged. There was no dowry system at that time; a girl came with two garments and a few ornaments only. According to *Dharmashastras*, "Brahma Vivah" is the best marriage among all.

2. *Daiva Vivaha*: If the girl is groomed with ornaments and married to a priest during a sacrifice, it is called *Daiva Vivah*. In this type of marriage the girl's family wait for a reasonable period for a suitable man for their daughter but when nobody turns up they go looking for a groom in such places where a sacrifice is being conducted. According to the *Dharmashastra, Daiva marriage* is considered inferior to Brahma marriage because it is considered degrading for the womanhood to look for groom.

3. *Arsha Vivaha*: In this type of marriage, the bridegroom gives a cow and a pair of bull to the guardian of girl. Marriages of this type used to happen because the parents of the bride couldn't afford the expense of their daughter's marriage at the right time according to the brahma rite. So the girl is married off to an old sage. The cows, which were taken in exchange of the bride shows that even the groom does not have any remarkable qualities. According to Sastras, noble marriages had no monetary or business transactions so this kind of marriages were not considered noble.

4. *Prajapatya Vivaha*: In this type of marriage, the bride's father goes in search for a groom for his daughter. The protection of the bride or daughter is handed over by the father to the bridegroom during the *Panigrahan* ceremony or the acceptance of the bride's hands. The actual wedding ceremony takes place after *Panigrahan*.

5. *Gandharva Vivaha*: However when a man and a woman marry with each others consent but may not have the consent of their family then this wedding is called *Gandharva Vivah* or 'love marriage'.

6. *Asura Vivaha*: In the Asura type of marriage the groom is not at all suitable for the bride . In no way is he a match for the girl but willingly gives as much wealth as he can afford to the bride's parents and relatives. In Arsha type cows are given in exchange for the bride but there is no compulsion like the Asura type. Even the groom is also not so rich and powerful like his counterpart in Asura type.

7. *Rakshasa Vivaha*: In the case where the bride is willing however, the family of the bride are not, the bride is forcefully taken from the family. A famous example is Lord Krishna takes Rukmini.

8. *Paishacha Vivaha*: In the case where the bride is intoxicated, possessed or not in a conscious state of mind when being married and thus is married unwillingly, is an example *Paishacha vivaha*, which has been outlawed by Manu.

Hindu Marriage Customs

Historically the so called vedic marriage was but one of the few different types of Hindu marriage customs. Love marriage was also seen in historical Hindu literature and has been variously described in many names: e.g. Gandharva vivaha etc. In certain poor vaishnav communities still there is a custom called kanthi-badal which is exchange of bead-garlands as a very simplified form of ritual in solitude in front of an idol of Krishna, considered a form of acceptable love marriage.

According to Hindu *Shastra,* there are four stages of life, of which *Grahastha Ashram* or married life signifies the second stage. It begins, when a man and a woman come together and marry. In India, marriage is treated as an institution, which teaches the actual values of life. Every stage in life has its own charm and a married life is no exception. In India, a marriage is usually arranged by the respective parents of the bride and the groom and follows various steps. Marriage among Hindus is not only considered a union of two souls, but of two families.

A Hindu wedding not only involves the bride and groom but the entire community, friends, family and relatives as everybody participates in their coming together of the to-be couple. The first and the foremost step is the selection of the bride and the bridegroom. While in love marriages, a boy and a girl themselves select their life partner, it is crucial when it comes to arranged marriages. Talking about arranged marriages in the Hindu custom, the parents select the prospective bride/groom for their son/daughter.

Ring Ceremony

After the selection procedure is over, the family members of both the girl and boy ask the priest to suggest an auspicious date for the engagement of the two also known as *misri* or *ring* ceremony. Since India boasts of diverse cultures and traditions, the engagement ceremony rituals differ from region to region and community to community. However, the basic of all the rituals, mentioned here, form an indispensable part of Hindu wedding. In the betrothal ceremony, the to-be bride and the groom exchange wedding rings among each other. Sweets and garlands are also exchanged among the couple.

After the festive spirit of engagement, the next important ritual is the mehndi party. It is believed that the color of mehndi signifies the essence of love in a marriage, so it is put on bride's hand to strengthen that bond of love. The bride's family and friends mainly celebrate this ceremony. The female friends and family members of the bride rejoice and celebrate this occasion, as henna gets painted on her hands and feet. Apart from the bride, the family members also get their hands painted with henna. Singing traditional songs and dancing to the beat of music forms a major part of this ritual.

Among the other important rituals is the Sangeet party, wherein all the family members and friends of the bride and groom celebrate, by singing and dancing the night away. Along with song and dance there are arrangements for food and drink. A large affair, Sangeet party is most popular among Punjabis, Marwaris and Gujaratis, although most of the regions today also practice this ritual. Ghari puja is also another important religious ceremony, which is performed on the eve of the wedding day at the groom and bride's place separately.

Beautification Process of Bridge and Bridegroom

On the morning of the wedding day, *Pithi* or *Haldi*, the cleansing ceremony is practiced during which the bride and bridegroom are pasted with turmeric powder in their respective homes, as a part of their beautification process. Talking about the actual marriage ceremonies, the Hindu wedding mostly takes place in a mandap or a tent, which is beautifully decorated with flowers. The main Hindu wedding ceremony is a long and elaborate affair, which lasts for several hours and is attended by a large number of relatives, friends, acquaintances and so on.

One of the most significant rituals the bride and the groom perform is the *Saptapadi* or saat phere around a scared fire and light, which is symbolic to God. While the bride and the groom take the seven circles, the priest or purohit recites the mantras and speak of the real essence and significance of marriage. It is also during this time that the groom fills vermillion in the center parting of the bride and puts mangalsutra around her neck. Both sindoor and mangalsutra have strong religious implications and are sacred symbols of a married woman. These were some of the rituals and customs, which were generally followed in all the Hindu marriages.

Talking about the varied customs and rituals followed, Hindu weddings extend up to four to five days. The ceremonies practiced are essentially divided into three parts—pre-wedding customs, wedding day ceremony and post-wedding rituals. The rituals and customs performed in each of the three phases have a deep significance and meaning. The pre wedding celebrations mainly includes engagement, sangeet, mehendi, haldi and tilak. Coming to the wedding day ceremonies, it involves different traditional rituals, each having its own meaning and role. One of the most important rituals of Hindu wedding is the seven rounds or *sapta padi* taken together, around the sacred fire, by the bride and the groom, while the seven vows or promise are read by the priest or purohit.

Seven Vows for Long-lasting Relationship

The bride and the bride groom take the vows before God, symbolized by fire and light. These seven promises taken together by the bride and groom build's the foundation of their relationship and marriage. It speaks of the loyalty, love, and commitment they would eventually share in their married life. Thereafter, post wedding ceremonies are performed, which mostly include *vidaai* and reception.

This is the most emotional moment of the wedding, when the bride takes leave from her parents and other family members and takes her first step towards her new life in her husband's house. On reaching the new home, there are a number of ceremonies that are performed, right from welcoming the new bride to playing games and making merry.

Hindu Marriage Rituals

According to Hindu *Sastra,* there are four stages of life, of which *Grahastha Ashram* or married life signifies the second stage. It begins, when a man and a woman come together and marry. In India, marriage is treated as an institution, which teaches the actual values of life.

A Hindu marriage symbolizes not just coming together of two individuals, but also the bonding of understanding, commitment, mutual love, oneness and spiritual growth. Traditionally, Hindu marriagc is much more than just celebration and fun. It demands sacrifice, companionship, dedication, and devotion from both the partners.

Each and every rituals and customs associated with marriage portrays the real essence of wedding. Traditionally, there are five signs of marital status of women, according to Hindu culture—mangalsutra, toe rings, kumkum, bangles and a nose ring. Talking about mangalsutra, the word denotes a significant meaning. While *mangal* means aupiscious, *sutra* can be deciphered as a thread.

Significance of Mangalsutra *in Hindu Marriage*

Mangalsutra, as such, is not just a jewelry item, but a sacred thread of love and goodwill worn by married women, as a symbol of their successful marriage. An inevitable part of Hindu marriage ceremony, *mangalsutra* refers to a revered symbol of wedlock. India being a land of diversity, different regions in the country have assigned different names for this scared symbol. While it is known as the thaaly or *maangalyam* in Kannada, *Telugu* and Tamil in Southern India, people in the northern part of India cails it *mangalsutra.* It is believed that the concept of this sacred thread had its roots laid down in South India. Having immense significance and importance, it traveled to North India as well and today, forms an imperative part of the wedding ceremony.

Mangalsutra is the token of dignity and love given to a bride by her groom. On the wedding day, the groom ties the Mangalsutra around the neck of the bride, while the priest recites Vedic hymns and prays. It signifies the union of the bride and the groom, amidst the presence of deities, who are believed to be attending the marriage. In some regions, the groom ties first and his sisters tie the rest. Talking about its appearance, this sacred thread is made of two strings of small black beads with a locket or pendant. Sometimes, it is also made of small beads of gold and black beads, with gold and diamond pendant.

Considered auspicious for married women, *mangalsutra* is believed to have divine powers. Each of the black beads in the *mangalsutra*, signify protection from evil power and are believed to protect the marriage of a couple, essentially the life of the husband. Hindu women feel superstitious, when this scared thread breaks or gets lost. In the present times, *mangalsutra* are boasts of various designs and patterns. While the Gujaratis and Marwaris often go for a diamond pendant, Maharashtrians have a pendant that consists of one or two vatis and Bengalis in the meanwhile, have coral incorporated in the designing of the *mangalsutra*.

Present Scenario

Today, the concept of wearing a *mangalsutra* has changed considerably. It is more of a fashion statement than a symbol of marriage, thanks to modernization. With the progressive times, the wearing of mangalsutra in working women has considerably reduced. There is also a marked change in the style and making of *mangalsutra* over the years. Previously, women used to wear simple design *mangalsutra*, with small pendants, but now, the trend is to wear short length ones, that too with a single string. Instead of gold pendants, they prefer diamond ones. However, the black beads have still managed to remain constant. Whatever may be the reason to adore it, mangalsutra surely symbolizes the real essence and concept of a Hindu marriage.

Solah Shringar

Almost all the girls wish to look their best and epitomize beauty on their wedding day. In India, the beautification of the bride consists of sixteen parts and covers almost every part of the body, right from the head to the toe. To get detailed information about the solah shringar of an Indian bride, explore the following lines.

Solah Shringar

Bindi

The first *shringar* of the bride, bindi has a strong religious implication and is a sacred symbol of a married woman. To make the *bindi* look utmost attractive, you can even decorate it with red and white dots around it and along the eyebrows.

Sindoor

A sacred symbol of suhaag, sindoor or vermillion is applied on the center parting of the hair and is a part of the shringar of a married woman.

Maangteeka

A hair accessory, *Maangtika* is worn on the central parting of the hair of the bride. It is mostly made out of gold.

Anjana

Kajal or kohl is one of the most popular solah shringar. It is basically applied on the edges of the upper and lower eyelids, enhancing the bride's eyes and making it attractive and appealing.

Nath

Nath or the nose ring completes the look of the bride, making her look traditional and ethnic. Made of gold, it is generally worn on the left nostril and is supported by a gold chain, which extends just behind left ear.

Haar

After the face, next comes the neck of the bride. It is adored with beautiful haar or necklace, which is usually made of gold and embellished with diamonds, pearls or stones.

Karn Phool

Ear rings or *karn phool* adorn the ear of the bride. Mostly, the ear ring flaunted by the bride is made out of gold and is extremely beautiful and heavy.

Mehendi

Mehendi signifies the essence of love in wedlock and is essentially applied on the hands and feet of the bride, to strengthen that bond of love. It is one of the most special pre-wedding rituals in India.

Choodiyan

Bangles or *choodiyan* adore the wrist of the bride and are usally made of glass, laakh or gold. Conventionally, brides adore their wrist with red bangles.

Baajuband

Baajuband or more popularly known as armlets are worn on the upper arms of the bride and are similar to bangles in their appearance. Mughal, Rajasthani or Jaipuri are the most popular designs of baajuband.

Aarsi

The fingers of the bride are adored with exotic rings. Aarsi is the thumb ring which the bride wears. It mostly has mirror embedded on it and enable the bride to have a glimpse of herself as well as her life-partner

Keshapasharachana

Apart from the make-up, hair style plays an imperative role in determining the look of the bride. Mostly, the hair is tied in the braid style, with hair accessories and flowers accentuating the look.

Kamarband

Kamarband is a waist band that is tied on the waist line of the bride. Made up of gold, it is embellished with stones, diamonds and precious gems and is beautifully designed.

Payal & Bichuas

Made up of silver, it is a thick chain that is tied on the ankle and is adored with tiny bells that make enticing sound. Bichuas or toe rings are similar to rings worn in the fingers of the hand, but are worn in the fingers of each foot.

Itar

Itar is a special fragrance that is applied on to the bride. It emits a special aroma and that helps the bride stay fresh despite the long elaborate rituals performed.

Bridal Dress

Made in bright bridal colors, such as red, maroon, gold or green, bridal dress comprises of saree, lehenga and salwar kurta. It truly brings out the eternal beauty of the bride.

Symbolic Rituals Worn by Married Hindu Women

The married Hindu women in different parts of India follow different customs. Mostly Sindoor, Mangalsutra and Bangles are considered as signs of a married woman. In some places, in especially Eastern India, instead of Mangalsutra they put only vermilion on the hair parting, wear a pair of conch bangles (shankha), red bangles (pala) and an iron bangle on the left hand (loha) while their husband is alive.

In South India, a married woman is required to wear a necklace with a distinctive pendant called a thali and silver toe-rings. Both are put on her by the husband during the wedding ceremony. The pendant on the thali is custom-made and its design is different from family to family. Apart from this, the married woman also wears a red vermilion (Sindoor) dot on her forehead called Kumkum and (whenever possible) flowers in her hair and coloured glass Bangles.

The married woman is encouraged to give up all of these when her husband dies (although some choose not to). In the Kashmiri tradition, women wear a small gold chain (with a small gold hexagonal bead hanging from the chain) through their upper ear which is a sign of being married. The married woman in Kumaon Uttarakhand wear a yellow cloth called pichoda.

Hindu Marriage Act

The Hindu Marriage Act was established in 1955 as part of the Hindu Code Bills. Three other important acts were also created during this time and they include the Hindu Succession Act (1956), the Hindu Minority and Guardianship Act (1956), and the Hindu Adoptions and Maintenance Act (1956). All of these acts were put forth under the leadership of Jawaharlal Nehru, and were meant to modernize the then current Hindu legal tradition.

Purpose of Act

As part of the Hindu Code Bill, the Hindu Marriage Act was enacted by parliament in 1955. Its purpose was to regulate personal life among Hindus, especially their institution of marriage, its validity, conditions for in-validity, and applicability.

Applicability of Act

The bill was viewed as conservative, but it was also modern in the sense that it recognizes the modern offshoots of the Hindu religion (Jains, Buddhists) as specified in Article 44 of the Indian Constitution.

Hindu View of Marriage

According to the tenets of Hinduism, marriage is a sacred relationship, a sacrament, and a divine covenant meant for procreation and continuation of family lineage. In the traditional Hindu system of marriage, there is no role for the state as marriage remained a private affair within the social realm.Within this traditional framework reference, marriage is undoubtedly the most important transitional *point* in a Hindu's life and the most important of all the Hindu samskaras, or lifecycle rituals.

Conditions of Marriage

The conditions of marriage are specified in Section 5 as follows: the Act expressively prohibits polygamy by stipulating that a Hindu marriage can be solemnized between two Hindus if neither party has a living spouse at the time of marriage; the age of eligibility is fixed at 21 years of age for bridegrooms and 18 years of age for brides; and finally, the Act specifically prevents marriages between prohibited degrees of relationships.

Ceremonies of Marriages

Section 7 of the Hindu Marriage Act recognizes the ceremonies and customs of marriage. Hindu marriage may be solemnized in accordance with the customary rites and ceremonies of either party. Such rites and rituals include the Saptapadi-the taking of seven steps by the bridegroom and the bride jointly before the sacred fire. The marriage becomes complete and binding when the seventh step is taken.

Registration of Marriage

The registration of Hindu marriages is explained below:

(1) For the purpose of facilitating the proof of Hindu marriages, the State Government may make rules providing that the parties to any of such marriage may have the particulars relating to their marriage entered in such manner and subject to such conditions as may be prescribed in a Hindu Marriage Register kept for the purpose.

(2) Notwithstanding anything contained in sub-section (1), the State Government may, if it is of opinion that it is necessary or expedient so to do, provide that the entering of the particulars referred to in sub-section (1) shall be compulsory in the State or in any part thereof, whether in all cases or in such cases as may be specified, and where any such direction has been issued, any person contravening any rule made in this behalf shall be punishable with fine which may extend to twenty-five rupees.

(3) All rules made under this section shall be laid before the State Legislature, as soon as may be, after they are made.

Guardianship of Marriage

Section 6 of the Hindu Marriage Act specifies the guardianship for marriage. Wherever the consent of a guardian in marriage is necessary for a bride under this Act, the persons entitled to give such consent are the following: the father; the mother; the paternal grandfather; the paternal grandmother; the brother by full blood; the brother by half blood; etc. The Guardianship For Marriage was repealed in 1978 after the Child Marriage Restraint Amendment was passed.

Divorce

Divorce can be sought by husband or wife on certain grounds, including: adultery, cruelty, desertion for two years, religious conversion, mental abnormality, venereal disease, and leprosy. A wife can also present a petition for the dissolution of marriage on if the husband marries again after the commencement of his first marriage or if the husband has been guilty of rape, sodomy, or bestiality. It does permit one spouse to separate if he/she is unhappy, despite the fact that marriage is held to be divine, if he/she can prove or identify the circumstances that have made the union untenable. Newly married couples cannot file a petition for divorce within one year of marriage.

Future

As of late, there has been a realization that Hindu marriage, as a central element of society, cannot be subjected to legislative intervention; this realization has led to legislative inaction and a refusal by the state to get involved in the regulation of Hindu marriage. Derrett predicted in his later writings that despite some evidence of modernization, the dominant view in Hindu society for the foreseeable future would remain that marriage is a form of social obligation.

Muslim Marriage

Muslim wedding ceremony is celebrated with grandeur. Muslim wedding, known as 'Nikaah' in Urdu, can take place at any convenient time, because there is nothing like muhurat (the auspicious time) for the Muslims. Traditionally, the Muslim wedding is held at either the bride or the groom's home. However, in the present time, due to convenience and the availability of enough space to accommodate the long list of guests, Muslim weddings are organized in banquet halls, auditorium as well as community centers. Wherever the wedding is held, all the rituals of the three phases of wedding are strictly followed by the Muslims.

Muslim marriage and Islamic wedding customs are traditions and practices that relate to wedding ceremonies and marriage rituals prevailing within the Muslim world. Participants in these rites belong to communities of people who have Islam as their faith.

According to the teachings of the Quran, a married Muslim couple is equated with clothing. Within this context, both husband and wife act as each other's protector and comforter, just the way real garments "show and conceal" the body of human beings. Thus, they are meant "for one another".

Muslim wedding is divided into pre-wedding, wedding and post-wedding rituals. Pre-wedding rituals largely involve the exchange of sweets, fruits and visits to the bride and groom's houses. The pre-wedding rituals increase the level of excitement among the families of the bride and groom, who keenly look forward to the wedding day.

The wedding is organized in an elegant and charming way, while the culmination of the entire ceremony, known as post wedding rituals, is special in its own terms. If you are keen about knowing more about Muslim wedding, then go through our section, where we have provided detailed information on the rituals of Muslim wedding.

Muslim Pre-Wedding Rituals

Known as 'Nikah' in Urdu, the Muslim marriage is the most important ceremony for the Islam. It is a much awaited occasion, wherein the union of two souls is celebrated in an elegant and charming way. It is not just restricted to a single day. The formal procedures are divided into pre-wedding, wedding and post wedding, each being different from the other.

The pre-wedding rituals make a Muslim wedding a very fascinating event to watch. The pre-wedding rituals of the Islam marriage are broadly divided into four phases. Check out information on the pre-wedding Muslim rituals in the following lines.

Istikhara, Imam-Zamin and Magni

The first phase of the pre-wedding Muslim rituals is known as Istikhara, wherein the religious head takes the approval of the Almighty to perform the wedding. After the consent, the groom's mother pays a visit to the bride's house along with sweets and Imam-Zamin, a silver or goin coin wrapped in silken cloth.

The custom of tying the coin onto the upper portion of the bride's hand is called the Imam-Zamin ceremony. This is followed by Magni, which is a custom wherein the groom's family members pay a visit to the bride's house both the groom and the bride's family exchange sweets and fruits.

Manjha and Mehndi

At the Manjha ceremony, the bride wears yellow clothes and turmeric paste is applied all over her body. After the application of turmeric, the bride is not supposed to step out of the house. This is followed by Mehndi ceremony, which is one of the much awaited rituals of the Muslim wedding. Female relatives of the bride apply turmeric paste all over her body. The purpose is to make the bride's skin glow naturally. A professional or a relative applies Mehndi on the bride's hands and feet.

Muslim Wedding Rituals

Wedding is an important turning point in everyone's life. The ceremonious occasion is organized and celebrated in myriad ways all around the world. Different communities of the society have their own way of organizing the most important occasion. The wedding rituals are broadly divided according to the religions.

The Muslims all over the world have a unique way of tying the wedding knot. Most of the Muslim weddings in India, whether simple or extravagant, are arranged by following the age-old rituals. In the following lines, we have provided information on Muslim wedding rituals.

Muslim Marriage Customs

Welcoming The Baraat

To announce the arrival of groom's baraat at the doorsteps of the bridal residence or wedding venue, the musicians play traditional songs. The groom and the bride's brother share a drink of sherbet. The bride's sisters come up with different ideas of playing pranks with the guests. They attempt to slap the guests playfully, using flower batons.

Nikaah Ceremony

Nikaah is the wedding ceremony that can take place at some convenient venue or else at the bride or groom's residence. The ceremony is conducted by the Maulvi (priest). Close friends and relatives witness the happening of the event. The father of the bride and groom, addressed as Walis, have an important role to play in the performance of nikaah. The priest reads certain verses from the Quran. Thereafter, Ijab-e-Qubul (proposal and acceptance) takes place.

The groom's side sends the proposal and the bride's side gives her consent. For the legality of marriage, mutual consent is of prime importance. On the wedding day, the elderly members of both the families decide the amount of Mehar (nuptial gift). Mehar is a mandatory price that the groom's family must pay to the bride.

Nikaahnama

Nikaahnama is a legal document that must be duly signed by the bride, bridegroom, Maulvi and Walis for the marriage to be legal. It contains a set of terms and conditions that must be abided by both the parties.

Blessing The Groom

The bridegroom seeks the blessings from the older women. As a mark of respect, the groom offers them 'salaam'. People give their heartiest wishes to the newly wed.

Dinner, Prayers and Aarsimashaf

The guests are served a lavish dinner. Men and women are usually seated separately, for dining. After the dinner, the newly wed get the chance to sit together for the first time. The heads of the bride and groom are covered using dupatta. Thereafter, the newly wed read prayers, as per the instructions of the Maulvi. The Quran is placed between the bride and groom and they are allowed to look at each other only through mirrors.

Muslim Post-Wedding Rituals

In India, wedding is something that cannot be restricted to a single-day celebration. People in different communities, following different religions, have their own way of honoring the newly wed couple, post marriage. The post-wedding rituals followed by Muslims are divided into four phases, wherein the bride is bid goodbye by her family and is welcomed to her 'new home', by the groom's family.

All the four phases of the rituals are filled with touching moments. If you want to know more about post-wedding rituals followed by Muslims, then go through the following lines.

Muslim Post-Wedding Customs

Rukshat Ceremony

With tearful eyes, the bride's family and friends bid her goodbye, before she leaves for her house with her husband. The bride's father places his daughter's hand in the hand of his son-in-law and requests him to take good care of his dear daughter.

Welcoming The Bride

Giving a warm welcome to her daughter-in-law, the groom's mother raises the Quran above her head, as she enters her new home.

Chauthi Custom

Chauthi custom takes place on the fourth day after marriage, in which the bride visits her parental house.

Valimah Ceremony

Valimah ceremony is the lavish reception party that the groom's family hostsfor welcoming the bride. It is an occasion that aims to facilitate intimate relationships between the two families.

Arrange Marriages in Muslims

Arranged marriages although young people are at liberty to express their preferences and state what they are looking for in a prospective partner, it is not the usual practice for them actively to seek a partner for themselves. This is mostly done by their parents or other elders within the family. In other words, it is usually an 'arranged marriage'. Arranged marriage must fulfil the basic condition of the freely given consent of both the bride and the groom. A 'forced' marriage, where consent has not been given by either the bride or the groom, or is given only under excessive pressure, is a different matter; this would be contrary to the teachings of Islam, and would immediately call into question the validity of the marriage. Arranged marriages are the general custom among Muslims as the best way to find, vet and meet potential husbands or wives within the overall context of the Islamic way of life.

Community programs

There has been a recent[when?] emergence of events and programs held by community groups and organisations aimed at helping single Muslims to find prospective partners. These events and programs have mostly been found in non-Muslim countries, mainly in the USA and United Kingdom, due to the fact that there is growing concern from the organisers that the Muslim youth in non-Muslim countries are struggling to find prospective partners. The programs and events differ from traditional marriage bureaus and match making websites for the reason that participants can meet real people face to face and that the events do provide a platform for single Muslims to meet in a environment that is conducive to their faith.

Choice of partner

With regards to freedom of choice when marrying within their religion, Muslim men and women are given the right to choose who they want to marry. When marrying outside the religion, Muslim men may marry Christian or Jewish women but not other religions. Muslim women are not allowed to marry outside of Islam.

In relation to women, men are encouraged to get married to religiously devoted women.

Same-sex Marriage is not allowed in Islam.

Dowries in Muslim

At the wedding, a Muslim husband typically gives a gift, known as the Mahr or dower, to his wife. This type of dower, based on what was agreed upon by the couple, could be in the form of any item and "in any amount". An example is a cantar or a "great amount" of gold. However, the man can also marry a woman based on the amount of knowledge he has about the Quran, even though he has no material possessions.

After the consummation of their marriage, it is customary for the male spouse to give a wedding reception, known as the Walima, to family members and friends. Such a reception serves as a celebration of the couple's happiness.

In Islam, both husbands and wives are described to have equal duties and rights, although men are further described as having a "degree above" their wives. The Islamic rationale for this is that the husband is given authority within the household because he has received a heavier load of responsibilities, which include taking care of the woman who has become his wife, and that he also provides financial support to her. Wives are expected to respect their husbands wishes. On the other hand, men are expected to safeguard their women, because they were married to women with God's trust. Yet, both man and woman, once married, are expected to act as responsible guardians. Married men are to act as guardians of their families. The women, in turn, become guardians of the home and their children.

Marriage in Sikhism

Anand Karaj is the Sikh marriage ceremony, meaning "Blissful Union" or "Joyful Union", that was introduced by Guru Amar Das. The four Lavan (marriage hymns which take place during the marriage ceremony) were composed by his successor, Guru Ram Das. It was originally legalised in India through the passage of the Anand Marriage Act 1909 but is now governed by the Sikh Reht Maryada (Sikh code of conduct and conventions) that was issued by the Shiromani Gurdwara Prabandhak Committee (SGPC). It dictates that only those who follow the Sikh religion may marry under the ceremony, therefore, Sikhs cannot marry persons professing other religions under it. It also states that child marriage is invalid and that no account should be taken of the prospective spouse's caste. However, in practice, many Sikhs take preference in people from their caste.

Punjabis are large hearted people who love splendor and grandeur. They are also keen on festivals and celebrations. This nature of Punjabis also reflects in their marriage celebrations. Like other Indian weddings, a Punjabi marriage ceremony is very ritualistic but also full of fun and frolic. It is in fact one of the most colorful and musical marriage ceremonies in the country. Each ceremony is like an excuse for merriment. A Punjabi Wedding is very vibrant and celebrated like a big carnival, exhibiting splendid grandeur.

A Punjabi wedding ceremony begins with Roka which is very much like anengagementceremony where both the family for the first time formally announces the prospective marriage. The Roka is then followed by celebrations like 'Sagan' and 'Chunni Chadana' performed at the groom's and bride's family respectively. The joy of a Punjabi wedding begins with the Sangeet and Mehendi ceremony from where the real fun and frolic starts. Bhangras and Giddas make a Punjabi wedding more colorful. Like other Hindu weddings phere and kanyadaan are important rituals of a Punjabi Wedding. A Punjabi Wedding ceremony solemnizes with Mangal Pheras and the bride is departed to her in laws home that very day.

The Anand Karaj usually takes place at a Gurdwara, although not necessarily so; the marriage may also be conducted at the bride's residence or any other place where the Guru Granth Sahib (Sikh holy book) has been installed. If the marriage takes place somewhere other than a gurdwara, the place must be suitable and the Guru Granth Sahib must be installed following the proper procedure. Any Amritdhari (man or woman who is a strict adherent of Sikhism) may perform the marriage ceremony. In a recent verdict of the Sri Akaal Takht Sahib,i.e. a Hukumnama, Anand Karaj will take place only in the Gurudwara as Sri Guru Granth Sahib will not be taken to any marriage hall for that purpose.

"Anand Karaj" literally "joyful ceremonial occasion or proceedings" is the name given the Sikh marriage ceremony. For Sikhs, married status is the norm and the ideal; through it, according to their belief, come the best opportunities for serving God's purpose and the well being of humanity, and it affords the best means of fulfillment of individuality and attainment of bliss. Sikhism repudiates monkery, vows of celibacy, renunciation or the sannyasin state.

Important Features

The following are other important points that must be adhered to by the Sikh couple and their families:

- Marriage is a partnership of equals.
- No consideration is to be given to caste, social status, race or lineage.
- No dowry is allowed.
- No day is considered holier above any other, hence no astrological considerations are to be made and no superstitions are to be observed in fixing the date of the wedding.
- The religious ceremony to take place in a Gurdwara or in the presence of *Guru Granth Sahib.*
- Burden of the cost of the wedding to be shared as equally as possible.

The Anand Karaj ceremony is joyous and festive event in which families and friends from both sides are heavily involved. Most Sikh weddings take place in the morning and are completed before noon. Following the ceremony is a langar or a formal lunch. The wedding event can last for the whole day and may spill into the next day.

Most families combine the wedding ceremony with the engagement ceremony called the "Kurmai", where the Kurmai is held just before the wedding vows or Laava. The engagement ceremony can also be held as a separate event on a different day. It is usually conducted in the Gurdwara or at the home of the groom-to-be. It involves *Ardas*, *Kirtan*, *Sagaan* (Exchange of gifts) and Langar. In the "Sagaan" ceremony, the groom is presented with a kara, kirpan, Indian sweets, fresh fruits, dried fruits and nuts. The bride-to-be's family in turn are presented with garments and sweets for the bride-to-be.

Pre-Wedding Punjabi Ritual

Punjabi marriage traditions are very elaborate and ritualistic. They begin days before the actual wedding day in the form of pre-wedding ceremonies. Roka is the first pre-wedding ceremony where the two families formally meet to finalize the relationship between the two families. *Roka* is then followed by a series of colorful and interesting occasions like 'Sagan and *Chunni Chadhana*'.

Tahka (or Roka) is when the immediate family of both sides meets and blesses the union and the engagement is then announced.

A month or so before the big day...

- *Shri Akhand Path* is the continuous reading of the Guru Granth Sahib, the Path is usually held by the groom's side preceding the Kudmai.
- Kudmai (or *sagai* or *mangni*) is the engagement ceremony; it usually takes place on the third day of the Shri Akhand Path with friends and family of both sides.
- Chunni ceremony is where the ladies from the groom's side adorn the bride-to-be with vermillion, make-up, mehendi, jewelry, bangles, a bindi and a bright colored dupatta as a welcoming gesture. This ceremony can take place during the tahka or any other day preceding the wedding ceremony.
- *Mayaan*, a beautifying ritual performed (by the females in the brides family) by rubbing a mixture of about 11/2 cups of besan (gram flour) 2-3 tsps. of *Sandalwood* powder, 2 tsp butter or almond oil and 3 teaspoons of water on the bride.

The Week before...

- Sangeet: is a celebration of song and dance which usually takes place about a week before the wedding day. The event is celebrated on both the bride's and groom's side separately.
- Mehndi is where the bride, her female relatives and friends get together to have a henna party, usually two to three days before the wedding day.

The Night before...

- Churah: The bride's maternal uncle(s) adorn her wrists with bangles (traditionally ivory) the night before the wedding.
- Jago is a festive dance that also takes place a night or two before the wedding.

As the actual wedding day comes near, the celebrations become more vibrant and vivacious. *Sangeet* is held only few days before the wedding day and is the most amusing pre-wedding ceremony. Meheandi is held a night or two before the marriage day and is important part of the pre-wedding celebrations.

Roka Ceremony

Roka ceremony marks the beginning of a formal relationship between the two families. It is basically carried out to secure the commitment of both the parties. It is a small function involving the family members and close relatives of both the prospective bride and groom. The families involved exchange gifts, sweets, fruits and dry fruits.

Sagan Ceremony

Sagan ceremony can be held either at the groom's house or at a banquet hall. A havan is performed by a pundit. Thereafter, the prospective ride's father applies *Tilak* (made of kesar, rice grains and flower petals) on the boy's forehead. All the relatives and friends of the girl's side come forward to bless the prospective groom, offer sweets to him and give him cash/gifts.

Chunni Chadana

On the occasion of *chunni chadana*, groom's parents and close relatives visit the bride's house. The groom's sister or sister in law presents the girl a red sari, as a token of acceptance of the girl in their family. Thereafter, the girl is dressed in the clothes given by the boy's family.

The main ritual of the ceremony is when the girl's would be mother-in-law places a red *chunni* on the girl's head and gives her some traditional jewelry. Following this is a ritual in which the girl is fed boiled rice and milk by all the relatives of the boy that are present at the time. The ceremony comes to an end with the exchanging of rings between the prospective bride and groom.

Sangeet

Sangeet is the musical program, which is held at both the bride as well as groom's house. In the sangeet session, wedding folk songs are sung and all the relatives and friends dance to the tunes of the music. This ceremony is considered auspicious as the wedding songs are said to be full of blessings for the prospective couple. Also, this ceremony becomes amusing with interesting songs with teasing punches for the prospective couple and dance performances by every younger and elder member of the family.

Mehendi

Like other Hindu weddings, mehendi is also an important pre-wedding ritual of a Punjabi marriage. As a part of Kwar Dhoti, *Mehendi* is taken to the girl's place by the boy's sister and brother-in-law. This *Mehendi* is then applied to the girl's hands and feet in beautiful motifs. *Kwar Dhoti* also includes dry fruits, specifically dry dates. The girl eats half of a dry date and the other half is given to the boy, this ritual is said to increase the love between the two.

Takha: In this ceremony, the boy and the girl commit to enter a wedlock, and won't consider any more matrimonial proposals. Ardaas is done, followed by exchange of gifts.

Mangni/shagun: The engagement. Usually very high profile. This when the girls side of the family goes to the boys' side with gifts, jewellery, and other goods, to confirm the engagement.

Rokka: Official engagement ceremony when the bride and groom to be exchange rings and relatives and family and friends come give present/ money and blessing to the couple to be.

Dholki (sangeet): Can be one day or many days, usually high profile in a banquet hall, ladies sings traditional songs, and it is the eastern version of the western Bridal shower. Nowadays, people hire DJs and have a dance party followed by dinner.

ladies sangeet-is held for the bride and her bridesmaids-in the western countries they just do it in a banquet hall dance and do the jaago. But in Inidia it is done altogether with dholki and mehnd

Mehendi: The Mehendi ceremony takes place in the atmosphere of a party. The bride and other ladies get mendhi (henna designs) done, on their hands and feet (most ladies get it done only on their hands but the bride gets it done on both hands and feet). For the bride the mendhi is sent by the future mother-in-law.

Vatna/Butna: This ritual demands that the bride-to-be stay at home in her old clothes for a couple of days before her wedding. On the wedding day, before her bath, *butna* (a paste of powdered turmeric and mustard oil) is applied on her body by female relatives and friends. *Ubtan* is supposed to bring glow on the bride's and groom's body especially face. This tradition is also known as *shaint* in some cultures. After this ritual, bride and groom are constrained from meeting each other until the wedding ceremony. Both, the *ghara ghardoli* and the ubtan ceremonies are also performed for the groom at his house. Here the decorated pitcher of water (ghadoli) is brought for his bath by his bhabi (elder brother's wife).

The rut jugga ceremony is where the family dances and sings in the beautifully decorated wedding home. Rut Jugga is in the last hours of the night. They decorate copper or brass vessel called "gagger" with diyas (clay lamps) and fill them with mustard oil and light them.

The bride/bridegrooms maternal aunt (mammi) carries it on her head, and another lady will have a long stick with bells, and she will be shaking it. The ladies will then go into other friends and families homes and be welcomed by sweets and drinks, they will then dance there and move on. It is a loud ceremony, filled with joy, dancing, fireworks, and food. And if the family wishes the ladies' *dholki* (ladies night of singing) and mendhi will follow the mayian and dinner.

Punjabi Wedding Rituals

Punjabi Wedding ceremony is an interesting ceremony full of several rituals and customs. The wedding preparations start day before the actual wedding ceremony. Overall, a Punjabi wedding is very vibrant and colorful. The wedding ceremony starts from the Chuda ceremony and at the groom's place with Vatna ceremony.

Actual wedding takes place at the girl's residence. The date of the wedding is set by mutual consultation to suit both parties.

Astrological or horoscopic considerations are discountenanced in Sikh calculations. Matters such as the strength of the barat (the bridegroom's party), timing of arrival and departure, duration of stay, are also decided mutually so that the bride's parents may make suitable arrangements. Before setting out, the bridegroom may go to a gurdwara to make obeisance and offer ardas before the Guru Granth Sahib.

Rituals at the Marriage Venue

Milni Ceremony

When the groom's *barat* reaches the wedding venue, Milni ceremony is performed. The bride's close relatives give a warm welcome to the groom and his relatives with flower garlands. Rose water is sprinkled on them. In the Milni ceremony, the girl's relatives give *Shagun* (a token of good luck) to the groom's close relatives. It is done in the descending order, beginning from the elder most. Cash and clothes are gifted.

Varmala

Varmala is the actual beginning of marriage rituals on the involves the exchange of garlands between the bride and groom. Friends and relatives of the bride and groom indulge in teasing and fun, to celebrate this happy occasion. An auspicious time or muhurat is chosen for the performance of wedding ceremony.

At the time of *muhurat*, the *purohit* conducts a *puja* for the groom, in which the groom is asked to chant the first few mantras. It is during this time, when the bride's sisters indulge in stealing of shoes. It is a fun tradition, in which the girls charge a fee for agreeing to return the shoes.

Kanyadaan and Phere

The wedding is actually solemnized with four important rituals- the *kanyadaan*, in which the bride's father giving his daughter's hand to the groom, the *Mangalpheras* in front of the sacred fire, the *sindoor* ritual when the groom applies vermilion to the girl's hair partition and the *mangalsutra* when the groom ties a beaded necklace to the girl's neck. When all these rituals are over, the couple gets up to touch the feet of all the elder members in the family and seek their blessings for a happily married life.

Sarbala/Shabbala: A young nephew or cousin also dons similar attire. He is called the sarbala/shabbala (caretaker of the groom) and accompanies him .

Sehrabandi: The groom's sister ties *sehera* to his turban.

Varna: The groom's bhabi lines his eyes with *surma* (kohl). After this, the groom's sisters and cousins feed and decorate his mare. varna, a ceremony that is supposed to ward off the evil eye. The cash is given away to the poor.

Milni (means "Introductions") : The Ardas is performed by the priest (Giani) followed by the formal introductions of the main male players in the families. Example is both eldest *chachas* (father's younger brother) will come together and exchange garlands of flowers and money. After or during the wedding, ladies will do the same thing, but a much smaller affair.

Jaimala: After *milni*, the bride and groom come in the middle of the circle where the family is standing, and place a heavily made garland made of flowers on each other to state, they accept each other and will love and live together with one and other.

Kanyadaan:Bride's father puts a ring on the boy's finger and then he gives his daughter to the boy. This ritual is known as the *kanyadaan*. It is after the *kanyadaan* that the pheras begin.

Pheress/Lavan: In a Hindu Punjabi wedding, *agni* (sacred fire) is usually encircled seven times. In a Sikh Wedding, the Bride and Groom will walk in tow around the *Guru Granth Sahib* four times.

Juta chhupai. This is when the girl's young relatives grab the groom's untended shoes and hide it away to be returned after the ceremony for a fee which is *kalecharis* of gold for the bride's sisters and of silver for her cousins. This joyful custom is called *juta chhupai*.

Post-Wedding Punjabi Rituals

Punjabis love celebrations. Their marriage ceremonies are thus extremely grand and elaborate. Even after few days of marriage, the celebrations at the groom's and bride's places are on. The post wedding celebrations start right after the solemnization of marriage at the *mandap*. Preparations for *Vidaai* and *Ashwirwad* ceremony go hand in hand. Once the couple is blessed by all the elderly people at home, the brother of the bride accompanies the couple for Vidaai to the main exit of their home.

Punjabis love celebrations. Their marriage ceremonies are thus extremely grand and elaborate. Even after few days of marriage, the celebrations at the groom's and bride's places are on. The post weddingcelebrations start right after the solemnization of marriage at the Mandap. Preparations for *vidaai* and *ashwirwad* ceremony go hand in hand. Once the couple is blessed by all the elderly people at home, the brother of the bride accompanies the couple for Vidaai to the main exit of their home. The celebrations after *vidaai* takes place at the groom's place except for the pag phere Ceremony at the bride's home the next day after marriage.

Vidaai Ceremony

In the Vidaai ceremony, the bride departs from her parental house and bids goodbye to her parents, friends and relatives. While leaving the home, the bride throws back handful of puffed rice back at the main exit of her father's home as a token of her father's prosperity and good luck. Thereafter, she boards a beautifully decorated car and heads her way towards her new home.

Swagat Ceremony

After the marriage is over, the bride is welcomed at the groom's house. She is welcomed by her mother in law at the entrance of her new home by putting the *sarson ka tel* (mustard oil) on both the sides of the entrance door. Then, a traditional aarti of both the bride and the groom is performed. Thereafter, the newly wedded couple goes to the *pooja* room and seeks the blessings of God.

Mooh Dikhai Ki Rasm

Mooh dikhai is the formal introduction of the new bride to the rest of the family. The mother-in-law gives the bride jewelry, cash and gifts. It is a ceremony to facilitate intimacy. The other relatives also give presents and cash to the bride.

Reception Ceremony

To make the bride feel at home, the groom's parents usually throw a reception party. It is an occasion, where the newly wedded couple is given a warm welcome by all. It does not have an ancient origin. In fact, it is a western concept that is gaining popularity in India too.

Pag Phere

As a part of *phera dalna* ritual, the newly wedded couple visits the bride's house on the next day after marriage. Usually, the girl's brother comes to take them back to his home. The bride's parents prepare a special lunch. Also, the newly weds are given lots of gifts and sweets. This is actually a formal introduction of groom to the bride's family.

Rituals observed at the groom's house: *Pani vaarna*. The groom's mother performs the traditional aarti with a pitcher of water. She makes seven attempts to drink the water from the pitcher. The groom must allow her to succeed only at the seventh attempt. The bride must, with her right foot, kick the mustard oil that is put on the sides of the entrance door before she enters the house.

Phera Dalna: the newly weds visit the bride's parents on the day after the wedding. The bride's brother usually fetches them.

Christian Marriage

Civil laws recognize marriage as having social and political status. Christian theology affirms the secular status of marriage, but additionally views it from a moral and religious perspective that transcends all social interests.

While marriage is honored among Christians and throughout the *Bible*, it is not seen as necessary for everyone. Single people who either have chosen to remain unmarried or who have lost their spouse for some reason are neither incomplete in Christ nor personal failures. There is no suggestion that Jesus was ever married.

Divorce or dissolution of marriage is generally seen from a Christian perspective as less than the ideal, with specific opinions ranging from it being universally wrong to the notion that it sometimes is inevitable.

The *Bible* holds that sex is reserved for marriage. It says that sex outside of marriage is the sin of adultery (for the married person) if either sexual participant is married to another person. Voluntary sexual intercourse between persons not married to each other is considered the sin of fornication.

Ideas about roles and responsibilities of the husband and wife is the long-held male-dominant/female-submission view.

A small but growing number of Christian denominations conduct weddings between same-sex coupleswhere it is civilly legal. A few others perform ceremonies to bless same-sex unions without recognising them as marriage.

Christians believe that marriage is considered in its ideal according to the purpose of God. At the heart of God's design for marriage is companionship and intimacy. The biblical picture of marriage expands into something much broader, with the husband and wife relationship illustrating the relationship between Christ and the church.

It is also considered in its actual occurrence, sometimes involving failure. Therefore, the Bible speaks on the subject of divorce. The New Testament recognizes a place for singleness. Salvation within Christianity is not dependent on the continuation of a biological lineage.

Marriage in Buddhism

The Buddhist wedding does not even include any complex rituals. The Buddhist marriage is based more on faith and belief than any religious foundation. The most pleasant thing about a Buddhist wedding is that other than anymatrimonial customs and traditions, they are more inclined towards a sincere effort to create a harmonious relationship.

There is no compulsory ceremony in a Buddhist marriage, it is entirely up to the wish of a couple to go for a registered marriage at court or one of the few Buddhist temples licensed as a legal marriage venue.

However, in general a typical Buddhist wedding takes place in two parts, one of them is a Buddhist component and the other is a non-Buddhist component. The first one involves offering hearty prayers along with gifts to the almighty and monks. In this section, a couple is also meant to take vows of faithfulness and understanding. The non-Buddhist component engulfs all the traditional practices followed specifically by the family of the couple which may include a prayer in the spirit house, a feast or any gift exchange.

Pre-wedding Buddhist Rituals

A Buddhist marriage is the simplest possible marriage. There are no religious tangles or mandatory rules and regulations. The entire marriage ceremony is treated as a social affair unlike the other religions which also regard it as a religious affair. The only thing that a coupler needs to do for tying a nuptial knot is to go for a registered marriage at court or one of the few Buddhist temples licensed as a legal marriage venue.

There is no necessary involvement of monks or any religious preacher. However, in general people find it more auspicious to consult their priests before solemnizing any relationship and that is why before the marriage ceremony, pre wedding rituals like Horoscope Matching and Chessian Betrothal Ceremony takes place in almost all the Buddhist families.

Horoscope Matching

Horoscope matching is given due consideration among Buddhists. After having matched the horoscopes of the prospective bride and groom, the boy's family, in consultation with the lama (priest), selects an auspicious day for putting forward the proposal for marriage.

Chessian Betrothal Ceremony

Chessian is the betrothal ceremony, in which the maternal uncle of the bride'sparent is seated on a raised platform. The priest recites prayer and gives "madyan", a religious drink to everybody. This is followed by the fixing of wedding date in consultation with the astrologer.

Buddhist Wedding Rituals

In general, a Buddhist wedding ceremony takes place in a temple. Though there is no compulsion to match stars or find out auspicious time for it, people have general tendency to believe in this activity. Thus, on an auspicious time, both the bride and the groom bow in front of Buddha image. After this, they recite certain prayers and chants and light incense sticks and candles in front of the image. Then the parents of the couple put a loop of strings on their heads to connect them. After this, the couple makes offering to the monks such as flowers, food, sweets and medicines. At times, token money is also given to the temple.

The priest then places a thread on the heads of the monks. Recitations in Pali language are made to evoke blessings for the newly wed couple. The string is connected to a container that is sanctified after the ceremony. Also, a red paste is applied on the foreheads of the bride and the groom. Though Buddhist weddings are not very formal but their form has changed significantly. Initially monks did not attend the weddings as they are present during the funeral rites. Nowadays, the role of the monks in weddings has become quite profound, however not compulsory.

Many Buddhist families still believe in the solemnization of the marriage on their own. This marriage ceremony is generally followed by some family rituals of the involved families like a prayer in the spirit house, a feast or any gift exchange. The couple can their directly leave for their new home from the marriage venue.

Modernity of Marriage

Many people believe that arranged marriage is the traditional form of marriage in India and that love marriage is a modern form that a few couples opt for, usually in urban areas. Love marriage differs from an "arranged marriage" in that the couple, rather than the parents, choose their own partner.

However, there are various instances from ancient scriptures of Hinduism, of romantic love marriages that were accepted in ancient times, for example Dushyanta and Shakuntala in the story of the mahabharata who undergo a love marriage. Somewhere in the course of time, arranged Marriages became predominant and love marriages became unacceptable. Despite some love marriages, the vast majority of Indians continue to have arranged marriages.

Divorce Laws in India

India has different divorce laws for different religions. Almost all the religions has their own divorce laws in India which are used amongs themselves. There are seperate laws for inter-cast or inter-religion marriages. Divorce laws in India for Hindus is described in Hindu Marriage Act, 1955. Hindu Marriage Act is also used for Sikhs, Buddhists and Jains as they don't have their own seperate marriage anddivorce laws. Here is the list of various divorce laws in India for various religions:

- Hindu (including Sikhs, Jains and Buddists) : Hindu Marriage Act, 1955
- Muslims : Dissolution of Muslim Marriages Act, 1939
- Christians : Indian Divorce Act, 1869
- Parsis : The Parsi Marriage and Divorce Act, 1936
- Inter-Cast of Inter-Religion : Special Marriage Act, 1954

Grounds for Divorce in India

In India divorce is granted mainly on 4 different grounds. (You can see the grounds for divorce for Muslims here (section number 2):

1. Adultery

2. Desertion
3. Cruelty
4. Impotency
5. Chronic Diseases

Divorce Procedure in India

Divorce in India is certainly not an easy procedure. The entire process of divorce that starts from coping up with emotional ups and downs to contesting for the long awaited divorce decree for several months is definitely a tough affair to get through. Before opting for a divorce you should be aware of the fact that a divorce procedure in India extents for almost a year and in some special cases of disputes the procedure may continue for years. The long distressing process of divorce will be easier for you to handle if you have a firm determination to get the divorce.

Due to existence of diverse religious faiths in India, the Indian Judiciary has implemented laws separately for couples belonging to different religious beliefs.

Divorce procedure in India is based on the following acts.

- The Hindu Marriage Act, 1955
- The Parsi Marriage and Divorce Act, 1936
- The dissolution of Muslim Marriage act, 1939
- The Parsi Marriage and Divorce Act, 1936
- The Special Marriage Act, 1956
- The Foreign Marriage Act, 1969

With the advancement of time and social awareness, several acts have been passed by the government to make the present day divorce procedure in India more progressive with respect to gender affairs and related sensitive issues. The Muslim Women Act 1986 was passed to protect the rights of Muslim women on divorce. For inter caste and inter-religion marriages the divorce laws are approved under The Special Marriage Act, 1956.

A contested divorce is filed on the grounds that are mentioned in the acts passed out separately for different Indian religions.

Getting a divorce through mutual consent should always be preferred over thecontested divorce as the procedure of getting a mutual divorce is simpler in comparison to that of the other. For a mutual divorce procedure in India, you can come to an agreement with your spouse where you may resolve all kinds of disputes regarding maintenance, custody of children and such.

Under Section 13B of the Hindu Marriage Act, a husband and wife can file a mutual divorce only when they have lived apart for at least a year. The couple must jointly mention about their inability to continue the marital relationship due to some unavoidable circumstances. Both the sides must voluntarily agree to dissolve the marriage.

The filing of a mutual divorce by both the husband and the wife is termed as 'the first motion'. A couple can file for a second motion after a gap of six months. The six months time span is provided to the couple so that they get the time to re-consider their marriage.

A divorce decree can be passed before the completion of the six months term if all the mandatory requirements for the divorce are sufficed. If the divorce file is not withdrawn within eighteen months the court passes a divorce decree. Incase one of the sides withdraws his/her petition the court initiates to make an enquiry. If the concerned side disagrees to give the consent, the court holds no right to pass the divorce judgment.

Mutual Divorce in India

Mutual Divorce is to be filed by the couple only after they have lived apart for at least a year. A petition supported with affidavits for divorce should be filed in the district court by the both the spouses. The husband and the wife should jointly state to the court that they are unable to live together as they are facing immense difficulties in adjustment.

The filing of divorce petition by both the husband and the wife is legally known as the "The First Motion Petition for Mutual Consent Divorce". "The Second Motion Petition for Mutual Consent Divorce" mentioned in the sub-section (2) of Section 13 B is filed when the couple reappears to the court for the second time after a period of six months. If the judge is satisfied after a hearing from both the husband and wife, the court announces a mutual divorce decree.

If the couple fails to appear in the court after six months and not later than eighteen months from the date of first motion, the divorce petition becomes null and void. Either of the couple can withdraw his/her petition within the six months term.

A judgment for mutual divorce is passed out only if all the necessary agreements required for a mutual divorce in India are strictly maintained. The husband and the wife should come to terms of settlement regarding the following issues.

- Custody of Child
- Return of Dowry Articles / Istridhan of Wife
- Lump Sum Maintenance Amount of Wife
- Litigation Expenses

For a mutual divorce in India, we would always suggest you to consult an experienced lawyer who will effectively guide you to get the divorce through a mutual agreement done between you and your spouse.

Even though India still boasts of that nearly hundred percent of the marriages are a success, rapid urbanization and awareness of various rights are now instigating thedivorce rate to shoot up. Empowerment of women has initiated the dissolution of marriage in urban areas as financially educated women are now open to the option of ending the relationship rather than to bear life long abuses silently. The campaigns on gender equality are now giving rise to ego clashes between the husband and wife, especially if the wife too is the bread earner of the family.

Around 20 years back India had a negligible divorce rate of around 5%. But based on the increasing number of divorce being filed today, the divorce rate in India is expected to rise up at a faster rate by the ensuing year.

Divorce Under Hindu law

The Hindu Marriage Act, 1955 came into existence, eight years after the independence of the country. Divorce between two persons married under the Hindu Marriage Act is also governed by the same Act. Section 13 of the Hindu Marriage Act deals with the grounds on which the parties can seek a decree of divorce from a competent court having jurisdiction to entertain such petition.

Grounds for Divorce (under Section 13)

A petition for divorce may be presented by either the husband or wife for dissolving the marriage on the following grounds:

That the other party:

1. Has after the marriage had voluntary sexual intercourse with any other person; or
2. Has after the marriage treated the petitioner with cruelty
3. Has deserted the petitioner for a continuous period of not less than two years immediately preceding the presentation of the petition,
4. Has ceased to be a Hindu by conversion to another religion,
5. Has been incurably of unsound mind or has been continuously or intermittently from a mental disorder that the petitioner cannot reasonably be expected to live with such a person,
6. Has been suffering from a virulent and incurable form of leprosy,

7. Has been suffering from venereal disease in a communicable form
8. Has renounced the world by entering any religious order.
9. Has not been heard of as being alive for a period of seven years or more by persons who would have naturally heard of it, had that party been alive.

No petition for divorce can be filed by either party unless one year has elapsed since the date of marriage.

Under Section 14 of the Hindu Marriage Act. 1955, no petition for divorce can be filed within one year of the marriage. But in case the petitioner's case is of exceptional hardship, High Court is empowered to grand leave to file the case before the expiry of one year.

Additional grounds for divorce by a wife

In addition to the grounds stated above a wife may also present a petition for the dissolution of her marriage on the following grounds.

1. Where the marriage was solemnized before the commencement of this Act, and the husband had married again before such commencement or that any other wife of the husband whom he had married before such commencement was alive at the time of the marriage. In such a case its necessary that the other wife is alive at the time of presentation of the petition.
2. That the husband has after the marriage been guilty of rape, sodomy or bestiality.
3. That her marriage whether consummated or not was solemnized before she attained the age of 15 years and she has repudiated the marriage after attaining that age but before attaining the age of 18 years.

Divorce by mutual Consent

Where both the parties mutually agree that they want to divorce a petition may be presented on the ground that they have been living separately for a period of one year or more, that they have not been able to live together and that they have mutually agreed that the marriage should be dissolved.

Thereafter both the parties have to make a motion to the court not earlier than 6 months and not later than 18 months from the date of presentation of the petition and the court after hearing the parties and on being satisfied will pass a decree of divorce.

Filing of Petition

Every petition shall be presented to the District Court within the jurisdiction of which-

1. The marriage was solemnized
2. The other party at the presentation of the petition resides; or
3. The parties to the marriage last resided.

Divorce under Muslim law

Muslims are governed by their personal laws under which "Nikah" (i.e. marriage) is a contract and may be permanent or temporary and permits a man 4 wives if he treats all of them equally. To have a valid "Nikah" under the Muslim Law, presence of a Qazi (Priest) is not necessary.

Merely a proposal in the presence and hearing of two sane males or one sane male and two sane female adults, all Muslims and acceptance of the said proposals at the same time constitute a valid Nikah under the Muslim Personal Law. A husband can divorce his wife without any reasons merely by pronouncing thrice the word "Talak". However for a Muslim woman to obtain divorce certain conditions are necessary.

5

KINSHIP SYSTEM IN INDIA

Kinship system is defined as the system of social relationships that constitute kinship in a particular culture, including the terminology that is used and the reciprocal obligations that are entailed. Kinship is a relationship between any entities that share agenealogical origin, through either biological, cultural, or historical descent. And descent groups, lineages, etc. are treated in their own subsections.

Kinship is one of the most basic principles for organizing individuals into social groups, roles, categories, and genealogy. Family relations can be represented concretely (mother, brother, grandfather) or abstractly after degrees of relationship. A relationship may have relative purchase (e.g., father is one regarding a child), or reflect an absolute (e.g., status difference between a mother and a childless woman). Degrees of relationship are not identical to heirship or legal succession. Many codes of ethics consider the bond of kinship as creating obligations between the related persons stronger than those between strangers, as in Confucian filial piety.

Kinship systems are mechanisms that link conjugal families (and individuals not living in families) in ways that affect the integration of the general social structure and enhance the ability of the society to reproduce itself in an orderly fashion. Kinship performs these social functions in two ways. First, through relationships defined by blood ties and marriage, kinship systems make possible ready-made contemporaneous networks of social ties sustained during the lifetimes of related persons and, second, they enable the temporal continuity of identifiable family connections over generations, despite the limited lifespan of a family's members.

Modernity, Family Patterns and Kinship Systems

There are at least three ways to develop historical typologies related to kinship and family. One way is to hypothesize a linear historical progression, which includes a family type existing at the beginning point in time, a particular historical process that will act upon the family and kinship structures (e.g., urbanization or industrialization), and a logical outcome at the end of the process.

A second approach builds upon the above approach by positing a transitional family type that emerges during the historical process and gives way in the final stages of the process to another family type. A third approach, which includes devising a family type based upon a configuration of attributes peculiar to a particular historical era (e.g., the Victorian family, the American colonial family), implies that any historical era represents a unique convergence of diverse factors.

Bipolar Typologies

By and large, sociologists have drawn a connection between kinship and family on the basis of a distinction between traditionalism and modernity. Generally, this distinction draws upon Henry Maine's depiction of the transformation of social relations in early societies. Maine argued that social relations changed from those based on ascriptive status (deriving from birth) to relations created and sustained through voluntary contractual arrangements. Maine's theory has evoked a series of typologies that, in large measure, refine the status- contract distinction. For instance, an ideal type developed by Ferdinand Toennies has provided a backdrop for later typologies. The Toennies typology itself refers to a shift from Gemeinschaft (community) as a form of social organization based upon an existential will (Wessenwille), which is suited to feudalism and peasant society, to Gesellschaft (society) as a social form based upon rational will (Kurwille), which fits an urban environment under modem capitalism. Contemporary family typologies, in building upon Toennies's conceptual scheme, portray a weakening of kinship obligations and constraints.

One position, rooted in George P. Murdock's (1949) analysis of cross-cultural archives, has resulted in the main sequence theory of social change in kinship structure (Naroll 1970). Main sequence theory pertains to the way differential gender contributions to production of material resources affects the use of kindred as human resources/ property.

This theory holds that basic changes in kinship are initiated by a shift in the relative importance of men and women to the economic life of the society. First, there is a modification in the economic division of labor by gender. (For example, in hoe cultures, women tend to do the farming; when plows are introduced, men become the farmers.) Second, the shift in sexual division of labor generates a change in married couples' choices of residence, the major alternatives being near the husband's relatives (patrilocal), the wife's (matrilocal), or anywhere the couple desires (neolocal). Third, the change in choice of residential site affects the line of descent and inheritance favored in the kinship system: the husband's side (patrilineal), the wife's (matrilineal), or both sides (bilateral). (In line with the shift in residence, plow cultures show a greater inclination toward patrilinearity than do hoe cultures.) Fourth, the transfer to lineage affiliation generates a change in kinship terminology, particularly in ways that show tribal or clan membership, or, in modern societies, the dissolution of larger kinship structures.

As applied to the emergence of modernity, main sequence theory predicts a continual emancipation from kinship constraints. An increase in the proportion of women in the labor force will produce a trend toward neolocal residence, which in turn will lead to increased emphasis upon bilaterality, weakening sibling ties and obligations to both sides of the extended family, and in the long run to changes in kin terminology and identity.

In a variation of main sequence theory, urban sociologists such as Wirth (1956) and Burgess and associates (1963) wrote on the effects of transferring the economic base of societies from the land to urban centers. The theme of their work is to be found in the German proverb "Stadt Luft macht frei" ("city air makes one free"). For example, Burgess and associates described a progression from what they named the institutional family to the companionship family. In this conceptualization, the institutional family, embedded in a larger kinship group, is characterized by patriarchy, clearly defined division of household labor by sex, and high fertility. Its unity is derived mainly from external constraints-social mores, religious authority, fixity in location, position in the social structure, and the value of familism (i.e., values giving priority to the collective welfare of the family over that of individual members). Burgess and associates regarded the institutional family as an adaptation to relatively immobile, rural, agricultural societies and believed its way of life was fixed over time.

By way of contrast, urban society, which is characterized by mobility, anonymity, and change, makes inoperative the social control mechanisms developed to maintain stable, rural societies. With the withering of these external controls on rural family life, Burgess, Locke, and Thomes proposed that the companionship family is bound together by internal forces-mutual affection, egalitarianism, a sense of belonging, common interests- and affords freedom from the demands of traditional family and kinship ties.

Unlike the urban sociologists, structural functionalists such as Talcott Parsons (1954) place considerable emphasis on the interaction of subsystems in the larger social system. In part, structural functionalists are concerned with economic and kinship factors in structuring nuclear family relationships. Parsons described American kinship as "a 'conjugal' system in that it is made up exclusively of interlocking conjugal families" and is multilineal (i.e., bilateral) in descent. Parsons associates kinship solidarity with unilineal descent, that is, with a "structural bias in favor of solidarity with the ascendant and descendant families in any one line of descent". The absence of such bias in the American descent system, Parsons suggests, is in large measure responsible for "the structural isolation of the individual conjugal family" (i.e., its autonomy).

The importance Parsons attributes to unilinearity as a factor in facilitating strong dependence upon kin ties is exemplified by his highlighting two exceptions to the structural isolation of the conjugal family in America-the upper-class elements, whose status depends on the continuity of their patrilineages' solidarity, and the lower-class elements, in which there is "a strong tendency to instability of marriage and a 'mother-centered' type of family structure". However, Parsons regards the urban middle class as characterizing "the focal American type of kinship." Since in the middle class the residence of the conjugal family typically is neolocal, and the conjugal family is economically independent of "the family of orientation of either spouse," the role of the conjugal family in U.S. society can be, for theoretical purposes, understood as master of its own destiny, rid of the impediments of extended-family ties.

In reaction to those sociologists who see modernity as inimical to bonds of kinship, other social scientists turn their attention to the attenuated functions of kinship in contemporary society. Just as Goode (1963) notes a "fit" between the needs of modern capitalist society for a socially and geographically highly mobile population and the flexibility of the isolated conjugal family system, the revisionists indicate a similar fit between the existence of a highly mobile population and the presence of kin who give emergency aid and social support to relatives.

The revisionists shift our attention away from constraints imposed by kinship loyalties and obligations and direct it instead to sources of services, goods, and emotional support that cannot readily be supplied by bureaucracies, markets, or other agencies. In his typology, Litwak (1960a, 1960b) distinguishes the isolated nuclear family (without kiship resources) from the traditional extended family (implying a hierarchy of authority), on the one hand, and from the modified extended family (which consists of a network of related but autonomous nuclear families), on the other. Although, the revisionists have not destroyed the foundation of the bipolar family typologies, they do focus on a previously neglected area of analysis.

Three-Stage Typologies

Some modernization typologies introduce a third, transitional stage between traditional and modern kinship and family structures. These typologies accept the position that initially there is an emancipation from traditional kinship constraints and obligations, but they also propose that at some point new values of modernity emerge to fill the vacuum left by the dissipation of the old kinship constraints. For example, building on the work of LePlay, Zimmerman and Frampton (1966) offer a scheme of transformation in which families change from a patriarchal form to a stem-family structure and thence to an unstable family type. Zimmerman and Frampton begin with the premise that each social organization derives its "essential character" from a triad of "imperishable institutions"-family, religion, and property.

However, in their view, "familism is necessary in all complete social organization to a degree more imperative than the need for property". Zimmerman and Frampton regard the patriarchal family as the most familistic form. The patriarchal type is rooted in idealistic religious values and is characterized by a common household of a patriarch and his married sons and their families, wherein the property is held in the name of the "house," with the father as trustee. They identify the patriarchal form as having been prevalent among agriculturists in the Orient, in rural Russia, and among Slavonic peasants.

With urbanization and industrialization, however, the unstable family becomes predominant. Zimmerman and Frampton associate the unstable family with materialism and individualism and the resulting atomization of social life. Individuals are "freed from all obligations toward their parents and relatives", and the identity of each conjugal family as a social unit ends with the death of the parents and the dispersal of the children.

The stem family represents a transitional state between the patriarchal and unstable forms. The stem family extends branches into urban centers while retaining its roots in the ancestral lands. As a result, the stem family provides a balance between the security of the traditional influences and resources of the "house" and the freedom and resources of the cities. However, historical researchers yield less idyllic descriptions of the stem family than the Zimmerman and Frampton portrait.

A less romantic depiction of a transitional family type is drawn by Lawrence Stone (1975) in his typology of the English family's movement from feudalism to modernity. Stone posits the existence of a dual historical process. He places the decline of the importance of kin ties in the context of the emergence of a powerful, centralized state, and he then regards the rise of the modern family as an ideological emergence accompanying the development of capitalism.

Problem of Structure in Modernity Typologies

Typologies depicting historical transformations in family and kinship place much emphasis on the "fit" between the needs of modern industrial society and the presence of the conjugal family type. Despite this conjecture, Parsons (1954, p. 184) suggests that in western society an "essentially open system" of kinship, with its "primary stress upon the conjugal family" and its lack of larger kin structures, has existed for centuries, long before the modern period. Like Macfarlane (1986), Parsons dates its establishment in late medieval times "when the kinship terminology of the European languages took shape."

Moreover, Goode's (1963) analysis of family trends in eleven societies indicates that acceptance of modern, conjugal family ideology may precede economic and industrial development rather than come as a subsequent adaptation. Such findings cast doubt on the validity of the dichotomy between traditional societies and modernity as providing a theoretical basis for the typologies discussed above.

Parsons argues that:

1. there is an incompatibility between corporate kinship and multilineal systems, and
2. in large measure, this incompatibility accounts for the prevalence of highly adaptable, structurally independent conjugal households in modern societies.

However, findings by Davenport (1959), Mitchell (1963), Pehrson (1957), Peranio (1961), and others that corporate structures of kinship (such as clans) do exist in some multilineal kinship systems undercut

Parsons's argument that such structures are to be found only in unilineal systems. Nevertheless, if multilateral kinship systems can accommodate corporate structures, then they can also include other kinship elements that sustain loyalties to descent groups and facilitate segmentation of the society.

The Problem of Connecting Kinship and Family in Modernity Typologies

Revisionists of the isolated conjugal family position have presented considerable evidence of residual elements of kinship ties in contemporary society. However, they do not adequately explain the connections between types of kinship systems and variation in performance of family functions in different parts of the social structure. Their main concern is with changes in kinship and family, changes that are consistent with the general loosening of tradition in modern society. But their focus on emancipation from tradition diverts their attention from

1. the influence of emerging ethnic, religious, or class interests upon patterns of integration of family networks in the larger social structure and
2. the temporal dimensions of kinship, which go beyond living kin to departed ancestors and generations yet to come.

Additionally, given the fact that the family-kinship typologies described above have their roots in the distinction between tradition and modernity, they overlook those nonindustrial, primarily nonurban societies in which families approach the companionship model as well as those ethnic and religious segments of industrial, primarily urban societies where strong familistic tendencies persist.

Except for Stone (1975) and Zimmerman and Frampton (1966), these typologies are based on the concept of emancipation from tradition, and they do not deal explicitly with the emergence of new family values (other than flexibility and freedom). Most of all, their emphasis on emancipation from the constraints of tradition precludes their explaining why cohesive forces of family and kinship may remain strong (or increase in strength) in the face of an economic and social environment that is hostile to stable family life. Exceptions are Sennett 1970 and Harris and Rosser 1983.

Critical Commentary on Historical Typologies

Family typologies describing historical trends from one period of history to another are vulnerable to criticism of their teleological assumptions. Criticisms often involve:

1. the definition of polar concepts and
2. the problem of inevitability.

Definition of polar concepts?

The definition of polar concepts depends upon the value commitments of the analyst. For example, those analysts who view trends in kinship and family as movement toward liberation from traditional constraints and from obstacles to personal independence define the original state as confining and generally unjust and the future state as enabling emancipation from these obsolete social structures.

Family-theorist Ernest Burgess and associates (1963) view the evolution of family structure as going "from institution to companionship"-from external community constraints upon family relations to voluntaristic unity that derives from affection, domestic peace, and common goals. Similarly, Marxists define the transition as being away from family structures required to sustain an economic system based on unearned rewards of the dominant class and suppression of the laboring class.

Their claim is that following the rise of future true communism, the dissolution of economic classes would liberate family life from the constraints and suffering imposed by economic-position; for Frederick Engels, under true communism, family life would be liberated from economic demands, and, founded on personal bonds, families would endure only as long as these bonds lasted.

By way of contrast, analysts favoring traditional values define the trend in family life as a steady decay of family structure. Pitirim Sorokin, upon whose work Zimmerman and Frampton base their typology, notes that "the family as a sacred union of husband and wife, of parents and children, will continue to disintegrate . . . . The home will become a mere overnight parking place mainly for sex-relationship." From another perspective, the behaviorist John Watson (1927) predicted that "in fifty years [1977], unless there is some change, the tribal custom of marriage will no longer exist. Family standards have broken down . . . The mystery and beauty of marriage and the rearing of children has pretty well broken down." In the Aldous Huxley's science fiction novel *Brave New World* (1955), all functions now performed by families would be community undertakings, and the word "mother" would be regarded as obscene.

The distinction between typologies focusing on personal liberation and those portraying decay highlights the fact that each approach deals with partial realities. Liberation typologies tend to slight disruptive activities of emerging family structure (e.g., spouse abuse, child abuse, splitting into factions, isolation from resources of kin and family).

Instead, they tend to associate these activities with traditional family structures. In the Soviet Union, family problems were generally attributed to survivals of the traditional pre-Revolution family forms. Decay typologies do the opposite. They tend to underestimate unifying elements and personal satisfactions associated with the emerging family types and to overestimate the chaos associated with these types.

Problem of inevitability?

Some typologies posit a straight-line progression from a beginning state to an end state, while others at least imply a degree of indeterminacy in movement. For any particular typology, the degree of indeterminacy depends on the analyst's conception of history. For example, the Burgess institution-to-companionship family typology assumes there to be a major historical evolution from fairly isolated rural communities to societies with a high degree of industrialization; the family and kinship institutions evolve through a long series of adaptations to keep up with the industrialization of societies and a movement from a rural to an urban way of life.

Similar typologies-like Toennies's Gemeinschaft to Gesellschaft ([1887] 1957) and Redfield's folk society to civilization (1947)-are based on comparable assumptions deriving from the dictum of Henry Maine, namely, that, as an overarching historical trend, the basis for social relations has been evolving from status to contract.

Despite the inevitability of trends implicit in the definition of polarities of family and kin structure in typologies of liberation (or decay), with the passage of time, definitions of polarities change. For example, analysts have redefined the concept of companionship as an end-state. In the 1940s, Burgess regarded the future end-state as one in which the husband and wife

1. would be married without interference from family and community constraints,
2. would remain united through affection and common interests,
3. would maintain an equality in decision making and other aspects of family status, and
4. would orient their parenthood toward producing children with healthy personalities.

But variations in family life included under the "companionship family" definition have been broadly expanded over time. By the end of the twentieth century, the end-state of the companionship family (as well as the unstable-family concept) has been redefined to include a diversity of household arrangements, such as

1. couples living together without formal marriage;
2. same-sex couples and their children (by adoption or by birth from previous or supplementary liaisons); and
3. voluntary single-parent households.

Given these modifications in the concept of the companionship family, the very nature of the typology has been transformed. As a result, it is difficult to determine what family and kinship theorists will consider to be the evolutionary outcome twenty-five years from the present.

According to Murdoch's (1949) depiction of main sequence theory (described earlier), the changing pattern of employment has facilitated the widespread movement of women into broad sectors of occupations. This change has affected the composition of residences and, subsequently, will affect the descent structure and eventually kinship terminology. Evidence of this development can readily be seen. Around 1960, in an offhand comment during a lecture, Murdoch predicted that the control over wealth in America

1. would flow increasingly into the hands of women,
2. would at some point create shifts in household patterns, and
3. in the long run would produce a kinship structure dominated by women.

Regardless of the accuracy of Murdoch's prediction, changes in practices pertaining to kinship are appearing in various ways:

1. Newspapers obituaries have routinely begun to include "life companions" (of either gender) in the list of related survivors;
2. public policy pertaining to health insurance coverage has been modified in some communities to include unmarried domestic partners;
3. in some countries (e.g., Russia, Israel), intestacy laws have been amended to include unrelated household residents;
4. the issue of legally recognizing same-sex marriages (or domestic partners) as a valid arrangement has emerged in a wide range of communities.

Unlike the theoretical inevitability of collectively rational adaptations assumed by evolutionary theorists, the typologies formulated by cyclical theorists lead away from regarding their end-states as inevitable. In their portrayal of historical processes, the cyclical theorists have the burden of explaining conditions for triggering reversals in historical cycles. These reversals imply that critical periods arise through cultural innovations and conflicts.

The effects of novelty and conflict in these critical periods introduce an indeterminancy into the historical process. This indeterminacy brings to the foreground the problem of the inhibition of change: What introduces a new cycle, and what brings the cycle to a halt? For example, as discussed earlier, Zimmerman and Frampton (1947) see the history of the family as a series of repetitive cycles: a decay from corporate family forms (based on idealistic values) to unstable, chaotic families (based on materialistic values and individualism), followed by a regeneration of familism. Their scheme of analysis explains the oscillations between various degrees of familism and individualism in terms of a conflict between maintaining an enduring, traditional social structure and attending to persistent personal yearnings. The idealism of religious or ascetic values facilitates social stability in corporate family settings. However, the stifling of personal aims and desires, without idealism, encourages the adoption of materialistic values and sensuality associated with the unstable family. Hence, there is no guarantee that an old cycle will end or that new ideals supporting familism will again emerge.

A Trans-historical Typology of kinship and family systems

For well over a millennium, church intellectuals have been aware of variations in marital selection and their implications for family structure and kinship ties as well as for social structure. Early in the fifth century, in his De Civitate Dei (City of God), Saint Augustine of Hippo noted that in early biblical times demographic insufficiencies made it necessary for Jews to practice kinship endogamy. However, he proposed that marrying close relatives, and thereby creating multiple family ties with the same people, restricted the potential expanse of social circles that could be tied into a coherent community. Kinship endogamy tends to divide societies into segments.

On the other hand, marrying persons from previously unrelated families would "serve to weld social life securely" by binding diverse peoples into an extensive web of relationships. Later, in the twelfth century, Gratian suggested that God commanded the Hebrews to select relatives as mates "because the salvation of man was realized in the pure Jewish race" but that the Christian faith, which could be readily spread through teaching, made kinship endogamy obsolete.

Gratian's argument suggests that the differences between Judaic and Christian marriage systems have broad implications for contemporaneous functions of kinship as well as for temporal functions, connecting past and future generations. The discussion that follows presents a kinship and family typology derived ultimately from Augustine's and Gratian's depictions of marriage systems as well as from issues pertaining to descent. This typology involves theoretical concerns drawn from sociology and anthropology.

Contemporaneous and Temporal Functions of Kinship Systems

Both marriage systems and descent rules affect the character of links between contemporaneous networks of families. A major controversy that at one time occupied many social anthropologists was whether marriage systems (i.e., marital alliances between groups) are more fundamental in generating forms of social organization than are descent rules or vice versa.

At stake in the controversy was the issue of whether the social solidarity undergirding descent rules is more fundamental than the ideas of reciprocity and exchange involved in marriage systems. In the end, Africanists favored descent rules, while Asianists leaned toward marital alliances. In their assessment of the controversy, Buchler and Selby (1968) found evidence for the validity of both views.

However, despite the chicken-and-egg character of the controversy, the alliance-descent issue highlights the contradictory nature of kinship structure. This contradiction is depicted in the opposing views of structuralists such as Claude Levi- Strauss (1963), who supports the alliance position, and functionalists such as Meyer Fortes (1969), who argues for the descent position.

Alliance theories of kinship systems identify the primary function of kinship as the integration of networks of related families into the contemporaneous social fabric. Alliance adherents begin with marriage as the central element in structuring the way kinship operates. To alliance theorists, the significance of marriage lies in the idea that marriage is essentially a mode of exchange whose primary reason for existence is to inhibit conflict in society. In their view, kin groups exist as organized entities to effect marital exchanges. According to Levi-Strauss, the leading figure in alliance theory, "exchange in human society is a universal means of ensuring the interlocking of its constituent parts". In unilineal systems, women are exchanged for equivalent valuable property, services, or both; in bilateral systems (which by their nature become multilateral in the long run), commitments to each other's relatives are exchanged. In bilateral kinship, bride and groom are of presumably equivalent value. Thus, in general, alliance theorists regard descent groupings primarily as a necessary ingredient for sustaining the marriage exchange system over the generations.

Descent Theory of Kinship

The descent theory of kinship systems rests on the assumption that the continued welfare of kindred over the generations is the primary function of kinship. In particular, Fortes regards "filiation"- being ascribed the status of a child of one's parents, with all the lifetime rights and obligations attached to that status as the "crucial relationships of intergenerational continuity and social reproduction". He proposes that, as a concomitant of filiation, "the model relationship of kinship amity is fraternity, that is sibling unity, equality, and solidarity", and he provides a biblical example of the tie between David and Jonathan.

On the one hand, alliance theory postulates that the basic drive in kinship organization is derived externally, from the kind of alliances appropriate to the structure of power in the community. Collectively, marital alliances create between families a network of links that integrate them in reference to overarching religious, economic, and political institutions. On the other hand, descent theory ascribes the bases of organization to internal demands, structural factors in the persistence of the kindred: rules governing residential location, division of labor and authority among members, and the various economic and political functions to be performed by the kinship system.

Given the contradiction in the impulse for kinship organization, there is an apparent "impasse between the alliance and filiation point of view". What appears to be at issue is the depiction of the kinds of reciprocity norms that define the character of kinship. Descent theory presumes that an axiom of amity (i.e., prescriptive altruism or general reciprocity) is basic to the coherence of kin groups; alliance theory holds that balanced reciprocity (i.e., the rightness of exchanges for overt selfinterest, opportunistic individualism, or noumenal norms) is in the final analysis the glue that integrates families and kin groups into a coherent whole.

The contradiction is apparent in many ways. For example, in biblical references and religious writings, the Ten Commandments enjoin one to honor parents and, conversely, to "cleave" to one's spouse and maintain peace in the household. In terms of kinds of reciprocity, one commandment involves unconditional giving or honoring, while the other concerns maintaining domestic peace (implying fair give-and-take).

Similarly, contemporary writers on marriage generally find the concept of balanced reciprocity appropriate in describing the quality of husband-wife ties. For example, Walster and Walster (1978) report that marriages work best when both husband and wife (as well as lovers) believe that each is receiving a fair exchange for what he or she offers in the relationship. Moreover, in their review of research on the quality of marriage, Lewis and Spanier (1982) note the importance of the symmetry of exchange in establishing and maintaining strong marital ties. However, in the socialization of children and in the allocation of resources, the rule of amity (or prescriptive altruism) is supposed to prevail. For example, parents are ordinarily expected to make "sacrifices" for their children when necessary; to do otherwise is to be a "bad" parent. In the American court system, the general rule for the disposition of children in cases of divorce, child neglect or abuse, or adoption is that the court should base its decision on the welfare of the child rather than on the interests of the parents or other parties.

To some extent, the descent-marriage contradiction can be obscured by compartmentalizing marital, parental, and filial conduct and by dividing responsibilities of husband and wife. However, conflicts in norms for dealing with family members and kindred may occur for several reasons, but they occur principally because of scarcities of time and resources required to carry out duties and obligations in the face of a wide range of simultaneous and conflicting demands.

Since the resulting dilemmas are widespread in the society, there is a need for a general rule. Because contradictory alliance and descent impulses are operative, each group is pushed to establish a coherent kinship scheme that gives priority to one impulse over the other or at least establishes some form of compromise between them.

There is evidence that rules governing marital functions conflict with those pertaining to descent functions, paralleling the alliance-descent controversy in kinship systems. Where descent functions are given precedence in family organization, marital functions are subordinated (and vice versa). *Examples of this inverse relationship are*:

1. if husband-wife unity is central, then the unity between siblings is peripheral (and the reverse), and
2. if marriage between close affines is forbidden, first-cousin marriage is permitted (and vice versa).

These examples are discussed in the sections that follow.

Marital Unity Versus Unity of the Sibling Group

Comparisons between societies indicate that ties between siblings have an inverse relationship to husband-wife ties. Where descent is valued over alliance or marriage in kinship relations, brother-sister bonds are particularly close, while the husband-wife relationship is relatively distant. In such family systems whether or not its therapeutic implications are true, parents are expected to remain together for the sake of the children, and this expectation expresses the priority of descent over marital ties. Conversely, in family systems where the marriage function is more valued, the husband-wife relationship is intense (e.g., the importance of the give-and-take of love and of companionship for marriage) and the brother-sister relationship is competitive, distant, or both and the incest taboo justifies their apartness.

In societies where priority is given to marital bonds over descent ties, the presence of children is of less importance in dissolving an unhappy marriage, and there is greater ambiguity about what is best for the children. The mere fact that the strength of brother-sister ties and that of marital ties vary inversely in different societies lends support to the proposition that there is a contradiction in the family system between its marital functions and its descent functions.

Affines and Cousins in American Marriage Law

The opposition between marital and descent functions in the family is also illustr ated by the inverse relationship in American law of marriages considered to be incestuous: As a general tendency, states that forbid second marriages between a person and certain affines (such as that person's parents-in-law and sons- or daughters-in-law) allow first cousins to marry, while those that permit marriage between close affines forbid first-cousin marriage. If the preferred function of marriage is to reinforce close consanguineous kinship ties, then this pattern of marital prohibitions signals a subordination of affinal bonds to those of consanguinity.

Marrying into the family of the former spouse will not reinforce any of the other existing bonds of consanguinity. Consequently, although first-cousin marriage is to be permitted in order to reinforce intimate kinship ties, marriage with close affines should be avoided. However, if marriage is considered to be primarily a mechanism for creating new bonds between previously unrelated families, then a second marriage into the same family merely serves to maintain the affinal bonds initiated in the first marriage.

Social Structure and Kinship Systems

The presence of contradictory impulses in organizing kinship ties produces a predicament in establishing priorities between them. This contradiction evokes a question: Which circumstances lead some societies (and ethnic and religious subgroups) to give priority to descent and others to favor alliance assumptions in their kinship and family organization (Farber 1975)? In their analyses of the relationship between kinship organization and social structure, both Paige (1974) and Swanson (1969) distinguish between societies that feature the legitimacy of special interests-factionalism-in organizing social life and those that feature the importance of common interests-communalism- as an organizing theme.

Factions are a means for gathering forces and mobilizing members for conflict or competition with other factions. They emerge as a reaction to perceived danger to their well-being from other groups. Factions emerge where either :

1. special interest groups vie for superiority over other groups for access to power, wealth, or some other property, or
2. groups sense a danger to their continued autonomous existence as an ethnic or religious entity.

In kinship organization, the continual mobilization of family and kin results in the generation of norms that are centripetal in nature, that is, they facilitate the pulling inward of human, symbolic, and material resources. This centripetal tendency permits each kin group to separate itself from competing groups in order to endure. As a result, centripetal kin groups favor norms strengthening descent relationships over norms facilitating new alliances with other groups through marriage. Insofar as descent-group norms are rooted in the axiom of amity, one would expect centripetal kinship organization to feature the norm of prescriptive altruism over balanced reciprocities in kinship and family relations

Jewish family norms provide some insight into the relationship between centripetal kinship systems and the application of the axiom of amity. In its basic ideology and in the code of laws supporting that ideology, Judaism assigns a major significance to the concept of nurturance. Since nurturance is a central feature of maternal giving, it can be regarded as a metaphor for the axiom of amity.

"Kinship system" as systemic pattern

The concept of "system of kinship" tended to dominate anthropological studies of kinship in the early 20th century. Kinship systems as defined in anthropological texts and ethnographies were seen as constituted by patterns of behavior and attitudes in relation to the differences in terminology, listed above, for referring to relationships as well as for addressing others. Many anthropologists went so far as to see, in these patterns of kinship, strong relations between kinship categories and patterns of marriage, including forms of marriage, restrictions on marriage, and cultural concepts of the boundaries of incest. A great deal of inference was necessarily involved in such constructions as to "systems" of kinship, and attempts to construct systemic patterns and reconstruct kinship evolutionary histories on these bases were largely invalidated in later work. However, anthropologist Dwight Read later argued that the way in which kinship categories are defined by individual researchers are substantially inconsistent. This occurs when working within a systemic cultural model that can be elicited in fieldwork, but also allowing considerable individual variability in details, such as when they are recorded through relative products.

Descent and Family

Descent, like family systems, is one of the major concepts of anthropology. Cultures worldwide possess a wide range of systems of tracing kinship and descent. Anthropologists break these down into simple concepts about what is thought to be common among many different cultures.

Descent groups

A descent group is a social group whose members claim common ancestry. A unilineal society is one in which the descent of an individual is reckoned either from the mother's or the father's line of descent. With matrilineal descent individuals belong to their mother's descent group. Matrilineal descent includes the mother's brother, who in some societies may pass along inheritance to the sister's children or succession to a sister's son. With patrilineal descent, individuals belong to their father's descent group. Societies with the Iroquois kinship system, are typically uniliineal, while the Iroquois proper are specifically matrilineal.

In a society which reckons descent bilaterally (bilineal), descent is reckoned through both father and mother, without unilineal descent groups. Societies with the Eskimo kinship system, like the Eskimo proper, are typically bilateral. The egocentrid kindred group is also typical of bilateral societies.

Some societies reckon descent patrilineally for some purposes, and matrilineally for others. This arrangement is sometimes called double descent. For instance, certain property and titles may be inherited through the male line, and others through the female line.

Societies can also consider descent to be ambilineal (such as Hawaiian kinship) where offspring determine their lineage through the matrilineal line or the patrilineal line.

Lineages, clans, phratries, moieties and matrimonial sides

A lineage is a unilineal descent group that can demonstrate their common descent from a knownapical ancestor. Unilineal lineages can be matrilineal or patrilineal, depending on whether they are traced through mothers or fathers, respectively. Whether matrilineal or patrilineal descent is considered most significant differs from culture to culture.

A clan is a descent group that claims common descent from an apical ancestor (but often cannot demonstrate it, or "stipulated descent"). If a clan's apical ancestor is nonhuman, it is called a totem. Examples of clans are found in the Chechen, Chinese, Irish, Japanese, Polish, Scottish, Tlingit, andSomali societies. In the case of the Polish clan, any notion of common ancestry was lost long ago.

A phratry is a descent group containing at least two clans which have a supposed common ancestor.

If a society is divided into exactly two descent groups, each is called a moiety, after the French word for half. If the two halves are each obliged to marry out, and into the other, these are called matrimonial moieties. Houseman and White have discovered numerous societies where kinship network analysis shows that two halves marry one another, similar to matrimonial moieties, except that the two halves—which they call matrimonial sides—are neither named nor descent groups, although the egocentric kinship terms may be consistent with the pattern of sidedness, whereas the sidedness is culturally evident but imperfect.

The word deme is used to describe an endogamous local population that does not have unilineal descent. Thus, a deme is a local endogamous community without internal segmentation into clans.

Nuclear family

The Western model of a nuclear family consists of a couple and its children. The nuclear family is ego-centered and impermanent, while descent groups are permanent lasting beyond the lifespans of individual constituents and reckoned according to a single ancestor.

Kinship calculation is any systemic method for reckoning kin relations. Kinship terminologies are native taxonomies, not developed by anthropologists. Beanpole family is a term used to describe expansions of the number of living generations within a family unit, but each generation has relatively few members in it.

Legal ramifications

Kinship and descent have a number of legal ramifications, which vary widely between legal and social structures.

Next of Kin traditionally and in common usage refers to the person closest related to you by blood, such as a parent or your children.

In legal terms, for example in intestacy, it has come to mean the person closest to you, which is generally the spouse if married, followed by the natural children of the deceased.

Whilst someone is alive they may nominate any person close to them to be their next of kin. The next of kin is usually asked for as a contact in case of accident, emergency or sudden death. It does not involve completing any forms or registration in the UK, and may be a friend or carer unrelated to you by blood or marriage.

Most human groups share a taboo against incest; relatives are forbidden from marriage but the rules tend to vary widely when one moves beyond the nuclear family. At common law, the prohibitions are typically phrased in terms of "degrees of consanguinity."

More importantly, kinship and descent enters the legal system by virtue of intestacy, the laws that at common law determine who inherits the estates of the dead in the absence of a will. In civil lawcountries, the doctrine of legitime plays a similar role, and makes the lineal descendants of the dead person forced heirs. Rules of kinship and descent have important public aspects, especially undermonarchies, where they determine the order of succession, the heir apparent and the heir presumptive.

Kinship Terminology

Archaeologist Lewis Henry Morgan (1818-1881) performed the first survey of kinship terminologies in use around the world. Although much of his work is now considered dated, he argued that kinshipterminologies reflect different sets of distinctions. For example, most kinship terminologies distinguish between sexes (the difference between a brother and a sister) and between generations (the difference between a child and a parent). Moreover, he argued, kinship terminologies distinguish between relatives by blood andmarriage (although recently some anthropologists have argued that many societies define kinship in terms other than "blood").

Morgan made a distinction between kinship systems that use classificatory terminology and those that use descriptive terminology. Morgan's distinction is widely misunderstood, even by contemporary anthropologists. Classificatory systems are generally and erroneously understood to be those that "class together" with a single term relatives who actually do not have the same type of relationship to ego. (What defines "same type of relationship" under such definitions seems to be genealogical relationship. This is problematic given that any genealogical description, no matter how standardized, employs words originating in a folk understanding of kinship.) What Morgan's terminology actually differentiates are those (classificatory) kinship systems that do not distinguish lineal and collateral relationships and those (descriptive) kinship systems that do. Morgan, a lawyer, came to make this distinction in an effort to understand Seneca inheritance practices. A Seneca man's effects were inherited by his sisters' children rather than by his own children. *Morgan identified six basic patterns of kinship terminologies*:

- Hawaiian: only distinguishes relatives based upon sex and generation.
- Sudanese: no two relatives share the same term.
- Eskimo: in addition to distinguishing relatives based upon sex and generation, also distinguishes between lineal relatives and collateral relatives.
- Iroquois: in addition to sex and generation, also distinguishes between siblings of opposite sexes in the parental generation.
- Crow: a matrilineal system with some features of an Iroquois system, but with a "skewing" feature in which generation is "frozen" for some relatives.
- Omaha: like a Crow system but patrilineal.

Morgan identified six basic patterns of kinship terminologies:

- *Hawaiian kinship*: the most classificatory; only distinguishes between sex and generation. Thus, siblings and cousins are not distinguished (the same terms are used for both types of relatives).
- *Sudanese kinship*: the most descriptive; no two types of relatives share the same term. Siblings are distinguished from cousins, and different terms are used for each type of cousin (i.e. father's brother's children, father's sister's children, mother's sister's children and mother's brother's children).
- *Eskimo kinship*: has both classificatory and descriptive terms; in addition to sex and generation, it also distinguishes between lineal relatives (those related directly by a line of descent) and collateral relatives (those related by blood, but not directly in the line of descent). Lineal relatives have highly descriptive terms; collateral relatives have highly classificatory terms. Thus, siblings are distinguished from cousins, while all types of cousins are grouped together. The system of English-language kinship terms falls into the "Eskimo" type.
- *Iroquois kinship*: It has both classificatory and descriptive terms; in addition to sex and generation, it also distinguishes

between siblings of opposite sexes in the parental generation. A genealogical relationship traced through a pair of siblings of the same sex is classed as a blood relationship, but one traced though a pair of siblings of the opposite sex can be considered an in-law relationship. In other words, siblings are grouped together with parallel cousins, while separate terms are used forcross-cousins. Also, one calls one's mother's sister "mother" and one's father's brother "father". However, one refers to one's mother's brother and one's father's sister by separate terms (often the terms for "father-in-law" and "mother-in-law", since cross-cousins can be preferential marriage partners).

- *Crow kinship*: like Iroquois, but further distinguishes between mother's side and father's side. Relatives on the mother's side of the family have more descriptive terms, and relatives on the father's side have more classificatory terms. Thus, Crow kinship is like Iroquois kinship, with the addition that a number of relatives belonging to one's father's matrilineage are grouped together, ignoring generational differences, so that the same term is used for both one's father's sister and one's father's sister's daughter, etc.
- *Omaha kinship*: like Iroquois, but further distinguishes between mother's side and father's side. Relatives on the mother's side of the family have more classificatory terms, and relatives on the father's side have more descriptive terms. Thus, Omaha kinship is like Iroquois, with the addition that a number of relatives belonging to one's mother's patrilineage are grouped together, ignoring generational differences, so that the same term is used for both one's mother's brother and one's mother's brother's son, etc.

The basic principles of Crow and Omaha terminologies are symmetrical and opposite, with Crow systems having a matrilineal emphasis and Omaha systems a patrilineal emphasis.

Western kinship

Most Western societies employ Eskimo kinshipterminology. This kinship terminology commonly occurs in societies based on conjugal (or nuclear) families, where nuclear families have a degree of relative mobility. *Members of the nuclear use descriptive kinship terms*:

- Mother: a female parent
- Father: a male parent

- Son: a male child of the parent(s)
- Daughter: a female child of the parent(s)
- Brother: a male child of the same parent(s)
- Sister: a female child of the same parent(s)
- Grandfather: father of a father or mother
- Grandmother: mother of a mother or father
- Cousins: two people that share the samegrandparent(s)

Such systems generally assume that the mother's husband has also served as the biological father. In some families, a woman may have children with more than one man or a man may have children with more than one woman. The system refers to a child who shares only one parent with another child as a "half-brother" or "half-sister." For children who do not share biological or adoptive parents in common, English-speakers use the term "stepbrother" or "step-sister" to refer to their new relationship with each other when one of their biological parents marries one of the other child's biological parents. Any person (other than the biological parent of a child) who marries the parent of that child becomes the "stepparent" of the child, either the "step-mother" or "step-father." The same terms generally apply to children adopted into a family as to children born into the family.

Typically, societies with conjugal families also favorneolocal residence; thus upon marriage a person separates from the nuclear family of their childhood (family of orientation) and forms a new nuclear family (family of procreation). However, in the western society the single parent family has been growing more accepted and has begun to truly make an impact on culture. The majority of single parent families are more commonly single mother families than single fathe.. These families face many difficult issues besides the fact that they have to rear their children on their own, but also have to deal with issues related to low income.

Many single parents struggle with low incomes and must cope with other issues, including rent, child care, and other necessities required in maintaining a healthy and safe home. Members of the nuclear families of members of one's own (former) nuclear family may class as lineal or as collateral. Kin who regard them as lineal refer to them in terms that build on the terms used within the nuclear family:

- Grandparent
- Grandfather: a parent's father
- Grandmother: a parent's mother
- Grandson: a child's son
- Granddaughter: a child's daughter

For collateral relatives, more classificatory terms come into play, terms that do not build on the terms used within the nuclear family:

- Uncle: father's brother, mother's brother, father's sister's husband, mother's sister's husband
- Aunt: father's sister, mother's sister, father's brother's wife, mother's brother's wife
- Nephew: sister's son, brother's son, wife's brother's son, wife's sister's son, husband's brother's son, husband's sister's son
- Niece: sister's daughter, brother's daughter, wife's brother's daughter, wife's sister's daughter, husband's brother's daughter, husband's sister's daughter

When additional generations intervene (in other words, when one's collateral relatives belong to the same generation as one's grandparents or grandchildren), the prefixes "great-" or "grand-" modifies these terms. Also, as with grandparents and grandchildren, as more generations intervene the prefix becomes "great-grand-," adding an additional "great-" for each additional generation. Most collateral relatives have never had membership of the nuclear family of the members of one's own nuclear family.

Cousin: the most classificatory term; the children of aunts or uncles. One can further distinguish cousins by degrees of collaterality and by generation. Two persons of the same generation who share a grandparent count as "first cousins" (one degree of collaterality); if they share a great-grandparent they count as "second cousins" (two degrees of collaterality) and so on. If two persons share an ancestor, one as a grandchild and the other as a great-grandchild of that individual, then the two descendants class as "first cousins once removed" (removed by one generation); if they shared ancestor figures as the grandparent of one individual and the great-great-grandparent of the other, the individuals class as "first cousins twice removed" (removed by two generations), and so on.

Similarly, if they shared ancestor figures as the great-grandparent of one person and the great-great-grandparent of the other, the individuals class as "second cousins once removed". Hence one can refer to a "third cousin once removed upwards."

Cousins of an older generation (in other words, one's parents' first cousins), although technically first cousins once removed, are often classified with "aunts" and "uncles." Similarly, a person may refer to close friends of one's parents as "aunt" or "uncle," or may refer to close friends as "brother" or "sister," using the practice of fictive kinship. English-speakers mark relationships by marriage except for wife/husband with the tag "-in-law." The mother and father of one's spouse become one's mother-in-law and father-in-law; the female spouse of one's child becomes one's daughter-in-law and the male spouse of one's child becomes one's son-in-law.

The term "sister-in-law" refers to three essentially different relationships, either the wife of one's sibling, or the sister of one's spouse, or, in some uses, the wife of one's spouse's sibling. "Brother-in-law" expresses a similar ambiguity. The terms "half-brother" and "half-sister" indicate siblings who share only one biological or adoptive parent.

Cognatic kinship

It is a mode of descent calculated from an ancestor or ancestress counted through any combination of male and female links, or a system of bilateral kinship where relations are traced through both a father and mother.

Fictive Kinship

It is a term used by anthropologists and ethnographers to distinguish between forms ofkinship or social ties that are based on neither consanguinal (blood ties) nor affinal ('by marriage') ties. To the extent that consanguinal and affinal kinship ties might be considered real or true kinship, the term fictive kinship would be used to refer to those kinship ties that are fictive in the sense of not-real. Invoking the concept as an cross-culturally valid anthropological category therefore rests on the presumption that the inverse category of '(true) kinship' built around consanguinity and affinity is similarly cross-culturally valid. Use of the term was common until the mid-to-late twentieth century, when anthropology effectively deconstructed and revised many of the concepts and categories around the study of kinship and social ties.

Stemming from anthropology's early connections to legal studies, the term fictive kinship may also be used in a legalistic sense, and this use continues in societies where these categories and definitions regarding kinship and social ties have legal currency; e.g. in matters of inheritance.

As part of the deconstruction of kinship mentioned above, anthropologists now recognize that, cross-culturally, the kinds of social ties and relationships formerly treated under the category of 'kinship' are very often not necessarily predicated on blood ties or marriage ties, and may rather be based on shared residence, shared economic ties, or familiarity via other forms of interaction.

Milk kinship

Milk kinship, formed during nursing by a non-biological mother, was a form of fostering allegiance with fellow community members. This particular form of kinship did not exclude particular groups, such that class and other hierarchal systems did not matter in terms of milk kinship participation.

Traditionally speaking, this practice predates the early modern era, though it became a widely used mechanism for developing alliances in many hierarchical societies during the early modern period. Milk kinship used the practice of breast feeding by a wet nurse to feed a child either from the same community, or a neighbouring one. This wet nurse played the strategic role in forging relations between her family and the family of the child she was nursing, as well as their community.

6

CASTE SYSTEM OF INDIA

Indian society has consisted since ancient times of several thousand tribal and occupational groups or communities called Jati. The phrase "Caste System" conflates the reality and theory—the reality of the Jati system prevalent throughout the Indian society since ancient times and the varna(class/group), theoretical scheme based on idealised self-identification in Brahminical traditions.

The caste system of India is probably one of the most ill-understood entities known. It is also the source for differing emotions, actions, reactions and behaviour among different people for a plethora of reasons and even non reasons.

The word 'caste' is the English language translation of the Portuguese word 'casta' which literally means 'breed or lineage'. When the Portuguese arrived in India in 1498, they found what was to them, a perplexing system of stratification and discrimination prevailing amongst the people of India. Unable to explain this system to their rulers in Portugal, the first Portuguese sea-farers to India called it 'casta'. In order to have a better picture of the caste system of India, it is important to review the events occurring in the northwest corner of the Indian sub-continent about 3000 years prior to the arrival in India of the Portuguese explorer, Vasco da Gama.

Original Inhabitants of India

The original inhabitants of India are described as being the negrito people. They continue to live in the hills as well as villages and cities of

India as 'scheduled tribes'. There also were Alpine, Mongoloid and Paleo-Mediterranean people.

In the northwest corner of the Indian sub-continent, in what today is Sind-Pakistan and the Indian State of Saurashtra, existed a very highly developed and sophisticated civilization—the (Sindhus) Indus Valley civilization of Harrapa and Mohenjo Daro. The people who lived in these cities were the original Negritos(Naga) and the Dravidians, the highly intelligent but smaller and dark brown descendants of Mediterranean origin.

Recent excavations reveal the high level of sophistication of these Harappan cities which eventually succumbed to a variety of factors including drought, famine . These set of events were probably the initial catalysts for the Dravidian move to their present 'home' in South India. The Nagas moved inland and into the hills.

Around 1500 BC, there was another development occurring several hundred thousand miles west and north-west of the Indus valley. The nomadic, Caucasian, well built but rustic, cattle rearing people from the region around the Caspian Sea were restless. They were looking for newer and greener pastures. They began migrating to different parts of what is now Europe, the Middle East and the Indian subcontinent.

The Sanskrit speaking people, the Aryans traveled towards the Indus Valley. Initial migration appears to have been in the form of a few 'scout' or pioneer groups. A full scale migration occurred within the following decades. The Aryans with their superior physique and their horse driven chariots established unquestionable superiority over the Dravidian and tribal population of the Indus Valley.

The central government in Delhi has organized a reservation of seats in colleges and positions in the employment sector for individuals from the hitherto-discriminated-against Untouchables and Scheduled Tribes. This issue has sparked off widespread discontent and needs to be looked at again. The reservation policy is a form of reverse discrimination and will eventually backfire on the country's development. Judging by the fact that it is a 'hot' political issue, the likelihood of any changes in this reverse discrimination are highly unlikely, at least in the foreseeable future.

The ugly head of 'caste' rears itself ever so often at the time of marriage. This will continue not only in the system of arranged marriages but also in the non-arranged ones.

"Caste was originally an arrangement for the distribution of functions of society, just as much as class in Europe, but the principle on which the distribution was based in India was peculiar to this country.

Jati in Caste System

The Indian caste system is a system of social stratification and social restriction in India in which communities are defined by thousands of endogamous hereditary groups called Jatis.

The Jatis were hypothetically and formally grouped by the Brahminical texts under the four well known categories (the varnas): viz Brahmins (priests), Kshatriyas (kings, warriors, law enforcers, administrators), Vaishyas (traders, bankers), and Shudras (Artisans, labourers, agriculturists, cattle raisers, craftsmen, service providers). Certain people like foreigners, nomads, forest tribes and the chandalas (who dealt with disposal of the dead) were excluded altogether and treated as untouchables. Although identified with Hinduism, in the past (1883 year data) [Full citation needed] the caste-like systems were also observed among followers of other religions in the Indian subcontinent, including some groups of Muslims and Christians, most likely due to common cultural elements. Theoretically, all foreigners are considered to be casteless; in the 18th century, the high-caste Brahmins avoided undertaking sea trips, as they considered the European merchants as untouchable.

Jati (the word literally means 'birth') is the term used to denote clans, tribes, communities and sub-communities in India. It is a term used across religions. In Indian society each jati typically has an association with a traditional job function or tribe, although religious beliefs (e.g. Sri Vaishnavism or Veera Shaivism) or linguistic groupings define some jatis. A person's surname typically reflects a community (jati) association. In any given location in India 500 or more jatis may co-exist, although the exact composition will differ from district to district.

The British, since 1901, for the purposes of the Decennial Census, fitted all the Jatis into one or the other of the varna categories as described in Brahminical literature, ignoring that there are many Jatis that would straddle two Varnas, based on occupation. As a community in south India put it,"We are soldiers and saddle makers too".

The Indian society since pre-historic times had a complex, inter-dependent and cooperative political economy. One non-sacred text, the Laws of Manu, c. 200, codified the social relations between communities from the perspective of the Varna castes. Although this book was almost unknown south of the Vindhyas, it gained prominence when the British administrators and western scholars used it exclusively to gain an understanding of traditional Hindu law in India.

Varna in Caste System

Varna refers to the categorization of the Hindu society by four castes, hypothesized by the Brahmins and their sacred texts. This quadruple division is not to be confused with Jati or even the much finer division of the contemporary caste system in India. The four varnas, or chatur varna, are mentioned in ancient texts in the following (stratified) order, from top to bottom:

1. Brahmins: vedic priests.
2. Kshatriya: kings, governors and professional soldiers.
3. Vaishyas: bankers and merchants
4. Shudras: cattle keepers, agriculturists, labourers, artisans and service providers.

The first three varna are considered Arya, and thus allowed to participate in *Vedic rituals* from which the *Shudra varna* is excluded, although it was the largest segment of the population.

Separate and shunned by the society, including by the Shudras, were the "untouchables" such as the Dalit and the *Chandaal*, who had to deal with the disposal of dead bodies and are described as dirty and polluted. There was a belief that one's Karma in the past, resulted in one's condition in this birth. "Now people here whose conduct is good can expect to quickly attain a pleasant birth, like that of a Brahmin, the *Kshatriya*, or the *Vaishya*. But people of evil conduct can expect to enter a foul womb, like that of a dog, a pig, or a Chandaal".

The varna system of the Brahminical society is described in the various *Puranas* and *Smritis*, among others. *Manusmriti*, is one of numerous *Dharmashastra* texts reflecting the laws and society of Maurya period India and being a reference work for the Brahmins of Bengal especially, was relied upon by the British colonial administrators and scholars based in Calcutta, the capital city. Manusmriti was almost unknown south of the Vindhyas.

Religious Form of Caste System

In Hinduism there exists four castes arranged in a hierarchy. Anyone who does not belong to one of these castes is an outcast. The religious word for caste is 'Varna'. Each Varna has certain duties and rights. Each Varna members have to work in certain occupation which only that Varna members are allowed. Each Varna has certain type of diet. The highest Varna is of the Brahman. Members of this class are priests and the educated people of the society. The Varna after them in hierarchy is *Kshatria*. The members of this class are the rulers and aristocrats of the society. After them are the Vaisia.

Members of this class are the landlords and businessmen of the society. After them in hierarchy are the *Sudra*. Members of this class are the peasants and working class of the society who work in non-polluting jobs. The caste hierarchy ends here. Below these castes are the outcasts who are untouchable to the four castes. These untouchables worked in degrading jobs like cleaning, sewage etc.

The first three castes had social and economical rights which the *Sudra* and the untouchables did not have. The first three castes are also seen as 'twice born'. The intention in these two births is to the natural birth and to the ceremonial entrance to the society at a much later age.

Each Varna and also the untouchables are divided into many communities. These communities are called Jat or Jati (The caste is also used instead of Jat). For example the Brahmans have castes called Gaur, Kokanastha, Sarasvat, Iyer and others. The outcasts have Jats like Mahar, Dhed, Mala, Madiga and others. The Sudra is the largest Varna and it has the largest number of communities. Each Jat is limited to professions worthy of their Varna. Each Jat is limited to the Varna diet. Each Jat members are allowed to marry only with their Jat members. People are born into their caste and it cannot be changed.

This is the how the caste system is supposed to be in its religious form. But in reality it is much more complicated and different from its religious form.

Modern Status of Caste system

The modern Hindu caste system recognizes many more social groupings not mentioned in the Hindu scriptures and only theoretically accepts the necessity of following prescribed duties. Caste politics is a controversial issue in the contemporary Republic of India.

The caste system is still socially relevant in India, even when the topic is avoided by general rhetoric. Caste has become an important factor in the politics of rural India, although elections in the first decade of the present century seem to have diminished a hold that was very much evident in the previous few decades.

The Government of India has officially documented castes and sub-castes, primarily to determine those entitled for reservation (positive discriminationin education and jobs) through the census. The Indian reservation system, though limited in scope, relies entirely on quotas. The

Government lists consist of Scheduled Castes, Scheduled Tribes and Other Backward Classes:

Scheduled Castes (SC)

Scheduled castes generally consist of "Dalit". The present population is 16% of the total population of India (around 165 million). For example, the Delhi state has 49 castes listed as SC.

Scheduled Tribes (ST)

Scheduled tribes generally consist of tribal groups. The present population is 7% of the total population of India i.e. around 70 million.

Other Backward Classes (OBC)

The Mandal Commission covered more than 3000 castes under OBC Category, regardless of their affluence or economic status and stated that OBCs form around 52% of the Indian population. However, the National Sample Survey puts the figure at 32%. There is substantial debate over the exact number of OBCs in India; it is generally estimated to be sizable, but many believe that it is lower than the figures quoted by either the Mandal Commission or the National Sample Survey.

The caste-based reservations in India have led to widespread protests, such as the 2006 Indian anti-reservation protests, with many complaining of reverse discrimination against the forward castes (the castes that do not entitled for the reservation).

The government is carrying out Caste Census for 2011. It will help in verifying the claims and counterclaims by various sections of the society about their actual numbers. It would also help the government to re-examine and even undo some of the policies which were formed in haste like Mandal commission and bring more objectivity to the policies with contemporary realities. Others believe that there is actually no social stigma at all associated with belonging to a backward caste, and that because of the huge constitutional incentives, in the form of educational and job reservations, a large number of people will falsely declare themselves to be from a backward caste, to avail of the benefits. This will not only result in a marked inflation of the backward castes numbers, but also lead to enormous administrative and judicial resources being devoted to social unrest and litigation, if such dubious caste declarations are challenged.

The leaders of independent India decided that India will be democratic, socialist and secular country. According to this policy, there is a separation between religion and state. Practicing untouchability or discriminating a person based on his caste is legally forbidden. Along with this law the government allows positive discrimination of the depressed classes of India.

The Indians have also become more flexible in their caste system customs. In general the urban people in India are less strict about the caste system than the rural. In cities one can see different caste people mingling with each other, while in some rural areas there is still discrimination based on castes and sometimes also on untouchability. Sometimes in villages or in the cities there are violent clashes which, are connected to caste tensions. Sometimes the high castes strike the lower castes who dare to uplift their status. Sometimes the lower caste get back on the higher castes.

In modern India the term caste is used for Jat and also for *Varna*. The term, caste was used by the British who ruled India until 1947. The British who wanted to rule India efficiently made lists of Indian communities. They used two terms to describe Indian communities. Castes and Tribes. The term caste was used for Jats and also for *Varnas*. Tribes were those communities who lived deep in jungles, forests and mountains far away from the main population and also communities who were hard to be defined as castes for example communities who made a living from stealing or robbery. These lists, which the British made, were used later on by the Indian governments to create lists of communities who were entitled for positive discrimination.

The castes, which were the elite of the Indian society, were classified as high castes. The other communities were classified as lower castes or lower classes. The lower classes were listed in three categories. The first category is called Scheduled Castes. This category includes in it communities who were untouchables. In modern India, untouchability exists at a very low extent. The untouchables call themselves Dalit, meaning depressed. Until the late 1980s they were called Harijan, meaning children of God. This title was given to them by Mahatma Gandhi who wanted the society to accept untouchables within them.

The second category is Scheduled Tribes. This category includes in it those communities who did not accept the caste system and preferred to reside deep in the jungles, forests and mountains of India, away from the main population. The Scheduled Tribes are also called Adivasi, meaning aboriginals.

The third category is called sometimes Other Backward Classes or Backward Classes. This category includes in it castes who belong to *Sudra* Varna and also former untouchables who converted from Hinduism to other religions. This category also includes in it nomads and tribes who made a living from criminal acts.

According to the Central government policy these three categories are entitled for positive discrimination. Sometimes these three categories are defined together as Backward Classes. 15% of India's population are Scheduled Castes. According to central government policy 15% of the government jobs and 15% of the students admitted to universities must be from Scheduled Castes. For the Scheduled Tribes about 7.5% places are reserved which is their proportion in Indian population. The Other Backwards Classes are about 50% of India's population, but only 27% of government jobs are reserved for them.

Along with the central government, the state governments of India also follow a positive discrimination policy. Different states have different figures of communities entitled for positive discrimination based on the population of each state. Different state governments have different lists of communities entitled for positive discrimination. Sometimes a specific community is entitled for rights in a particular state but not in another state of India.

In modern India, new tensions were created because of these positive discrimination policies. The high caste communities feel discriminated by the government policy to reserve positions for the Backward Classes. In many cases a large number of high caste members compete for a few places reserved for them. While the Backward Classes members do not have to compete at all because of the large number of reserved places for them compared to the candidates.

Sometimes in order to fill the quota, candidates from the lower classes are accepted even though they are not suitable. Sometimes some reserved positions remain unmanned because there were few candidates from the lower classes causing more tension between the castes. Between the lower castes there are also tensions over reservation.

In the order of priority for a reserved place of the Backward Classes, candidate from the Scheduled castes is preferred over a candidate from the Scheduled Tribes who is preferred over a candidate from the other Backward Classes. As stated earlier Other Backward Classes are about 50% of India's population but only 27% of the Other Backward Classes are entitled for positive discrimination according to central government policy. Some Other Backward Classes communities are organizing politically to be recognized as Backward Classes entitled for positive discrimination.

The Scheduled Tribes who are seen as the aborigins of India got ownership and certain rights over Indian land. Many communities in India claim also to be aborigins of India and they are claiming the same rights as the Scheduled Tribes.

The caste identity has become a subject of political, social and legal interpretation. Communities who get listed as entitled for positive discrimination do not get out of this list even if their social and political conditions get better. In many cases the legal system is involved to decide if a certain person is entitled for positive discrimination.

But with all this positive discrimination policy, most of the communities who were low in the caste hierarchy remain low in the social order even today. And communities who were high in the social hierarchy remain even today high in the social hierarchy. Most of the degrading jobs are even today done by the Dalits, while the Brahmins remain at the top of the hierarchy by being the doctors, engineers and lawyers of India.

Forward Caste

Forward Caste is also known as Forward Class, Forward Community, and General Class. It is a term used in India to denote groups of people who do not qualify for any of the positive discriminationschemes operated by the government of India. These schemes are known as Reservation Benefits. Those groups who do so qualify are listed as Other Backward Castes or Scheduled Castes and Scheduled Tribes and they can take advantage of defined quotas for education benefits, government employment and political representation. The lists of Forward, Other Backward and Scheduled Castes, and Scheduled Tribes are compiled irrespective of religion. The lists are subject to change from time to time, dependent upon social, educational and economic factors.

However, although lists are produced for those groups entitled to take advantage of the quotas, there is no such list for the Forward Caste group; if a person does not belong to any of the listed groups then that person is by default a member of a group classed as Forward Caste.

Population of Forward Class

Estimates put the forward castes population at anywhere from 5-15%. However, a national sample survey estimates Forward Caste population almost same as backward castes at around 36%. Family health survey combined forward castes population along with all communities of other religions. If you exclude backward castes of other religions, then it is around 38.6% which is more than backward castes population. State wise forward caste population can be found from the chart.

Economic and Educational Status of Forward Caste

Forward Castes will have to compete only in the open category, as they are considered socially, educationally, and economically advanced. Currently the reservation proportion stands at 50% in central-government educational institutions and central-government jobs. However, in certain states such as Tamil Nadu, the reservation percentage stands at around 69%.

Economic Status

The 1998-1999 National Sample Survey calculated the economic status of forward communities separately for rural/urban areas in various income brackets. It shows

- Only 6.4% of forward Castes in rural areas appear in upper income bracket with per capita monthly income stands at above Rs 925 per month.
- 30% of rural population is made up of forward Castes.
- More than 65% of forward Castes per capita income stands below Rs 525 per month.

For urban areas

- Only 5.6% of forward Castes appear in the upper-income bracket with per capita income at or above Rs. 1925 per month (around US $40).
- More than 25% of forward Castes per capita income stands below Rs. 500 per month (around $10)

Educational status

- More than 30% of forward Castes above 15 years of age are illiterate.
- Only 8% of forward Castes are graduates.
- Around 85% of forward Castes above 15 years of age have done equal to or below secondary education (10 Years of education).

Impact of Seat Reservation on Forward Castes

After the implementation of OBC reservation, only 50% of seats are available in open competition. All communities can compete in open competition which means forward castes must secure between 72% and 78% of the 'open competition' seats in order to maintain their representation in keeping with their estimated population of 36-39%, whereas other communities will get major chunk of seats through exclusive reservations. This has resulted in protests from forward caste community members and supporters from other communities under the banner of Youth for Equality. They have pointed out following as reasons for their protests.

- The Government has implemented reservations for the Scheduled castes and Scheduled Tribes for the last 64 years, however the social and economic situation of these groups has not shown much improvement. This might be interpreted as an indication of the ineffectiveness of reservation in higher educational institutions as a means of achieving social equality.
- Any difference between proportion of different communities in Higher educational institutions is mainly because of difference in primary school enrollment. This fact was also confirmed in National sample surveys and pointed out by Oversight committee in its final report. Government should attack the cause instead of providing reservation at higher education level
- Already 24% of college seats are with Other backward Castes. Providing another 27% seats will deprive chances of forward Castes.
- Reservation on the basis of caste is cornered only by rich and affluent. For example daughter of former President of India got admission into Indian Foreign Services denying opportunity to another poor person from her own community.

The Government of India decided to introduce 27% reservations for other backward Castes all over India. Many states does not have even 27% of other backward Caste population as per national sample surveys. This includes major Indian states like Jammu & Kashmir, Himachal Pradesh, Goa, Maharashtra, Punjab, West Bengal. Central government, however, excluded 27% reservations to other backward Castes to the areas with high tribal populations.

Scheduled Castes and Scheduled Tribes

The Scheduled Castes (SCs), also known as the Dalit, and the Scheduled Tribes (STs) are two groupings of historically disadvantaged people that are given express recognition in the Constitution of India. During the period of British rule in the Indian sub-continent they were known as the Depressed Classes.

The Scheduled Castes and Scheduled Tribes make up around 15% and 7.5% respectively of the population of India, or around 24% altogether, according to the 2001 Census. The proportion of Scheduled Castes and Scheduled Tribes in the country's population has steadily risen sinceindependence in 1947.

The Constitution (Scheduled Castes) Order, 1950 lists 1,108 castes across 25 states in its First Schedule, while the Constitution (Scheduled Tribes) Order, 1950 lists 744 tribes across 22 states in its First Schedule.

Since Independence, the Scheduled Castes have benefited by the "Reservation" policy. This policy was made an integral part of the Constitution by the efforts of Dr. Bhimrao Ambedkar, regarded as the father of the Indian Constitution, who participated in Round Table Conferences and fought for the rights of the Depressed Classes. The Constitution lays down general principles for the policy of affirmative action for the SCs and STs.

Constitutional Framework

The Constitution provides a framework with a three pronged strategy to improve the situation of SCs and STs.

1. *Protective Arrangements* : Such measures as are required to enforce equality, to provide punitive measures for transgressions, to eliminate established practices that perpetuate inequities, etc. A number of laws were enacted to operationalize the provisions in the Constitution. Examples of such laws include The Untouchability Practices Act, 1955,Scheduled Caste and Scheduled Tribe (Prevention of Atrocities) Act, 1989, The Employment of Manual scavengers and Construction of Dry Latrines (Prohibition) Act, 1993, etc.

2. *Affirmative action* : Provide positive preferential treatment in allotment of jobs and access to higher education, as a means to accelerate the integration of the SCs and STs with mainstream society. Affirmative action is also popularly referred to as Reservation.

3. *Development* : Provide for resources and benefits to bridge the wide gap in social and economic condition between the SCs/STs and other communities.

National Commissions

To effectively implement the various safeguards built into the Constitution and other legislations, theConstitution, under Articles 338 and 338A, provides for two statutory commissions - the National Commission for Scheduled Castes, and National Commission for Scheduled Tribes.

Sachar Committee Report

According to the 61st Round Survey of the NSSO, almost nine-tenths of Buddhists in India belonged to scheduled castes of the Constitution while one-third of Christians belonged to scheduled tribes. Major part of scheduled castes were Hindus by religion but belonged to castes and tribes having low population. The Sachar Committee report of 2006 also confirmed that members of scheduled castes and tribes of India are not exclusively adherents of Hinduism.

Religion	Scheduled Caste	Scheduled Tribe
Buddhism	89.50%	7.40%
Christianity	9.00%	32.80%
Sikhism	17.0%	0.90%
Hinduism	22.20%	9.10%
Gond	-	15.90%
Jainism	-	2.60%
Islam	0.80%	0.50%

Scheduled Castes and Tribes (Prevention of Atrocities) Act, 1989

The Scheduled Castes and Tribes (Prevention of Atrocities) Act, 1989 was enacted by the Parliament of India (Act 33 of 1989), to prevent atrocities againstscheduled castes and scheduled tribes. The Act is popularly known as POA, the SC/ST Act, the Prevention of Atrocities Act, or simply the Atrocities Act.

Article 17 of Indian Constitution seeks to abolish 'untouchability' and its practice in any form is forbidden. It is basically a "statement of principle" that needs to be made operational with the ostensible objective to remove humiliation and multifaceted harassments meted to the Dalits and to ensure their fundamental and socioeconomic, political, and cultural rights.

This is to free Indian society from blind and irrational adherence to traditional beliefs and to establish a bias free society. For that, Untouchability (Offences) Act 1955 was enacted. However, lacunae and loopholes impelled the government to project a major overhaul of this legal instrument. From 1976 onwards the Act was revamped as the Protection of Civil Rights Act. Despite various measures adopted to improve the socio-economic conditions of the SCs and STs they remain vulnerable and are subject to various offences, indignities and humiliations and harassment. When they assert their rights and against the practice of

Untouchability against them the vested interest try to cow them down and terrorize them. Atrocities against the SCs and STs, still continued.

The normal provisions of the existing laws like, the Protection of Civil Rights Act 1955 and Indian Penal Code have been found inadequate to check these atrocitiescontinuing the gross indignities and offences against Scheduled Castes and Tribes.

Recognizing these, the Parliament passed 'Scheduled Caste and Scheduled Tribe (Prevention of Atrocities) Act', 1989 & Rules, 1995. The statement of objects and reasons appended to the Bill while moving the same in the Parliament, reads "despite various measures to improve the socioeconomic conditions of SCs & STs, they remain vulnerable. They are denied a number of civil rights; they are subjected to various offences, indignities, humiliations and harassment. They have, in several brutal incidents, been deprived of their life and property. Serious atrocities are committed against them for various historical, social and economic reasons."

The preamble of the Act also states that the Act is "to prevent the commission of offences of atrocities against the members of Scheduled Castes and Tribes, to provide for Special Courts for the trial of such offences and for the relief and rehabilitation of the victims of such offenses and for matters connected therewith or incidental thereto."

Thus objectives of the Act clearly emphasize the intention of the Government to deliver justice to these communities through proactive efforts to enable them to live in society with dignity and self-esteem and without fear or violence or suppression from the dominant castes. The practice of untouchability, in its overt and covert form was made a cognizable and non compoundable offence, and strict punishment is provided for any such offence.

The SCs and STs (Prevention of Atrocities) Act, 1989 with stringent provisions (which extends to whole of India except the State of Jammu & Kasmhir) was enacted on 9 September 1989. Section 23(1) of the Act authorises the Central Government to frame rules for carrying out the purpose of the Act. Drawing power from this section, the Scheduled Castes and the Scheduled Tribes (Prevention of Atrocities) Rules of 1995 were framed. The rules for the Act were notified on 31 March 1995.

The purpose of the Act was to help the social inclusion of Dalits into Indian society, but the Act has failed to live up to its expectations admitted by the Union Minister for Home Affairs in Parliament on 30 August 2010.

Defining "Atrocity"

The term 'atrocity' was not defined until this Act was passed by the Parliament in 1989. In legal parlance, the Act understands the term to mean an offence punishable under sections 3(1) and 3(2).

In specific terms, following are the definitions of "atrocity":

1. Atrocity is "an expression commonly used to refer to crimes against Scheduled Castes (SCs) and Scheduled Tribes (STs) in India".
2. It "denotes the quality of being shockingly cruel and inhumane, whereas the term 'crime' relates to an act punishable by law".
3. It implies "any offence under the Indian Penal Code (IPC) committed against SCs by non-SC persons, or against STs by non-ST persons. Caste consideration as a motive is not necessary to make such an offence in case of atrocity".
4. It signifies "crimes which have ingredients of infliction of suffering in one form or the other that should be included for reporting". This is based on the assumption that "where the victims of crime are members of Scheduled Castes and the offenders do not belong to Scheduled Castes caste considerations are really the root cause of the crime, even though caste considerations may not be the vivid and minimum motive for the crime".

Basic Features of the Act

The provisions of SC/ST Act and Rules can be divided into three different categories, covering a variety of issues related to atrocities against SC/ST people and their position in society.

- The first category contains provisions of criminal law. It establishes criminal liability for a number of specifically defined atrocities, and extends the scope of certain categories of penalizations given in the Indian Penal Code (IPC).
- The second category contains provisions for relief and compensation for victims of atrocities.
- The third category contains provisions that establish special authorities for the implementation and monitoring of the Act.

The basic features of the Act are:

1. Creation of new types of offences not in the Indian Penal Code (IPC) or in the Protection of Civil Rights Act 1955 (PCRA).
2. Commission of offences only by specified persons (atrocities can be committed only by non-SCs and non-STs on members

of the SC or ST communities. Crimes among SCs and STs or between STs and SCs do not come under the purview of this Act).

3. Defines various types of atrocities against SCs/STs (Section 3(1)i to xv and 3(2)i to vii).
4. Prescribes stringent punishment for such atrocities (Section 3(1)i to xv and 3(2)i to vii).
5. Enhanced punishment for some offences (Section 3(2)i to vii, 5).
6. Enhanced minimum punishment for public servants (Section 3(2)vii).
7. Punishment for neglect of duties by a public servant (Section 4).
8. Attachment and forfeiture of property (Section 7).
9. Externment of potential offenders (Section 10(1), 10(3), 10(3)).
10. Creation of Special Courts (Section 14).
11. Appointment of Special Public Prosecutors (Section 15).
12. Empowers the government to impose collective fines (Section 16).
13. Cancellation of arms licences in the areas identified where an atrocity may take place or has taken place (Rule 3iii) and seize all illegal fire arms (Rule 3iv).
14. Grant arms licences to SCs and STs (Rule 3v).
15. Denial of anticipatory bail (Section 18).
16. Denial of probation to convict (Section 19).
17. Provides compensation, relief and rehabilitation for victims of atrocities or their legal heirs (Section 17(3), 21(2)iii, Rule 11, 12(4)).
18. Identification of atrocity prone areas (Section 17(1), 21(2)vii, Rule 3(1)).
19. Setting up deterrents to avoid committing of atrocities on the SCs amongst others (Rule 3i to 3xi).
20. Setting up a mandatory, periodic monitoring system at different levels (Section 21(2)v):
    (a) District level (Rule 3xi, 4(2), 4(4), 17).
    (b) State level (8xi, 14, 16, 18).
    (c) National level (Section 21(2), 21(3), 21(4)).

Together with the rules, it provides a framework for monitoring the state response to the atrocities against Scheduled Castes and Scheduled Tribes. According to the Act and Rules, there are to be monthly reports from the District Magistrates, quarterly review meetings at the district level by the District Monitoring and Vigilance Committee (DVMC) and half yearly reviews by a 25 member State Monitoring and Vigilance Committee (SVMC) the chaired by the Chief Minister. The performance of every Special Public Prosecutor (SPP) will also have to be reviewed by the Director of Public Prosecutions (DPP) every quarter. Annual reports have to be sent to the central government by 31 March every year.

Other Backward Class (OBC)

Backward class people is a collective term, used by the Government of India, for castes which are economically and socially disadvantaged. They typically include the Other Backward Classes (OBCs). According to *The Times of India* on 31 August 2010, even after 17 years, at most 7% of seats have been filled by OBCs, regardless of their 27% reservation. This difference between proportion of different communities in higher educational institutions is mainly because of difference in primary school enrolment. Political parties in India have attempted to use these communities as votebanks.

The Central Government of India classifies some of its citizens based on their social and economic condition as Scheduled Caste (SC), Scheduled Tribe (ST), and Other Backward Class (OBC). The OBC list presented by the commission is dynamic (castes and communities can be added or removed) and will change from time to time depending on social, educational and economic factors. For example, the OBCs are entitled to 27% reservations in public sector employment and higher education. In the constitution, OBCs are described as "socially and educationally backward classes", and government is enjoined to ensure their social and educational development.

Until 1985, the affairs of Backward Classes were looked after by the Backward Classes Cell (BCC) in the Ministry of Home Affairs. With the creation of a separate Ministry of Welfare in 1985 (renamed asMinistry of Social Justice and Empowerment on 25 May 1998) the matters relating to Scheduled Castes, Scheduled Tribes, Other Backward Classes (OBCs) and Minorities were transferred to the new Ministry.

The Backward Classes Division in the ministry looks after the policy, planning and implementation of programmes relating to social and economic empowerment of OBCs. It also looks after matters relating to two institutions set up for the welfare of OBCs: National Backward Classes Finance and Development Corporation (NBCFDC) and the National Commission for Backward Classes (NCBC).

First Backward Classes Commission

The First Backward Classes Commission was set-up by a presidential order on 29 January 1953 under the chairmanship of Kaka Kalelkar. The commission submitted its report on 30 March 1955. It had prepared a list of 2,399 backward castes or communities for the entire country and of which 837 had been classified as the "most backward". *Some of the most notable recommendations of the commission were*:

1. Undertaking caste-wise enumeration of population in the census of 1961;
2. Relating social backwardness of a class to its low position in the traditional caste hierarchy of Indian society;
3. Treating all women as a class as "backward";
4. Reservation of 70 per cent seats in all technical and professional institutions for qualified students of backward classes; and
5. Reservation of vacancies in all government services and local bodies for other backward classes.

The commission in its final report recommended "caste as the criteria" to determine backwardness. But this report was not accepted by the government as it feared that the backward classes excluded from the caste and communities selected by the commission may not be considered and the really needy would be swamped by the multitude and would hardly receive special attention.

Mandal Commission

The National Sample Survey puts the figure at 32%. There is substantial debate over the exact number of OBCs in India, with census data compromised by partisan politics. It is generally estimated to be sizable, but lower than the figures quoted by either the Mandal Commission or and National Sample Survey.

27 percent of reservation was recommended owing to the legal constraint that the total quantum of reservation should not exceed 50 percent. States which have already introduced reservation for OBC exceeding 27 per cent will not be affected by this recommendation. With this general recommendation the commission proposed the following overall scheme of reservation for OBC:

1. Candidates belonging to OBC recruited on the basis of merit in an open competition should not be adjusted against their reservation quota of 27 per cent.
2. The above reservation should also be made applicable to promotion quota at all levels.

3. Reserved quota remaining unfilled should be carried forward for a period of three years and de-reserved thereafter.
4. Relaxation in the upper age limit for direct recruitment should be extended to the candidates of OBC in the same manner as done in the case of SCs and STs.
5. A roster system for each category of posts should be adopted by the concerned authorities in the same manner as presently done in respect of SC and ST candidates.

These recommendations in total are applicable to all recruitment to public sector undertakings, both under the central and state governments as well as to nationalised banks. All private sector undertakings which have received financial assistance from the government in one form or other should also be obliged to recruit personnel on the aforesaid basis.

All universities and affiliated colleges should also be covered by the above scheme of reservation. Although, education is considered an important factor to bring a desired social change, "educational reform" was not within the terms of reference of this commission. To promote literacy the following measures were suggested:

1. An intensive time-bound programme for adult education should be launched in selected pockets with high concentration of OBC population.
2. Residential schools should be set up in these areas for backward class students to provide a climate specially conducive to serious studies. All facilities in these schools including board and lodging should be provided free of cost to attract students from poor and backward class homes.
3. Separate hostels for OBC students with above facilities will have to be provided.
4. Vocational training was considered imperative.
5. It was recommended that seats should be reserved for OBC students in all scientific, technical and professional institutions run by the central as well as state governments. The quantum of reservation should be the same as in the government services, i.e. 27 per cent.

Obligation of the Government

Under Article 340 of the Indian Constitution, it is obligatory for the government to promote the welfare of the Other Backward Classes (OBC). Article 340(1) states, " The president may by order appoint a commission, consisting of such persons as he thinks, fit to investigate the conditions of socially and educationally backward classes within the territory of India and the difficulties under which they labour and to make recommendations as to the steps that should be taken by the union or any state to remove such difficulties and as to improve 'their condition and as to the grants that should be made, and the order appointing such commission shall define the procedure to be followed by the commission."

Article 340(2) states, "A commission so appointed shall investigate the matters referred to them and present to the president a report setting out the facts as found by them and making such recommendations as they think proper."

Supreme Court conclusions from *Ashoka Kumar Thakur vs. Union of India* :

1. The Constitution (Ninety-Third Amendment) Act, 2005 does not violate the "basic structure" of the Constitution so far as it relates to the state maintained institutions and aided educational institutions. Question whether the Constitution (Ninety-Third Amendment) Act, 2005 would be constitutionally valid or not so far as "private unaided" educational institutions are concerned, is left open to be decided in an appropriate case.
2. The "Creamy layer" principle is one of the parameters to identify backward classes. Therefore, principally, the "Creamy layer" principle cannot be applied to STs and SCs, as SCs and STs are separate classes by themselves.
3. Preferably there should be a review after ten years to take note of the change of circumstances.
4. A graduation (not technical graduation) or professional course deemed to be educationally forward.
5. Principle of exclusion of Creamy layer applicable to OBC's.
6. The Central Government shall examine as to the desirability of fixing a cut off marks in respect of the candidates belonging to the Other Backward Classes (OBCs)to balance reservation with other societal interests and to maintain standards of excellence. This would ensure quality and merit would not suffer. If any seats remain vacant after adopting such norms they shall be filled up by candidates from general categories.
7. So far as determination of backward classes is concerned, a Notification should be issued by the Union of India. This can be done only after exclusion of the creamy layer for which necessary data must be obtained by the Central Government

from the State Governments and Union Territories. Such Notification is open to challenge on the ground of wrongful exclusion or inclusion. Norms must be fixed keeping in view the peculiar features in different States and Union Territories. There has to be proper identification of Other Backward Classes (OBCs). For identifying backward classes, the Commission set up pursuant to the directions of this Court in Indra Sawhney 1 has to work more effectively and not merely decide applications for inclusion or exclusion of castes.

8. The Parliament should fix a deadline by which time free and compulsory education will have reached every child. This must be done within six months, as the right to free and compulsory education is perhaps the most important of all the fundamental rights (Art.21 A). For without education, it becomes extremely difficult to exercise other fundamental rights.
9. If material is shown to the Central Government that the Institution deserves to be included in the Schedule (institutes which are excluded from reservations) of The Central Educational Institutions (Reservation in Admission) Act, 2006 (No. 5 of 2007), the Central Government must take an appropriate decision on the basis of materials placed and on examining the concerned issues as to whether Institution deserves to be included in the Schedule of the said act as provided in Sec 4 of the said act.
10. Held that the determination of SEBCs is done not solely based on caste and hence, the identification of SEBCs does not violate Article 15(1) of the Constitution.

Caste systems among Non-Hindus

The caste system is not constrained to Hindus society, but it is prevalent in non-Hindus also. The short of these caste systems in other religions are given below:

Christians

In some parts of India, Christians are stratified by sect, location, and the castes of their predecessors, usually in reference to upper class Syrian Malabar Nasranis. Christians in Kerala are divided into several communities, including Syrian Christians and the so-called "Latin" or "New Rite" Christians.

Syrian Christians

Syrian Christians derive status within the caste system from the tradition that they are converted High caste Hindus such as Namboodiris, Nairs and Jews (Israelites), who were evangelized by St. Thomas. Writers Arundhati Roy and Anand Kurian have written personal accounts of the caste system at work in their community. Syrian Christians, especially Knanaya Christians, tend to be endogamous and not intermarry with other Christian castes. This is because they wish to preserve their Jewish heritage.

The Latin Rite Christians were among the scheduled castes in the coastal belt of Kerala, where fishing was the primary occupation. They were actively converted by missionaries in the 16th and 19th centuries. These missionary activities were carried out by Western Latin Rite missionaries who did not understand the significance of the caste system in India; none of the Syrian churches had participated in such activities among the scheduled castes of India because they were aware of the prejudices of the caste system. The government of India later granted this group OBC status. Very rarely are there intermarriages between Syrian Christians and Latin Rite Christians.

Mass Conversion of Hindus into Christianity

In the Indian state of Goa, mass conversions were carried out by Portuguese Latin missionaries from the 16th century onwards. The Hindu converts retained their caste practices. The continued maintenance of the caste system among the Christians in Goa is attributed to the nature of mass conversions of entire villages, as a result of which existing social stratification was not affected. The Portuguese colonists, even during the Goan Inquisition, did not do anything to change the caste system.

Thus, the original Hindu Brahmins in Goa now became Christian Bamonns and the Kshatriyabecame Christian noblemen called Chardos. The Christian clergy became almost exclusively Bamon.Vaishyas who converted to Christianity became Gauddos, and Shudras became Sudirs. Finally, theDalits or "Untouchables" who converted to Christianity became Maharas and Chamars, the latter an appellation of the anti-Dalit ethnic slur Chamaar.

Muslims

The Sachar Committee's report commissioned by the government of India and released in 2006 documents the continued stratification in Muslim society, though stratification is not as rigid as the Hindu system, nor is it condoned by Islam.

Among Muslims, those who are referred to as Ashrafs are presumed to have a superior status derived from their foreign Arab ancestry, while the Ajlafs are assumed to be converts from Hinduism, and have a lower status. However, this may be more accurately described as ethnocentrism, since no prohibitions or rules are imposed on Aljafs, or their mingling with Ashrafs. In addition, the Arzal caste among Muslims was regarded by anti-caste activists like Ambedkar as the equivalent of untouchables, due to their low socioeconomic status.

In the Bengal region of India, some Muslims stratify their society according to 'Quoms,' though this is a description of their menial labour, and is not a rigid strata of society in strictly the same manner as a caste. While many scholars have asserted that the Muslim "castes" are not as acute in their discrimination as those of the Hindus, some like Ambedkar argued that the social evils in Sub-continental Muslim society were "worse than those seen in Hindu society", which maybe due to the influence of Hindu society in which they dwell.

Sikh

The Sikh Gurus criticized the hierarchy of the caste system. While some castes were widely perceived as being better or higher than others, they preached that all sections of society were valuable and that merit and hard-work were essential aspects of life.

In the Shiromani Gurdwara Prabandhak Committee, out of 140 seats, 20 are reserved for low caste Sikhs. However, the quota system has attracted much criticism due to the lack of meritocracy, since merit is considered the single most important component of winning a seat.

Buddhists

The Buddha specifically denounced the caste system and there was no practice of caste amongst his immediate followers. So the rest of this section has a questionable status. The Buddhists also had a caste system. Savarkar believed that the status of the backward castes (e.g. Chamar) that performed non-violence only worsened. When Ywan Chwang traveled to South India after the period of the Chalukyan Empire, he noticed that the caste system had existed among the Buddhists and Jains.

Jains

Jains also had castes in places such as Bihar. For example, in the village of Bundela, there were several "jaats" (groups) amongst the Jains.

A person of one "jaat" cannot intermingle with a Jain or another "jaat". They also could not eat with the members of other "jaats".

Baha'i

The Baha'i faith has grown to prominence in India, since its philosophy of the unity of humanity attracted many of the lower castes.

Hindu Reform Movements

Several contemporary groups, collectively termed as Hindu reform movements which strive to introduce regeneration and reform to Hinduism. Although these movements are very individual in their exact philosophies they generally stress the spiritual, secular and logical and scientific aspects of the Vedic traditions, creating a form that is egalitarian that does not discriminate based on Jati(caste or subcaste), gender, or race. Thus, most modern Hindu reform movements advocate a return to supposed ancient, egalitarian forms of Hinduism, and view aspects of modern Hinduism, such as discrimination and the caste system, as being corrupt results from colonialism and foreign influence.

Active Hindu communities are to be found in all parts of the world. There are groups in India that are actively engaged in getting women and those from socially disadvantaged jatis to become priests of Vedic ritual.

One of the foremost movements in breaking the caste system and educating the downtrodden was the Lingayat movement spearheaded by Basavanna in the 12th century in Anubhava Mantapa in Kalyani ofKarnataka. The less accessible Vedas were rejected and parallel Vachanas were compiled.

The new movements look up to Swami Vivekananda; Rabindranath Tagore; Ramana Maharshi; Shri Aurobindo (for his Integral Yoga); Maharishi Dayananda Saraswati, A.C. Bhaktivedanta Swami Prabhupada (founder of the modern Hare Krishna movement); Swami Sivananda, Swami Rama Tirtha;Narayana Guru,Jagadguru Swami Sathyananda Saraswathi, Paramhansa Yogananda; Shrii Shrii Anandamurti. More recently, the work of Maharishi Mahesh Yogi, Shirdi Sai Baba, Sathya Sai Baba, Swami Muktananda, Swami Chinmayananda Saraswati, Swami Dayananda Saraswati, Shriram Sharma Acharya, Pramukh Swami Maharaj, Sri Sri Ravi Shankar, and Mata Amritanandamayi has inspired millions to create new centers of spiritual development. In the intellectual field, the writings of Ananda Coomaraswamy, Ram Swarup, Sita Ram Goel, Subhash Kak, Frank Morales and David Frawley have been influential.

In social work, Mahatma Gandhi, Vinoba Bhave, Baba Amte and Shrii Shrii Anandamurti have been most important. Sunderlal Bahuguna created the chipko movement for the preservation of forestlands according to the Hindu ecological ideas.

The Rashtriya Swayamsevak Sangh or (RSS) was founded by Keshav Baliram Hegdewar in 1925. The goal was to unite Hindus, make them rise over their caste differences and work to achieve a Hindu Rashtra; the ideology of the Sangh, closely associated with political Hinduism, came to be known asHindutva.

7

RELIGION IN INDIAN SOCIETY

India is the birth place of Hinduism, Buddhism, Jainism and Sikhism, collectively known as Indian religions. Indian religions, also known as Dharmic religions are a major form of world religions along with Abrahamic ones. Today, Hinduism and Buddhism are the world's third- and fourth-largest religions respectively, with over 2 billion followers altogether, and possibly as many as 2.5 or 2.6 billion followers. India is also the birthplace for the Lingayat and Ahmadiyya faiths.

Religion and Indian Society

India is one of the most religiously diverse nations in the world, with some of the most deeply religious societies and cultures. Religion still plays a central and definitive role in the life of many of its people.

The religion of 80% of the people is Hinduism. Islam is practiced by around 13% of all Indians. Sikhism, Jainism and especially Buddhism are influential not only in India but across the world.Christianity, Zoroastrianism, Judaism and the Bahá'í Faith are also influential but their numbers are smaller. Despite the strong role of religion in Indian life, atheism and agnostics also have visible influence along with a self-ascribed tolerance to other people.

In recent years, particularly in cities, some of these lines have blurred and sometimes even disappeared.

Important family relations extend as far as gotra, the mainly patrilinear lineage or clan assigned to a Hindu at birth. In rural areas and sometimes in urban areas as well, it is common that three or four generations of the family live under the same roof. The patriarch often resolves family issues.

Throughout its history, religion has been an important part of the country's culture. Religious diversity and religious tolerance are both established in the country by lawand custom. A vast majority of Indians associate themselves with a religion.

According to the 2001 census, Hinduism accounted for 80.5% of thepopulation of India. Islam (13.4%), Christianity (2.3%) and Sikhism (1.9%) are the other major religions followed by the people of India. This diversity of religious belief systems existing in India today is a result of, besides existence and birth of native religions, assimilation and social integration of religions brought to the region by traders, travelers, immigrants, and even invaders and conquerors.

Zoroastrianism and Judaism also have an ancient history in India and each has several thousand Indian adherents. India has the largest population of people adhering to Zoroastrianism and Bahá'í Faith anywhere in the world. Many other world religions also have a relationship with Indian spirituality, like the Baha'i faith which recognizes Lord Buddha and Lord Krishna as manifestations of God Almighty.

Indian diaspora in the West have popularized many aspects of Hindu philosophy like yoga (meditation), Ayurvedic medicine, divination, vegetarianism, karma and reincarnation to a great extent. The influence of Indians abroad in spiritual matters has been significant as several organizations such as the Hare Krishna movement, the Brahma Kumaris, theAnanda Marga and others spread by Indian spiritual figures.

The Muslim population in India is the third largest in the world. The shrines of some of the most famous saints of Sufism like Moinuddin Chishti and Nizamuddin Auliya are in India and attract visitors from all over the world. India is also home to some of the most famous monuments of Islamic architecture like the Taj Mahal and the Qutb Minar. Civil matters related to the community are dealt with by the Muslim Personal Law, and constitutional amendments in 1985 established its primacy in family matters.

The Constitution of India declares the nation to be a secular republic that must uphold the right of citizens to freely worship and propagate any religion or faith (with activities subject to reasonable restrictions for the sake of morality, law and order, etc.). The Constitution of India also declares the right to freedom of religion as a fundamental right.

Citizens of India are generally tolerant of each other's religions and retain a secular outlook, although inter-religious marriage is not widely practiced. Inter-community clashes have found little support in the social mainstream, and it is generally perceived that the causes of religious conflicts are political rather than ideological in nature.

The documented history of Indian religions begins with historical Vedic religion, the religious practices of the early Indo-Aryans, which were collected and later redacted into the Samhitas (usually known as the Vedas), four canonical collections of hymns composed in archaic Sanskrit. These texts are the central *shruti* (revealed) texts of Hinduism. The period of the composition, redaction and commentary of these texts is known as the Vedic period, which lasted from roughly 1500 to 500 BCE.

The late Vedic period (9th to 6th centuries BCE) marks the beginning of the Upanisadic or Vedantic period. This period heralded the beginning of much of what became classical Hinduism, with the composition of the Upanishads, later the Sanskrit epics, still later followed by the Puranas.

Certain scholarship holds that the practices, emblems and architecture now commonly associated with the Hindu pantheon and Jainism may go back as far as Late Harappan times to the period 2000-1500 BCE.

Denominations in Hinduism

Hinduism is divided into numerous denominations, primarily Shaivism, Shaktism, Vaishnavism, Smarta and much smaller groups like the conservative Shrauta. Hindu reform movements such as Ayyavazhi are more recent. About 90% of Hindus reside in the Republic of India, accounting for 83% of its population.

Sikhism was founded in the 15th century on the teachings of Guru Nanak and the nine successive Sikh Gurus in Northern India. The vast majority of its adherents originate in the Punjab region.

In India, religion is a way of life. It is an integral part of the entire Indian tradition. For the majority of Indians, religion permeates every aspect of life, from commonplace daily chores to education and politics. Secular India is home to Hinduism, Islam, Christianity, Buddhism, Jainism, Sikhism and other innumerable religious traditions.

Hinduism is the dominant faith, practiced by over 80% of the population. Besides Hindus, Muslims are the most prominent religious group and are an integral part of, Indian society. In fact India has the second largest population of Muslims in the world after Indonesia.

Common practices have crept into most religious faiths in India and many of the festivals that mark each year with music, dance and feasting are shared by all communities. Each has its own pilgrimage sites, heroes, legends and even culinary specialties, mingling in a unique diversity that is the very pulse of society.

Common Traits of Indian Religions

Sometimes summarised as Dharmic religions or dharmic traditions though subtleties in the meaning of Dharma differs according to the religion, Hinduism, Buddhism, Jainism and Sikhism share certain key concepts, which are interpreted differently by different groups and individuals.

Common traits can also be observed in both the ritual and the literary sphere. For example, the head-anointing ritual of abhiseka is of importance in three of these distinct traditions, excluding Sikhism (in Buddhism it is found within Vajrayana). Other noteworthy rituals are the cremation of the dead, the wearing of vermilion on the head by married women, and various marital rituals. In literature, many classical narratives and purana have Hindu, Buddhist or Jain versions. All four traditions have notions of *karma*, *dharma*, *samsara*, *moksha* and various forms of Yoga. Of course, these terms may be perceived differently by different religions. For instance, for a Hindu, *dharma* is his duty. For a Jain, *dharma* is righteousness, his conduct. For a Buddhist, dharma is usually taken to be the Buddha's teachings. Similarly, for a Hindu, yoga is the cessation of all thoughts/ activities of the mind. For Jains, Yoga is sum total all physical, verbal and mental activities.

Rama is a heroic figure in all of these religions. In Hinduism, He is the God-incarnate in the form of a princely king; in Buddhism, he is a Bodhisattva-incarnate; in Jainism, he is the perfect human being. Among the *Buddhist Ramayanas* are: *Vessantarajataka*, *Reamker*, *Ramakien*, *Phra Lak Phra Lam*, *Hikayat Seri Rama* etc. There also exists the Khamti Ramayana among the Khamti tribe of Asom wherein Rama is an Avatar of a Bodhisattva who incarnates to punish the demon king Ravana. The *Tai Ramayana* is another book retelling the divine story in Asom.

Vedic period

The Vedic Period is most significant for the composition of the four *Vedas*, Brahmanas and the older *Upanishads* (both presented as discussions on the rituals, *mantras* and concepts found in the four Vedas), which today are some of the most important canonical texts of Hinduism, and are the codification of much of what developed into the core beliefs of Hinduism.

The Vedas reflect the liturgy and ritual of Late Bronze Age to Early Iron Age Indo-Aryan speaking peoples in India. Religious practices were dominated by the Vedic priesthood administering domestic rituals/rites and solemn sacrifices. The Brahmanas, Aranyakas and some of the older Upanishads are also placed in this period. Many elements of Vedic religion reach back to early Bronze Age Proto-Indo-Iranian times. The Vedic period is held to have ended around 500 BCE.

Vedanta

The period of Vedanta typically thought to have begun around 600 BCE, marked the end of the evolution of the main Vedic texts; it also accompanied the transformation of the semi-nomadic nature of the Indo-Aryan tribes to agriculture-based polities, as they increasingly formed permanent settlements in the Indo-Gangetic plain and other parts of Northern India. This period was foreshadowed by the Brahmanas that interpreted the four canonical Vedas in various fashions, which finally led to the Upanishads. While the ritualistic status of the four Vedas remained undiminished, the early Upanishads mainly relate to spiritual insights.

At this time, the concepts of reincarnation, *samsara*, *karma*, and *moksha* began to be accepted in ancient India within the sphere of the priestly establishment i.e. the Brahmana class.

Some scholars think that these new concepts developed by aborigines outside the caste system,others detect Sramana or even Ksatriya influence. These concepts were eventually accepted by Brahmin orthodoxy, and were to form much of the core philosophies of the later epics and Hinduism, as well as, against a different philosophical and religious background, in Buddhism and Jainism.

Hinduism: Religion of Gods & Goddesses

Hinduism is a religion with various gods and goddesses. According to Hinduism, three Lords rule the world. Lord Brahma: the creator; Lord Vishnu: the preserver and Lord Shiva: the destroyer. Lord Vishnu did his job of preserving the world by incarnating himself in different forms at times of crisis.

Hinduism does not have a "unified system of belief encoded in declaration of faith or a creed", but is rather an umbrella term comprising the plurality of religious phenomena originating and based on the Vedic traditions.

The characteristic of comprehensive tolerance to differences in belief, and Hinduism's openness, makes it difficult to define as a religion according to traditional western conceptions. To its adherents, Hinduism is the traditional way of life, and because of the wide range of traditions and ideas incorporated within or covered by it, arriving at a comprehensive definition of the term is problematic. While sometimes referred to as a religion, Hinduism is more often defined as a religious tradition. It is therefore described as both the oldest of the world's religions, and the most diverse. Most Hindu traditions revere a body of religious or sacred literature, the Vedas, although there are exceptions. Some Hindu religious traditions regard particular rituals as essential for salvation, but a variety of views on this co-exist.

Hinduism is sometimes characterized by the belief in reincarnation (*samsara*), determined by the law of *karma*, and the idea that salvation is freedom from this cycle of repeated birth and death. However, other religions of the region, such as Buddhism, Jainism and Sikhism, also believe in *karma*, outside the scope of Hinduism. Hinduism is therefore viewed as the most complex of all of the living, historical world religions. Despite its complexity, Hinduism is not only one of the numerically largest faiths, but is also the oldest living major tradition on earth, with roots reaching back into prehistory.

Radha Krishnon on Hinduism

A definition of Hinduism, given by the first Vice President of India, who was also a prominent theologian, Sarvepalli Radhakrishnan, states that Hinduism is not "just a faith", but in itself is related to the union of reason and intuition. Radhakrishnan explicitly states that Hinduism cannot be defined, but is only to be experienced. Similarly, some academics suggest that Hinduism can be seen as a category with "fuzzy edges", rather than as a well-defined and rigid entity. Some forms of religious expression are central to Hinduism, while others are not as central but still remain within the category.

Problems with the single definition of what is actually meant by the term 'Hinduism' are often attributed to the fact that Hinduism does not have a single or common historical founder. Hinduism, or as some say 'Hinduisms,' does not have a single system of salvation and has different goals according to each sect or denomination. The forms of Vedic religion are seen not as an alternative to Hinduism, but as its earliest form, and there is little justification for the divisions found in much western scholarly writing between Vedism, Brahmanism and Hinduism.

A definition of Hinduism is further complicated by the frequent use of the term "faith" as a synonym for "religion". Some academics and many practitioners refer to Hinduism using a native definition, as Sanatana Dharma, a Sanskrit phrase meaning "the eternal law", or the "eternal way".

The three Lords that rule the world have consorts and they are goddesses. Consort of God Brahma is Sarasvati; goddess of learning. God Vishnu's consort is Goddess Lakshmi; goddess of wealth and prosperity. God Shiva's consort is Goddess Parvati who is worshipped as Kali or Durga.

Along them there are a number of other gods and goddesses. To name a few of them, there is God Ganesh, who has an elephant's head and he is also a son of God Shiva and Goddess Parvati. Hanuman, who is an ape. Surya, Lord of sun. Ganga Ma, goddess of river Ganges. Samundra, Lord of the sea. Indra, king of the gods (but he isn't an important god). Prithvi, goddess of earth. Shakti, goddess of power. The Hindus call their goddesses 'Ma' meaning mother.

Some gods have more than one name. Lord Shiva is also known as Shankar, Mahadev, Natraj, Mahesh and many other names. Lord Ganesh is also called Ganpati. God Vishnu incarnated nine times to do his job and in his every appearance he had a different form which are also worshipped as gods. Among his appearances, he appeared as Lord Rama, Lord Krishna, Lord Narsimha, Lord Parsuram and Lord Buddha. Lord Krishna also has different names, Gopal; Kishan; Shyam and other names. He also has other titles with meanings like 'Basuri Wala' which means the flute musician and 'Makhan Chor' which means the butter stealer. There are also gods who can change their forms, for example: Goddess Parvati can change into Goddess Kali or Goddess Durga.

Not all of these gods are worshiped by all Hindus. Some Hindus worship only Lord Vishnu. Others worship only Lord Shiva. Others worship only the goddesses and call these goddesses collectively as Shakti meaning power. Many of these goddess worshipers worship Parvati in her images as Kali or Durga. People who worship Lord Shiva or Lord Vishnu also worship characters and images connected with these gods. Lord Vishnu worshipers (Vaishnaites) also worship his appearances. Lord Shiva's worshipers (Shaivites) also worship images of bull called Nandi, who was Lord Shiva's carrier and a unique stone design connected to Lord Shiva. There are also Hindus who worship all the gods.

There are some gods who are worshiped all over India like Rama and Krishna and other gods who are worshiped more in one region than the other like Lord Ganesh who is worshiped mainly in west India. Hindus also worship gods according to their personal needs. People who engage in wrestling, body building and other physical sports worship Lord Hanuman, who in Hindu legends was an ape with lot of physical strength. Businessmen worship Lakshmi, goddess of wealth.

Though Hindus worship different idols, many Hindus believe in one God and perceive in these different gods and goddesses as different faces of the same one God. Others believe that idolatry is the wrong interpretation of Hinduism.

Hindus believe in reincarnation. The basic belief is that a person's fate is determined according to his deeds. These deeds in Hinduism are called 'Karma'. A soul who does good Karma in this life will be awarded with a better life in the next incarnation. Souls who do bad Karma will be punished for their sins, if not in this incarnation then in the next incarnation and will continue to be born in this world again and again.

The good souls will be liberated from the circle of rebirth and get redemption which is called 'Moksha' meaning freedom. Hindus normally cremate their dead ones, so that the soul of the dead would go to heaven, except in a few cases of Hindu saints, who are believed to have attained 'Moksha'.

The main Hindu books are the four Vedas. They are *Rig Veda*, *Sama Veda*, *Yajur Veda* and *Atharva Veda*. The concluding portions of the Vedas are called Upanisads. There are also other holy books like *Puranas*, *Ramayana*, *Mahabharta* etc. The different gods and goddesses in the Hindu mythology are derived from these books. *Ramayana* and *Mahabharta* are the most popular Hindu epics.

The main story of *Ramayana* is the story of Lord Rama. Rama was born in a royal family and was suppose to be the king, but because of his step-mother, he was forced to exile from his kingdom for fourteen years. During this period his consort Sita was kidnapped by a demon called Ravan, who was king of Lanka. Rama with the help of his brother, Lakshman, and an army of monkeys under the leadership of Hanuman, rescued Sita. Many Indians believe that the present day Sri Lanka was then the kingdom of Lanka.

Mahabharta is a family epic. In this epic, the Pandva family and the Kaurav family who are cousins fight with each other for the control over a kingdom.

Pilgrimages and Customs

Hindus have many holy places. Badrinath, Puri, Dwarkha and Rameshwaram are four holiest places for the Hindus. Other holy places are Varanasi, Rishikesh, Nasik, Pushkar, Ujjain and other places. Some rivers are also holy to them. Among them are Godavri, Yamuna and above all Ganges which the Indians call Ganga. Another holy river is Sarasvati and it is invisible. Hindus also worship and respect some animals and birds like cobra, apes, peacocks and cow. Hindus also respect some trees and bush trees. The famous and the most respected bush tree is Tulsi.

Some of the Hindu customs, which exist or existed, do not have their bearing in Hindu scriptures but became part of Hinduism in different ways and fashion. For example, the Hindus see in cow a sacred animal. Religiously there is no reason to see cow as sacred and it is believed that cows were made 'sacred' to prevent their slaughter during periods of droughts and hunger. Cobra worship also is not found in Hindu scripts.

This custom became part of Hinduism when some Indian tribes who use to worship cobra adopted Hinduism. Burning of the widow on the dead husband's pyre also has no religious justification. This custom, outlawed in 1829, was probably brought to India by the Scythians invaders of India. Among the Scythians it was a custom to bury the dead king with his mistresses or wives, servants and other things so that they could continue to serve him in the next world. When these Scythians arrived in India, they adopted the Indian system of funeral, which was cremating the dead. And so instead of burying their kings and his servers they started cremating their dead with his surviving lovers. The Scythians were warrior tribes and they were given a status of warrior castes in Hindu religious hierarchy. The different castes who claimed warrior status or higher also adopted this custom.

There are four castes in Hindu religion arranged in a hierarchy. The highest caste is Brahmin, and they are the priest caste of Hinduism. After them are the *Kshatria*, who are the warrior castes. After them are the *Vaishya* caste , who are business people. And after them are the *Sudra*, who are the common peasants and workers. Below these four castes there are casteless, the untouchables. The four castes were not allowed to have any physical contact with the untouchables.

Religiously, people are born in a caste and it cannot be changed. Each caste has some compulsory duties, which its members must do. Each caste has professional limits which decides what profession each caste can follow. Each caste members can have social relations only with its caste members. Religiously this includes marraige and even eating only with caste members.

Origin of Hinduism

How did Hinduism originated is a difficult question. The accepted theory is that Hinduism was evolved after the historical meeting between the Aryans and Dravidians. Some claim that Hinduism is mainly an Aryan culture whereas the others claim that it is mainly a Dravidian culture. Religiously the Vedas were given by Brahma.

Before Hinduism, there existed another religion in India called Brahmanism and its followers were called Brahmins. The Brahmins were the spiritual and moral guides of the Indian society. The members of this religion were a close sect and others could not join it. The Brahmins slowly started accepting others into their religion and so was created Hinduism which included in it the customs which were not part of the Vedas. One of the reasons the Brahmins accepted others to their religion was the fear to loose their status as moral guides to priests of a new religion that started in India, namely Buddhism. The Brahmins even accepted Buddha as an incarnation of Lord Vishnu and part of his teachings and philosophy like non-violence into their religion.

The underlying tenets of Hinduism cannot be easily defined. There is no unique philosophy that forms the basis of the faith of the majority of India's population. Hinduism is perhaps the only religious tradition that is so diversified in its theoretical premises and practical expressions as to be called a "museum of religions". This religion cannot be traced to a specific founder nor does it have a "holy book" as a basic scriptural guide. The *Rig Veda*, *Upanishads* and the *Bhagwad Gita* can all be described as the sacred text of the Hindus.

Unlike most other religions, Hinduism does not advocate the worship of one particular deity. One may worship Lord Shiva or Vishnu or Rama or Krishna or some other gods and goddesses or one may believe in the 'Supreme Spirit' or the 'Indestructible Soul' within each individual and still be called a good Hindu. This gives an indication of the kind of contrasts this religion is marked by. At one end of the scale, it is an exploration of the 'Ultimate Reality'; at the other end there are cults that worship spirits, trees and animals.

Festivals and Ceremonies

There are festivals and ceremonies associated not only with gods and goddesses but also with the sun, moon, planets, rivers, oceans, trees and animals. Some of the popular Hindu festivals are Deepawali, Holi, Dussehra, Ganesh Chaturthi, Pongal, Janamasthmi and Shiva Ratri. These innumerable festive occasions lend Hinduism its amazing popular appeal and make the Indian tradition rich and colorful.

Hinduism is the predominant and indigenous religious traditionof the Indian Subcontinent. Hinduism is known to its followers asSan?tana

Dharma, amongst many other expressions. Generic "types" of Hinduism that attempt to accommodate a variety of complex views span folk and Vedic Hinduism to bhakti tradition, as inVaishnavism. Among other practices and philosophies, Hinduism includes a wide spectrum of laws and prescriptions of "daily morality" based on the notion of *karma, dharma*, and societal norms. Hinduism is a conglomeration of distinct intellectual or philosophical points of view, rather than a rigid common set of beliefs.

Hinduism is formed of diverse traditions and has no single founder. Among its direct roots is the historical Vedic religion ofIron Age India and, as such, Hinduism is often called the "oldest living religion" or the "oldest living major religion" in the world.

A large body of texts is classified as Hindu, divided into sruti ("revealed") and Smriti ("remembered") texts. These texts discusstheology, philosophy and mythology, and provide information on the practice of *dharma* (religious living). Among these texts, theVedas are the foremost in authority, importance and antiquity. Other major scriptures include the Upanishads, Puranas and theepics Mahabharata and Ramayana. The *Bhagavad Gita*, a syncretistic treatise from the Mahabharata, is of special importance. It combines Vedanta, Yoga, and some Samkhya philosophy into its discussion of good conduct and life.

Dharma

The concept of a "power" that is held to lie behind nature and that keeps everything in balance became a natural forerunner to the idea of Dharma. The idea of rta laid the cornerstone of dharma's implicit attribution to the "ultimate reality" of the surrounding universe, in classical Vedic Hinduism the following verse from the *Rig-Veda* is an example where *rta* is mentioned:

O Indra, lead us on the path of Rta, on the right path over all evils. -(RV 10.133.6)

The transition of the rta to the modern idea of dharma occurs in the Brihadaranyaka Upanishad. The Upanishads saw dharma as the universal principle of law, order, harmony, all in all truth, that sprang first from Brahman. It acts as the regulatory moral principle of the Universe. It is sat (truth), a major tenet of Hinduism. This hearkens back to the conception of the Rig Veda that "Ekam Sat," (Truth Is One), of the idea that Brahman is "Sacchidananda" (Truth-Consciousness-Bliss). Dharma is not just law, or harmony, it is pure Reality.

The word Sanatana means 'eternal', 'perennial', or 'forever'; thus, 'Sanatana Dharma' signifies that it is the dharma that has neither beginning nor end.

Beliefs of Hinduism

Hinduism refers to a religious mainstream which evolved organically and spread over a large territory marked by significant ethnic and cultural diversity. This mainstream evolved both by innovation from within, and by assimilation of external traditions or cults into the Hindu fold. The result is an enormous variety of religious traditions, ranging from innumerable small, unsophisticated cults to major religious movements with millions of adherents spread over the entire subcontinent. The identification of Hinduism as an independent religion separate from Buddhism or Jainism consequently hinges on the affirmation of its adherents that it is such.

Hinduism grants absolute and complete freedom of belief and worship. Hinduism conceives the whole world as a single family that deifies the one truth, and therefore it accepts all forms of beliefs and dismisses labels of distinct religions which would imply a division of identity. Hence, Hinduism is devoid of the concepts of apostasy, heresy and blasphemy.

Prominent themes in Hindu beliefs include (but are not restricted to), *Dharma* (ethics/duties), *Samsara* (The continuing cycle of birth, life, death and rebirth), *Karma* (action and subsequent reaction), *Moksha* (liberation from samsara), and the various Yogas (paths or practices).

Ceremonies and Customs

Guru Nanak Dev Ji taught that rituals, religious ceremonies, or idol worship is of little use and Sikhs are discouraged from fasting or going on pilgrimages. Sikhs do not believe in converting people but converts to Sikhi by choice are welcomed. The morning and evening prayers take about two hours a day, starting in the very early morning hours. The first morning prayer is Guru Nanak's *Jap Ji*. *Jap*, meaning "recitation", refers to the use of sound, as the best way of approaching the divine. Like combing hair, hearing and reciting the sacred word is used as a way to comb all negative thoughts out of the mind. The second morning prayer is Guru Gobind Singh's universal Jaap Sahib.

The Guru addresses God as having no form, no country, and no religion but as the seed of seeds, sun of suns, and the song of songs. The Jaap Sahib asserts that God is the cause of conflict as well as peace, and of destruction as well as creation. Devotees learn that there is nothing outside of God's presence, nothing outside of God's control. Devout Sikhs are encouraged to begin the day with private meditations on the name of God.

Upon a child's birth, the *Guru Granth Sahib* is opened at a random point and the child is named using the first letter on the top left hand corner of the left page. All boys are given the middle name Singh, and all girls are given the middle name Kaur (this was a once a title which was conferred on an indivdual at joining the Khalsa). Sikhs are joined in wedlock through the anand karaj ceremony. Sikhs are required to marry when they are of a sufficient age (child marriage is taboo), and without regard for the future spouse's caste or descent. The marriage ceremony is performed in the company of the Guru Granth Sahib; around which the couple circles four times. After the ceremony is complete, the husband and wife are considered "a single soul in two bodies."

According to Sikh religious rites, neither husband nor wife is permitted to divorce. A Sikh couple that wishes to divorce may be able to do so in a civil court but this is not condoned. Upon death, the body of a Sikh is usually cremated. If this is not possible, any means of disposing the body may be employed. The kirtan sohili and ardas prayers are performed during the funeral ceremony (known asantim sanskar).

Baptism and the Khalsa

Khalsa (meaning "Sovereign") is the collective name given by Gobind Singh to all Sikhs, male or female, who have been baptised or initiated by taking ammrit in a ceremony called ammrit sañcar. The first time that this ceremony took place was on Vaisakhi, which fell on 30 March 1699 at Anandpur Sahib in Punjab. It was on that occasion that Gobind Singh baptised the Pañj Piare-the five beloved ones, who in turn baptised Gobind Singh himself. The last name Singh is given to baptized Sikh males meaning lion and the last name Kaur is given to baptized Sikh females meaning princess/lioness.

Baptised Sikhs are bound to wear the Five Ks (in Punjabi known as pañj kakk? or pañj kakar), or articles of faith, at all times. The 5 items are: kes (uncut hair), kangha (small wooden comb), kara (circular steel or iron bracelet), kirpan (sword/dagger), and kaccha (special undergarment). The Five Ks have both practical and symbolic purposes.

Jainism

Jainism as a religious tradition was established in India about the same time as Buddhism. Mahavira, one of the jinas (conquerors) preached the Jain philosophy around the same time that Buddhism began.

Like Buddhism, Jainism rose against the corruption in the interpretation of Hinduism prevalent at the time. The underlying philosophy of Jainism is that renunciation of worldly desires and self-conquest leads to perfect wisdom. This faith believes in total abstinence and asceticism as practiced by the Jinas and theTirthankars ("crossing-makers"). The "crossing refers to the passage from the material to the spiritual realm, from bondage to freedom. Followers of this faith accept the popular gods of Hinduism but they are placed lower than the jinas.

The focus of this religion has been purification of the soul by means of right conduct, right faith and right knowledge. This faith also enunciates complete non-violence and the Jain monks can be seen with their nose and mouth covered by a cloth mask to ensure that they do not kill any germs or insects while breathing. Today, Jainism has more than three million adherents in India and finds wide acceptance because of its philosophy of sympathy for all living beings.

Jainism is an Indian religion that prescribes a path of non-violence towards all living beings. Its philosophy and practice emphasize the necessity of self-effort to move the soul towards divine consciousness and liberation. Any soul that has conquered its own inner enemies and achieved the state of supreme being is called a jina("conqueror" or "victor"). The ultimate status of these perfect souls is called siddha. Jainism is also referred to as shramana dharma (self-reliant) or the "path of the niganthas" (those without attachments or aversions) by ancient texts.

Jain doctrine teaches that Jainism has always existed and will always exist, although historians date the foundation of the organized or present form of Jainism to sometime between the 9th and the 6th century BC.

Like most ancient Indian traditions, Jainism has its roots from the Indus Valley Civilization, reflecting native spirituality prior to the Indo-Aryan migration into India. Other scholars suggested the shramana traditions were separate and contemporaneous with Indo-Aryan religious practices of thehistorical Vedic religion.

In the modern world, Jainism is a small but influential religious minority with as many as 4.2 million followers in India, and successful growing immigrant communities in North America,western Europe, the Far East, Australia and elsewhere. Jains have significantly influenced and contributed to ethical, politicaland economic spheres in India. Jains have an ancient tradition of scholarship and have the highest degree of literacy for a religious community in India and Jain libraries are the oldest in the country.

Jainism encourages spiritual development through cultivation of one's own personal wisdom and reliance on self control throughvows. The triple gems of Jainism - right vision or view (Samyak Darshana), right knowledge (Samyak Gyana) and right conduct (Samyak Charitra) - provide the path for attaining liberation from thecycles of birth and death. When the soul sheds its karmic bonds completely, it attains divine consciousness. Those who have attained moksha are called siddhas, while those attached to the world through their karma are called samsarin. Every soul has to follow the path, as explained by the Jinas and revived by the tirthankaras, to attain complete liberation or nirvana.

Jains do not believe in a creator deity that could be responsible for the manifestation, creation, or maintenance of this universe. The universe is self regulated by the laws of nature. Jains believe that life exists in various forms in different parts of the universe including earth. Jainism has extensive classification of various living organisms including micro-organisms that live in mud, air and water. All living organisms have soul and therefore need to be interacted without causing much harm.

Jains believe that to attain enlightenment and ultimately liberation from all karmic bonding, one must practice the following ethical principles not only in thought, but also in words (speech) and action . Such a practise through lifelong work towards oneself is called as observing the Mahavrata ("Great Vows"). These vows are:

- *Ahimsa* (Non-violence) - To cause "no harm" to living beings (on the lines of "live" and "let live"). The vow involves "minimizing" intentional as well as unintentional harm to another living creature. There should even be no room for any thought conjuring injury to others, let alone talking about it or performing of such an act. Besides, it also includes respecting the views of others (non-absolutism and acceptance of multiple views).
- *Satya* (Truthfulness) - To always speak of truth such that no harm is caused to others. A person who speaks truth becomes trustworthy like a mother, venerable like a preceptor and dear to everyone like a kinsman. Given that non-violence has priority, all other principles yield to it whenever there is a conflict. For example, in a situation where speaking truth would lead to violence, it would be perfectly moral to remain silent (for you are neither being untrue, nor causing violence by way of truth)
- *Asteya* (Non-stealing) - Not to take into possession, anything that is not willingly offered. It is the strict adherence to one's own possessions without desiring for the ones that belong to others. One should remain satisfied by whatever is earned

through honest labour. Any attempt to squeeze material wealth from others and/or exploit the weak is considered theft. Some of the guidelines for this principle follow as under:

- Always give people fair value for their labor or product.
- Not to voluntarily (or otherwise) take into possession, materials that are not earned or offered by others.
- Not to voluntarily (or otherwise) take materials into personal possession, that have been dropped off, or forgotten by others.
- Not to purchase materials as a result of being cheaper in value, if the resultant price reduction is a result of improper method of preparation. For instance, products made out of raw materials obtained by way of pyramid schemes, illegal businesses, stolen goods, etc., should be strictly prohibited

- *Brahmacharya* (Celibacy) - To exercise control over senses (including mind) from indulgence. The basic intent of this vow is to conquer passion, thus preventing wastage of energy in the direcition of pleasurable desires. During observance of this vow, the householder must not have a sensual relationship with anybody other than one's own spouse. Jain monks and nuns practice complete abstinence from any sexual activity.
- *Aparigraha* (Non-possession, Non-materialism) - To observe detachment from people, places and material things. Ownership of an object itself is not possessiveness; however, attachment to the owned object is possessiveness. For householders, non-possession is owning without attachment, because the notion of possession is illusory. The basic principle behind observance of this vow, lies in the fact that life changes. What you own today, may not be rightfully yours tomorrow. Hence the householder is encouraged to discharge his or her duties to related people and objects as a trustee, without excessive attachment or aversion. For monks and nuns, non-possession involves complete renunciation of property and human relations.

Jains hold that universe and its laws of nature are eternal, and have always existed in time. However, it constantly undergoes cyclical changes as per governing universal laws. The universe is occupied by both living beings (jiva) and non-living objects (Ajiva). The samsarin soul incarnates in various life forms during its journey over time. Human, sub-human (category catering to inclusion of animals, birds, insects and other forms of living creatures), super-human (heavenly beings) and hellish-beings are the four forms of samsarin soul incarnations. A living being's thoughts, expressions and actions, executed with intent of attachment and aversion, give rise to the accumulation of karma. These influxes of karma in turn contribute to determination of circumstances that would hold up in our future in the form of rewards or punishment. Jain scholars have explained in-depth methods and techniques that will result into clearance of past accumulated karmas as well as stopping the inflow of fresh karmas. This is the path to salvation.

A major characteristic of Jain belief is the emphasis on the consequences of not only physical but also mental behaviours. One's unconquered mind tainted with anger, pride (ego), deceit and greed joined with uncontrolled sense organs are powerful enemies of humans. Anger comes in way of good human relations, pride destroys humility, deceit destroys peace and greed destroys good judgement. Jainism recommends conquering anger by forgiveness, pride (ego) by humility, deceit by straight-forwardness and greed by contentment.

The principle of non-violence seeks to minimize karmas that limit the capabilities of one's own soul. Jainism views every soul as worthy of respect because it has the potential to become siddha (paramatma "highest soul"). Because all living beings possess a soul, great care and awareness is essential in one's actions. Jainism emphasizes the equality of all life, advocating harmlessness towards all, whether great or small. This policy extends even to microscopic organisms.

Jainism acknowledges that every person has different capabilities and capacities to practice and therefore accepts different levels of compliance for ascetics and householders. The Great Vows are prescribed for Jain monastics while limited vows are prescribed for householders. Householders are encouraged to practice five cardinal principles of non-violence, truthfulness, non-stealing, celibacy and non-possessiveness with their current practical limitations, while monks and nuns have to observe them very strictly. With consistent practice, it is possible to overcome the limitations gradually, accelerating spiritual progress.

Core Beliefs of Jainism

- Every living being has a soul.
- Every soul is potentially divine, with innate qualities of infinite knowledge, perception, power, and bliss (masked by its karmas).

- Therefore regard every living being as you do yourself, harming no one and being kind to all living beings.
- Every soul is born as a heavenly being, human, sub-human or hellish being according to its own karma.
- Every soul is the architect of its own life, here or hereafter.
- When a soul is freed from karmas, it becomes free and attains divine consciousness, experiencing infinite knowledge, perception, power, and bliss(Moksha).
- The triple gems of Jainism ("Right View, Right Knowledge and Right Conduct") provide the way to this realisation. There is no supreme divine creator, owner, preserver, or destroyer. The universe is self-regulated, and every soul has the potential to achieve divine consciousness (siddha) through its own efforts.
- Non-violence (to be in soul consciousness rather than body consciousness) is the foundation of right view, the condition of right knowledge and the kernel of right conduct. It leads to a state of being unattached to worldly things and being nonjudgmental and non-violent; this includes compassion and forgiveness in thoughts, words and actions toward all living beings and respecting views of others (non-absolutism).
- Jainism stresses the importance of controlling the senses including the mind, as they can drag one far away from true nature of the soul.
- Limit possessions and lead a life that is useful to yourself and others. Owning an object by itself is not possessiveness; however, attachment to an object is possessiveness. Non-possessiveness is the balancing of needs and desires while staying detached from our possessions.
- Enjoy the company of the holy and better-qualified, be merciful to afflicted souls, and tolerate the perversely inclined.
- Four things are difficult for a soul to attain: 1. human birth, 2. knowledge of the laws governing the souls, 3. absolute conviction in the philosophy of non-violence, and 4. practicing this knowledge with conviction in everyday life activities.
- It is, therefore, important not to waste human life in evil ways. Rather, strive to rise on the ladder of spiritual evolution.
- The goal of Jainism is liberation of the soul from the negative effects of unenlightened thoughts, speech, and action. This goal is achieved through clearance of karmic obstructions by following the triple gems of Jainism.

- Namokar Mantra is the fundamental prayer in Jainism and can be recited at any time of the day. Praying by reciting this mantra, the devotee bows in respect to liberated souls still in human form (arihants), fully liberated souls forever free from rebirth (siddhas), spiritual leaders (Acharyas), teachers, and all the monks and nuns. By saluting them saying "namo namaha", Jains receive inspiration from them to follow their path to achieve true bliss and total freedom from the karmas binding their souls. In this main prayer, Jains do not ask for any favours or material benefits. This mantra serves as a simple gesture of deep respect toward beings that are more spiritually advanced. The mantra also reminds followers of the ultimate goal of reaching nirvana ormoksha.
- Jains worship the icons of jinas, arihants and Tirthankaras, who have conquered their inner passions and attained divine consciousness, and study the Scriptures of these liberated beings.
- Jainism acknowledges the existence of powerful heavenly souls that look after the well-being ofTirthankaras. Usually they are found in pairs around the icons as male (yaksha) and female (yakshini) guardian deities. Even though they have supernatural powers, these deities are also souls wandering through the cycles of births and deaths just like most other souls. Over time, people began worshiping these deities as well.

Islam

Islamic religion is the second-most practiced religion in the Republic of India after Hinduism, with more than 13.4% of the country's population (over 138 million as per 2001 Census).

Islam came to India with the newly Islamised Arab merchants and traders on the Malabar Coast in the 7th century. Islam arrived in north India in the 12th century and has since become a part of India's rich religious and cultural heritage. Over the years, there has been significant integration of Hindu and Muslim cultures across India and the Muslims have played a prominent role in India's economic rise and cultural influence.

Matters of jurisdiction involving Muslims in India related to marriage, inheritance and wakf properties are governed by the Muslim Personal Law, and the courts have ruled that Sharia or Muslim law, holds precedence for Muslims over Indian civil law in such matters.

The Arab traders brought Islam to India in the early 8th century, but it was not until the 12th century that it became a force to reckon with in the Indian sub-continent. Unlike Buddhism, Jainism and Sikhism which emerged as offshoots of Hinduism, the concept, customs and religious practices of Islam were unique to this faith which professed universal brotherhood and submission to Allah - the God Almighty.

The Muslim invaders in the 12th century and the Mughal rulers in the 16th and 17th centuries helped in the spread of Islam in India. In its first phase, Islam was aggressive. But the mystics of Islam, or the Sufi saints, helped in spreading the message of peace and universal love.

The spirit of brotherhood propounded by Sufi saints and preachers like Kabir and Nanak helped in loosening the rigidity of the caste system. The interaction of the two faiths led to a synthesis of Hindu and Islamic elements in almost every sphere of life and culture. After an initial period of conflict and confrontation, today the two religions have accommodated and enriched each other.

Origin of Islamic Religion

Sources indicate that the castes among Muslims developed as the result of the concept of Kafa'a. Those who are referred to as Ashrafs are presumed to have a superior status derived from their foreign Arab ancestry, while the Ajlafs are assumed to be converts from Hinduism, and have a lower status. Actual Muslim social practice, including in India, points to the existence of sharp social hierarchies that numerous Muslim scholars have sought to provide appropriate Islamic sanction through elaborate rules of fiqh associated with the notion of kafa'a.

Most prominent Muslim scholars like Maulvi Ahmad Raza Khan Barelvi and Maulvi Ashraf Ali Faruqui Thanvi have championed the notion of caste superiority based on birth. It is argued that Muslims of Arab origin (Sayyeds and Shaikhs) are superior to non-Arab or Ajami Muslims, and so while a man who claims Arab origin can marry an Ajami woman, the reverse is not possible. Likewise, they argue, a Pathan Muslim man can marry a Julaha (Ansari) Mansuri (Dhunia,) Rayin (Kunjra) or Quraishi (Qasaior butchers) woman, but an Ansari, Rayin, Mansuri and Quraishi man cannot marry a Pathan woman since they consider these castes to be inferior to Pathans.

Many of these ulama also believed that it is best to marry within one own caste. The practice of endogamous marriage in one's caste is strictly observed in India. Interestingly, in three genetic studies representing the whole of South Asian Muslims, it was found that the Muslim population was overwhelmingly similar to the local non-Muslims associated with minor but still detectable levels of gene flow from outside, primarily from Iran and Central Asia, rather than directly from the Arabian Peninsula.

Law and Politics in Islam

Muslims in India are governed by "The Muslim Personal Law (Shariat) Application Act, 1937." It directs the application of Muslim Personal Law to Muslims in marriage, mahr (dower), divorce, maintenance, gifts, waqf, wills and inheritance. The courts generally apply the Hanafi Sunni law for Sunnis, Shia Muslims are independent of Sunni law for those areas where Shia law differs substantially from Sunni practice. The Indian constitution provides equal rights to all citizens irrespective of their religion. Article 44 of the constitution recommends a Uniform civil code. However, the attempts by successive political leadership in the country to integrate Indian society under common civil code is strongly resisted and is viewed by Indian Muslims as an attempt to dilute the cultural identity of the minority groups of the country. The All India Muslim Personal Law Board was established for the protection and continued applicability of "Muslim Personal Law" i.e. Shariat Application Act in India.

Islamic Traditions in South Asia

Sufism is a mystical dimension of Islam, often complimentary with the legalistic path of the sharia had a profound impact on the growth of Islam in India. A Sufi attains a direct vision of oneness with God, often on the edges of orthodox behavior, and can thus become a Pir (living saint) who may take on disciples (murids) and set up a spiritual lineage that can last for generations. Orders of Sufis became important in India during the thirteenth century following the ministry of Moinuddin Chishti (1142-1236), who settled in Ajmer, Rajasthan, and attracted large numbers of converts to Islam because of his holiness. HisChishtiyya order went on to become the most influential Sufi lineage in India, although other orders from Central Asia and Southwest Asia also reached India and played a major role in the spread of Islam. In this way, they created a large literature in regional languages that embedded Islamic culture deeply into older South Asian traditions.

Christianity

Christianity is India's third-largest religion, with approximately 24 million followers, constituting 2.3% of India's population. The works of scholars and Eastern Christian writings state that Christianity was introduced to India by Thomas the Apostle, who visited Muziris in Kerala in 52 AD to spread the gospel amongst Kerala's Jewish settlements. Although the exact origins of Christianity in India remain unclear it is widely believed that Christianity in India is almost as old as Christianity itself and spread in India even before it spread to many Christian nations of Europe.

Christians are found all across India and in all walks of life, with major populations in parts of South India, the Konkan Coast and the North-East. Indian Christians have contributed significantly to and are well represented in various spheres of national life. They include former and current chief ministers, governors and chief election commissioners. Indian Christians have one of the highest literacy, work participation and sex ratio figures among the various religious communities in India.

Most Christians in India are Catholics of the Latin Church. The state of Kerala is home to the Saint Thomas Christian community, an ancient body of Christians who are now divided into several different churches and traditions. There are two Eastern Catholic Saint Thomas Christian churches: the Syro-Malabar Catholic Church and the Syro-Malankara Catholic Church. There are also several Oriental Orthodox and independent churches in the Saint Thomas Christian community, including theMalankara Orthodox Syrian Church, the Malankara Jacobite Syrian Church and the Malankara Mar Thoma Syrian Church. Since the 19th century Protestant churches have also been present; major denominations include the Church of South India (CSI), the Church of North India (CNI), thePresbyterian Church of India, Baptists, Lutherans, Anglicans and other evangelical groups. The Christian Church runs thousands of educational institutions and hospitals contributing significantly to the development of the nation.

Christianity in India is as old as world Christianity. There are 25 million Christians in India which is just below 3% of the total population of the Country. Diversity of Christians is noticeable: Syrian Christians, Knanaya Christians, Goan Christians, Tamil Christians, Anglo-Indians, Naga Christians, etc are the main. They differ in language, social customs and economic prosperity. Christians play a decisive role in the fields of education, social work and even in politics.

Kerala is the cradle of Christianity in India. In the educational field, the work of the Christians of Kerala has been noteworthy and it is due to their efforts together with that of the government and of other religious and cultural groups that Kerala became the leading state in India for literacy.

Christianity first came to India by way of St. Thomas. He came to Kerala, in southwestern India, and founded the first church. Ironically, Shankaracharya, a Hindu reformer and seer, was born in Kerala some five hundred years after St. Thomas. St. Thomas ended up dying in the Chennai region (then known as Madras) of the Tamils.

Most Christians in India are Catholic (over 60 percent) and a majority of them are found in the south, particularly Kerala, Andhra Pradesh and Tamilnadu. Approximately on third of Kerala's population is comprised of Christians and they are involved in all aspects of society.

Contrary to popular belief, British rule had little to do with the growth of Christianity in India. The missionaries generally tended to turn public opinion, even those of the Indian Christians, against foreign rule. Bengali Christians in Calcultta were fairly important in their respective areas, whether it was in education, as a leader or an opinion-maker.

By tradition, Christianity is said to have arrived in India with Saint Thomas, one of the apostles of Jesus Christ, who spent some years in South India and possibly died there. However, others believe that the first missionary to arrive in the country was Saint Bartholomew. Historically, Christian missionary activity started with the advent of Saint Francis Xavier in 1544. He was followed by Portuguese missionaries at first and eventually by missionaries from other countries like Denmark, Holland, Germany and Great Britain. Throughout the 18th and 19th centuries Catholic as well as Protestant missionaries preached Christian doctrines in India and also made important contributions to social improvement and education in India.

Much of the modern influences in the Indian society can be attributed to the role of Christianity in India. Christian missionaries helped in setting up schools and colleges all over India and also spread the message of faith and goodwill in the country. Christianity and its teachings influenced a number of intellectuals and thinkers in India, including Mahatma Gandhi. Today, the Christians in India number about 30 million and consist of people from every denomination of Christianity.

Culture in Christianity

While Christians in India do not share one common culture, it is for the most part a blend of Indian and European cultures. It differs from one region to another depending on several factors such as the prevailing rite and tradition and the extent of time for which Christianity has existed in those regions. The St. Thomas Christians of Kerala (the first region in India to be proselytized by Christian missionaries) have a distinctively different culture when compared to Christians in other parts of the country.

Historical ties with the Syriac Orthodox Church and assimilation of Indian traditions have contributed to the development a unique culture among Kerala's Christians.The use of ornamental umbrellas for Christian religious festivities illustrates the indigenous character of Kerala's Christianity.

Goa was colonized by the Portuguese in 16th century AD; as a result of which Goan Chrisitans have adopted a more western culture. The dance, song and cuisine of Goa has been greatly influenced by the Portuguese. Contemporary Goan Christian culture can be best described as an increasingly anglicized Indo-Latin culture. Mangalorean Catholics are descended mainly from the Goan Catholicsettlers, who had migrated to South Canara from Goa, a state north of Canara, between 1560 and 1763 during the Goa Inquisition and the Portuguese-Maratha wars.

After migration to Mangalore, they adopted the local Mangalorean culture, but retained many of their Goan customs and traditions.Christianity in other parts of India spread under the colonial regimes of the Dutch, Danish, French and most importantly the English from the early 17th century to the time of the Indian Independence in 1947. Christian culture in these colonial territories has been influenced by the religion and culture of their respective rulers.

Contemporary Christian culture in India draws greatly from the Anglican culture as a result of the influence of the erstwhile British Raj. TheAnglican Book of Common Prayer is a widely used supplement for worship in the two major Protestant denominations: Church of South India and Church of North India. Today Christians are considered to be one of the most progressive communities in India. Urban Christians are to a greater extent influenced by European traditions which is considered an advantage in the business environment of urban India; this is given as an explanation for the large number of Christian professionals in India's corporate sector. The Christian church runs thousands of educational institutions which have contributed to the strengthening of Christian culture in India.

Religion plays a significant role in the daily life of Indian Christians. India ranks 15 among countries with highest church attendance. Religious processions and carnivals are often celebrated by Catholics. Cities with significant Christian populations celebrate patron saint days.

As in other parts of the world, Christmas is the most important festival for Indian Christians. Anglo-Indian Christmas balls held in most major cities form a distinctive part of Indian Christian culture. Good Friday is a national holiday. All Souls Day is another Christian holiday that is observed by most Christians in India. Most Protestant churches celebrate harvest festivals, usually in late October or early November.

Christian weddings in India conform to the traditional white wedding. However it is not uncommon for Christian brides particularly in the south to wear a traditional white wedding sariinstead of a gown. The vast majority of Protestant women and to a lesser extent Catholic women in India do not wear the bindi (red dot on the forehead) and can therefore be easily distinguished from their Hindu counterparts.

Zoroastrianism

Parsism or Zoroastrianism is about 2600 years old and finds its origin in Persia. The religion was founded by Spenta Zarathustra or Zoroaster, who is considered as the Prophet of the Parsis. Zoroastrian practice is based on the responsibility of every man and woman to choose between good and evil, and to respect God's creations. Prophet Zarathustra, who lived in Iran in 6000 BC, expounded a dualistic philosophy, based on the opposing powers of the good and the evil. Zarathustra preached the oneness of god and believed that Ahura Mazda was the one and only god, who is formless and has six great aspects called the Amesha-Spentas.

These are Ardibehest, Bahman, Shahrivar, Spendarmad, Khordad and Amardad. The mortals can worship Him in one of these forms. The Parsis believe that the Ahura Mazda is eternally in conflict with Angra Mainyu or Ahirman, who represents the evil force. Man has a free will to align himself to good or evil. Soul is immortal and upon death, the good go to Heaven and evil fall into Hell. The Parsis believe in the coming of the Saoshyant (Saviour) to the earth to defeat evil and further righteousness (Ashoi). They belief that when the Saoshyant comes, the final spiritual battle between the forces of good and evil will commence, resulting in the utter destruction of evil. Ristakhiz, the resurrection of the dead will take place—the dead will rise, by the Will of Ahura Mazda. The Final Judgement of all souls will commence, at the hands of Ahura Mazda the Judge (Davar) and all sinners punished, then forgiven, and humanity made immortal and free from hunger, thirst, poverty, old age, disease and death.

The Parsi place of worship is called the fire temple. Five daily prayers, usually hymns or Gathas uttered by Prophet Zarathustra are said in the home or the temple, before a fire, which symbolizes the realm of truth, righteousness and order. The fire-temples and rituals of the Yasna are sacred and are necessary for the religion, such as the Nirang-din ceremony, which creates the Holy Nirang. Fire is regarded as the son of Ahura Mazda, and represents god. In Zorastriniasm, Dakhma-nashini is the only method of corpse-destruction. This involves the destruction of the dead body in the stone-enclosed Dakhma, by the flesh-eating bird or the rays of the Sun.

Religious Scriptures

Zenda Avesta is the religious scripture of the Parsis. It contains the teachings, sermons and prayers composed by Prophet Zoroaster himself and also by his disciples and followers. Avestha is also the name of the language in which it is composed. It is divided into five parts: the Yasna (worship with ceremony and offerings), the Videvdad (laws against demons), the Yashts (worship), the Khordeh Avestha, which comprises of selected portions of the Avestha and forms the book of daily prayers of the Zoroastrians, and the five Gathas—Ahunavaiti, Ushtavaiti, Spenta-Mainyu, Vohu-Khshathra and Vashishta-Ishti, which contain the 17 hymns of God received by Prophet Zarathushtra by way of a Divine Revelation.

Principle Sects

There are three principle sects among the Parsis: Shahenshai, Kadmi and Fasli. The only difference between the three sects is the calendar they adhere to. The Faslis follow the traditional Persian calendar; the Shahenshais calculate their calendar from the last Sassanian king, Yazdegard III and the Kadmis claim their calendar is the oldest and most accurate.

Parsis of India

Parsi Reform Movement in India: Dababhai Naoroji, Naoroji Furdonji and others set up the Rehnumai Mazdayasan Sabha (Religious Reform Association) in 1851 to carry out campaigns against the strict orthodoxy in Zoroastrianism. They laid special emphasis on modernising the Parsis and raising the social status of women by providing for their education.

The first Zoroastrians to enter India arrived on the Gujarat coast in the 10th century and by the 17th century, most of them had settled in Bombay. Today, there are approximately 90,000 Parsisin India and are concentrated largely in Maharashtra and Gujarat.

The first Zoroastrians to enter India arrived on the Gujarati coast in the 10th century, soon after the Arabian conquest of Iran and by the 17th century, most of them had settled in Bombay. Zoroastrian practice is based on the responsibility of every man and woman to choose between good and evil, and to respect God's creations. The religion's founder, Zarathustra, who lived in Iran in 6000 BC was the first religious prophet to expound a dualistic philosophy, based on the opposing powers of good and evil.

Most Zoroastrians can be seen in Bombay today where they are known as Parsees. They have no distinctive dress and few houses of worship. Five daily prayers, usually hymns uttered by Zarathustra and standardized in the religious text Zenda Avesta, are said in the home or the temple, before a fire, which symbolizes the realm of truth, righteousness and order.

Basic beliefs of Zoroastrianism

Zoroastrians believe that there is one universal and transcendent God, Ahura Mazda. He is said to be the one uncreated Creator to whom all worship is ultimately directed. Ahura Mazda's creation—evident as asha, truth and order—is the antithesis of chaos, which is evident as druj, falsehood and disorder. The resulting conflict involves the entire universe, including humanity, which has an active role to play in the conflict.

The religion states that active participation in life through good thoughts, good words, and good deeds is necessary to ensure happiness and to keep chaos at bay. This active participation is a central element in Zoroaster's concept of free will, and Zoroastrianism rejects all forms of monasticism. Ahura Mazda will ultimately prevail over the evil Angra Mainyu or Ahriman, at which point the universe will undergo a cosmic renovation and time will end. In the final renovation, all of creation-even the souls of the dead that were initially banished to "darkness"-will be reunited in Ahura Mazda, returning to life in the undead form. At the end of time, a savior-figure (a Saoshyant) will bring about a final renovation of the world (frasho.kereti), in which the dead will be revived.

Parsis are a people who uprooted themselves and moved to a different world to save their religion. They migrated to India one thousand years ago. The Parsi experience is about dilemmas that most minority communities face; questions about religion and race, survival and extinction, assimilation and identity, tradition and the modern world. There are only 100,000 Parsis in the world today, mostly in India, particularly in Bombay. Demographically, they are a dying community-their deaths outweigh their births. Parsis like to quote a remark that Mahatma Gandhi once reportedly made, "In numbers Parsis are beneath contempt, but in contribution, beyond compare." Out of an Indian population of more than one billion, Parsis number a mere 76,000. Demographic trends project that by the year 2020, India will have achieved the dubious distinction of being the most populated country on earth with 1200 million people. At that point, Parsis who will number 23,000 or 0.0002 per cent of the population, will cease to be termed a community and will be labelled a 'tribe', as is any ethnic group below the 30,000 count.

8

SOCIAL CHANGE AND DEVELOPMENT

Social change is the result of a number of factors. Changes occur due to the process of formation, reformation or decay at various levels. In most of the cases, social changes occur as an imitation of the upper classes by their respective lower classes. In this process, there is always an internal conflict, continuously going on to excel others, which gives birth to unrest at mental level and a blind pursuit of availing luxuries of life, which generally end up on the form of confrontation and corruption. These changes are either positive or negative in nature. Social change in India serves the very purpose of focusing on all such important issues.

Definitions and Concepts of Social Change

Social Structure has been identified as:

- the relationship of definite entities' or groups to each other,
- enduring patterns of behaviour by participants in a social system in relation to each other, and
- institutionalised norms or cognitive frameworks that structure the actions of actors in the social system.

Social structure can also be divided into microstructure and macrostructure. Microstructure is the pattern of relations between most basic elements of social life, that cannot be further divided and have no social structure of their own (for example, pattern of relations between individuals in a group composed of individuals—where individuals have no social structure, or a structure of organizations as a pattern of relations between social positions or social roles, where those positions and roles have no structure by themselves). Macrostructure is thus a kind of 'second level' structure, a pattern of relations between objects that have their own structure (for example, a political social structure between political parties, as political parties have their own social structure).

Social change refers to an alteration in the social order of asociety. It may refer to the notion of social progress orsociocultural evolution, the philosophical idea that society moves forward by dialectical or evolutionary means. It may refer to a paradigmatic change in the socioeconomic structure, for instance a shift away from feudalism and towards capitalism. Accordingly, it may also refer to social revolution, such as the Socialist revolution presented in Marxism, or to other social movements, such as Women's suffrage or the Civil rights movement. Social change may be driven by cultural, religious, economic, scientific or technological forces.

More generally, social change may include changes in nature,social institutions, social behaviours or social relations.

One of the most obvious changes currently occurring is the change in population distribution. In the recent decades, developing countries became a larger proportion of world population, increasing from 68% in 1950 to 82% in 2010, while population of the developed countries has declined from 32% of total world population in 1950 to 18% in 2010. China and India continue to be the largest countries, followed by the US as a distant third.

However, population growth throughout the world is slowing. Population growth among developing countries has been slowing since the 1950s, and is now at 0.3% annual growth. Population growth among the less developed countries excluding the least developed has also been slowing, since 1960, and is now at 1.3% annual growth. Population growth among the least developed countries has not really slowed, and is the highest at 2.7% annual growth.

Social Structure and Development

Social structure is defined as relationships between different entities or groups or as enduring and relatively stable patterns of relationship emphasises the idea that society is grouped into structurally related groups or sets of roles, with different functions, meanings or purposes.

Social structure is a term used in the social sciences to refer to patterned social arrangements in society that are both emergent from and determinant of the actions of the individuals. The usage of the term "social structure" has changed over time and may reflect the various levels of analysis within differing sub-fields of sociology.

Meaning of Social Structure on Different Scales

1. On the Macro scale, it can refer to the system of socioeconomic stratification (e.g., the class structure), social institutions, or, other patterned relations between large social groups.
2. On the Meso scale, it can refer to the structure of social network ties between individuals or organizations.
3. On the Micro scale, it can refer to the way norms shape the behavior of actors within the social system.

One example of social structure is the idea of "social stratification", which refers to the idea that society is separated into different strata (levels), guided (if only partially) by the underlying structures in the social system. This approach has been important in the academic literature with the rise of various forms of structuralism. It is important in the modern study of organizations, because an organization's structure may determine its flexibility, capacity to change, and many other factors. Therefore, structure is an important issue for management.

Social structure may be seen to influence important social systems including the economic system,legal system, political system, cultural system, and others. Family, religion, law, economy and class are all social structures. The "social system" is the parent system of those various systems that are embedded in it.

1. Society: self contained, self sufficient population united by social relationships, bounded from other populations by geographic locations.
2. Stratification: unequal distribution of valued goods or holdings in a population (i.e. class, status, resources, grades, wealth, positional goods, etc.)
3. Network: pattern of relationships in a population of actors.
4. Social structure variables: pattern of relationships, size of institution, income distribution, and concurrency of social relationships.

Human Development and Social Structure

The relationship between human development and Social Structure. Sub-theme is variables of human development and social structure. Those are planning, social policy, human right, economic development, economic growth, education, woman workforce. Human development and social structure relations differ from to country the others. Different areas are; dissocial change, planning, social policy instruments, human right, economic development and economic growth, education, women workforce, unemployment and poverty.

Each country has its own way of social and political changes each have different priority. Planning has as different character also. Planning model absolutely differs from to country, e. g. Turkish, French and Dutch planning model and Russian planning models; .Economic growth does not means economic development. Education system has the most important role in developing countries. Woman participant workforce depends on social structure. So this matter should be discussed about developing countries. Poverty has two faces. (a) absolutely poverty, (b) relative poverty.

Social Structure as a Facilitator/Inhibitor

India contains a large number of different regional, social, and economic groups, each with distinctive or dissimilar customs and cultural practices. Region-wise, differences between social structures of India's north and south are marked, especially with respect to kinship systems and family relationships. Religious differences are pervasive throughout the country. There is the Hindu majority and the large Muslim minority or "second majority".

There are other Indian groups—Buddhists, Christians, Jains, Jews, Parsis, Sikhs, and practitioners of tribal religions-and hundreds of sub-religions or religious communities within larger communities like the Arya Samajis, Sanatanis among the Hindus; Shias and Sunnis among the Muslims; Monas and Keshdharis among Sikhs and hundreds of other castes, sub-castes, communities, vegetarians and non-vegetarians from each religion. Each group is proud of its faith and very sure of its superiority over other faiths.

A highly noticeable feature of India's social structure is highly inequitable division of the nation's wealth. Access to wealth and power varies sharply. Extreme differences in socio-economic status are glaringly visible among the smallest village communities to metropolitan cities and mega-towns. The poor and the rich live side by side in urban and rural areas. Prosperous, well-fed, perfumed men or women in chauffeured luxury cars passing and even living in narrow streets with poor, starving, ill-nourished, ill-clad or even half-naked men, women, children dwelling on their pavements and bathing in dirty water of its flowing or even clogged drains are common sights. Contrasting extreme poverty and enormous wealth and obvious class distinctions are egregiously visible in almost every settlement in India.

Urban-rural differences too are immense. Over 70 per cent of India's population lives in villages; agriculture still remains their mainstay. Mud houses, dusty lanes, grazing cattle, chirping and crying of birds at sunset and rising smell of dung and chulah-smoke are the usual settings for the social lives of most rural Indians. In India's metro cities, millions of people live among roaring vehicles, surging crowds, overcrowded streets, busy commercial establishments, loudspeakers blaring movie tunes or religious recitations, factories and trucks and buses breathing poisonous pollution into unhealthy lungs.

Gender distinctions are highly pronounced. The behaviour norms of men and women are very different, more so in villages. Prescribed ideal gender roles are fast losing to new patterns of behaviour among both sexes. Individually, both men and women behave in one way and collectively in quite another way. Public behaviour of both men and women is rude and unhelpful, but the same people when in individual situation and relationship can be very different. People occupying public positions are extremely unhelpful and even normal actions done toward others as part of normal routine are projected as personal favours.

Even senior citizens, retired persons, war widows do not get their pension approved for years! A clerk in a government office wields greater actual power than a decision-making executive and can withhold implementation of his superior's orders for ever. If the victim of delay approaches the court, the litigant is in for a shock after shock as the case gets adjourned endlessly and after years of attending court hearings gets an unimaginably skewed judgment written in a highly ambiguous language. Litigants pay high fees to lawyers and bribes to court staff and even to judges.

Surprisingly, observers tend to bypass these all-pervading differences of region, language, wealth, status, religion, urbanity, gender and absence of the rule of law but pay most devoted attention to that special and peculiar feature of Indian society: "Caste". The most loved and recognized identity of Indians is their caste. And, there are thousands of castes and caste-like groups. These are hierarchically ordered and named groups into which members are born. Caste members, as far as possible, marry within the caste or sub-caste and follow caste rules with respect to diet, ritual and aspects of life.

Yet, no generalisation can be made because, increasingly, caste-discipline is loosening and every individual is free to decide her or his own social ways and such an individual will always find small or big support and a milieu to evolve a suitable mode of living in spite of turning her/his back on caste and caste-ridden society, though at times, this can be a harrowing experience, especially in sub-caste communities where inter-caste and widow marriage is equated with community honour leading to honour-killing of the perceived violator of caste-norms, especially if the violator is weak. However, underlying norms of life, though honesty of thought and action may not be among them, are widely accepted in India.

Indian village life is neither simple nor inviting. That is why no villager who has come to the city goes back. Typical Indian villages have clustered dwelling patterns built very close to one another. Sociologists call them "nucleated settlements", with small and narrow lanes for passage of people and sometimes carts. Village fields surround these settlements. On the hills of central, eastern, and far northern India, dwellings are more spread out. In wet states of West Bengal and Kerala, houses are a little dispersed; in Kerala, some villages merge into the next village and visitor are not able to see divisions between such villages.

In northern and central India, neighbourhood boundaries can be vague. Houses of Dalits are ordinarily situated on outskirts of nucleated settlements. Distinct Dalit hamlets, however, are rare. Contrastingly, in the south, where socioeconomic divisions and caste pollution observances tend to be stronger than in the north, Dalit hamlets are set at a little distance from other caste neighbourhoods

Bigger land-owners do not cultivate lands but hire tenant farmers to do this work. Artisans in pottery, wood, cloth, metal, and leather, although diminishing, continue to eke out their existence in contemporary Indian villages like centuries past. Religious observances and weddings are occasions for members of various castes to provide customary ritual goods and services.

Accelerating urbanization is fast transforming Indian society. More than 26 per cent of the country's population is urban. India's larger cities have been growing at twice the rate of smaller towns and villages. About half of the increase is the result of rural-urban migration, as villagers seek better lives for themselves in the cities.

India can be superpower, only when its an Economical superpower for we have seen what happens when a nation tries to claim the status of the superpower on the basis of its milatry might alone (Former USSR)

And most of the recorded Human history, India had a lion's share of the global world economy. It shared the top spot with China for a very long time. And its economic model was suited for Agrarian society. Each village as a self supporting Agricultural unit, able to create Surplus and create derived demand for associated supply chain, demand chain and services.

It was Indian culture that catapulted the economic might, caste system created specialized skills and allowed every village to a self sufficient economic unit. It was cultural values of lesss material consumption that increased surplus and made Indian region an economic giant.

We were the great power with about 25% of world GDP, at the onset of the Industrial revolution in Europe and before advent of British into the Subcontinent as major political and milatry player.

Industrial revolution changed the game, and the economy truly became global slowly. the culture was responsible in a way for us to be a superpower. But the environment has now drastically changed, its game of volume, margins, market share, cost and access to the resources, Technology and innovation becoming powerful source for competitive advantage. If a species does not adapt, it pushes itself from the less dominating force in the environment.

We have moved away from the economic model of self-sufficient villages as economic units. Most of the developed economies or super power are not agrarian, as they have an opportunity cost associated with agrarian activities. They can use their energies for more value activities.

Science

We divide this topic in two sections—first what facilitates growth of India, then what inhibits it.

As Facilitator

1. Family is the core unit from which any community or society evolves. Indians acknowledge the power of family bonds and use them successfully to develop other connections, both in private and professional lives. Having in mind that communication skills are extremely important in today's globalized reality, this is an advantage for sure.
2. Patriotism - We have never seen Indian talking bad about his motherland, and probably that's why till today there is a Republic of India, not "united (more or less) states of India". Attachment to a home country is definetely what keeps people together.
3. Education. Here mostly about higher education and such a high interest in "hard science" (i.e. math, physics, biology, chemistry,

engineering). Whatever you mean by superpower, it can't be created without technology, and Indians know that very well.

4. "Adaptivity" and experience of "hard life" - many Indians experience very tough life conditions, due to various reasons, let it be economic, climatic etc. A person whose life was not a bunch of roses appreciates more what he has, and pushes himself to the limits to improve the situation for himself and the others.

As Inhibitor

1. Social structures in India. As far as a foreigner can see it, caste system and community separation didn't do any good to anyone so far. Social bias on a large scale, ostracizing people because of their skin colour, religion, gender, education, place of birth, parents' occupation and income, political affiliations, or even looks are things which constantly drag India down. Todays superpower can only be a modern community - not modern in a sense of blindly accepting everything and anything that comes, but with a huge dose of tolerance and understanding for what is different. Indians don't tolerate different, and bad news for them is, the world is becoming more and more heterogeneous, no one can escape that. If you don't, you are left far behind.

2. No rights for women - From the fact that parents prefer boys, though the appalling concept of a dowry, forced marriages, lack of knowledge about contraception, family planning, sex education, child protection, to no financial independence. Indian women live in the shade of their men and are considered of no use when on their own. Their education goes for nothing because they end up as housewives with no chance of any career. Indian women lack even basic knowledge of which rights they are missing and how to legally solve certain problems (e.g. domestic abuse). Those who decide about the shape of Indian society (men) don't realize that the country won't move forward unless women are free and powerful.

3. Intolerance for individuality. Indians, as a model example of a collective society, don't tolerate individuals. There is no freedom and no place for creativity, difference, opposition. Indians prefer to live as an overall mass, where each puzzle matches exactly the other, and people are assigned to earlier prepared for them roles, regardless of their personal wishes. Egoism is as present in Indian society as in any other country, just that it works in a different way. You need to be old enough and respected enough to rule over the others and manipulate within e.g. your children's

lives. If there is no place for self-expression and focus on personal goals, the society will remain this unhappy grey mass with no better perspectives for the future. These are the most important and that they play the most significant role when considering a journey towards superpower.

Development and Socioeconomic Disparities

India's North-Eastern part, comprising of seven states, is a lowly developed, tribal population dominated region in India. Inspite of the common Mongoloid origin and lifestyle of majority of the population residing here, sharp differences exist in the status of their socio-economic development

The incidence of uneven development is, in general, a special characteristic found among the developing nations. With the concentration of development around the center, the peripheries often do not receive even the percolated benefits of such lop-sided development. Though the Neoclassical theories postulate that it is through the mobility of capital stock, technology transfer and labour movement, the development gap between the center and the peripheries will eventually reduce, in reality such dynamics itself become a function of a set of other factors like the topography of the region, its geo-political sensitivity, political will of the authority and most important of all the awareness of people for development. The proposition of Growth Pole theory refers to the concentration of industries around a central core of other industries and acting as channel of growth in the area. However, it has not been much fruitful to reach its objective even in the developed economies.

On the other hand, the concept of development often confronts with conflict in the academic circle. In fact, the process of economic development itself has undergone paradigm-shifts over time. While, on the one side, such changes were inevitable as they were the timely responses to the contemporary necessities, on the other, the differences among the scholars originate mostly in the interpretation of the concept and in the outcome of various strategies implemented. With the introduction of globalization, the debate has become more intense.

In globalization, the market has emerged as the driving force of the economy and the development strategy initiated by this economy operates with its usual exclusion principle. The produce of development reaches that section of the society, which fits well in the market dynamics, ensuring survival of the fittest. However, the development ethicists have put strong objection to such exclusions. They argue that at least some of the development ideologies should address the problems of the excluded -

mostly the poor and the vulnerable section of the society. A complex and unresolved empirical question regarding the relative contributions of local and global factors to the wealth and poverty of the societies still exists. In this context, the role of different development agents becomes crucial. These agents at both governmental and non-governmental level have to shoulder the responsibilities of ensuring social upliftment and for that the best possible development strategy has to be devised.

Gender and Development

In recent decades, women's and girls' education and health levels have improved greatly. But in many parts of the world, women are still dying in childbirth, or not being born at all, at alarming rates. Women continue to lack voice and decision-making ability in the household and in society; and, their economic opportunities remain very constrained.

This inequality is manifestly unfair. It is also bad economics: under-investing in girls and women puts a brake on poverty reduction and limits economic and social development.

Culturally determined gender ideologies define rights and responsibilities and what is 'appropriate' behaviour for women and men. They also influence access to and control over resources, and participation in decision-making. These gender ideologies often reinforce male power and the idea of women's inferiority. Culture is sometimes interpreted narrowly as 'custom' or 'tradition', and assumed to be natural and unchangeable. Despite these assumptions, culture is fluid and enduring.

Gender and Development Approach

The main objectives of a Gender and Development approach (GAD) are to strengthen the effectiveness of development work in improving the situation of both women and men, and achieving progress towards social and gender equality. The focus is on social and gender equality as an objective, rather than women as a target group.

It focuses on the relationship between men and women in the community and on the unequal relations of power between them. The GAD approach aims for development that changes gender relations in order to enable women to participate and benefit on an equal basis with men. It is not a new approach but builds on the efforts and experience gained over the last three decades in development work to understand and improve the position of women and disadvantaged groups in the community.

Social and Gender Analysis

Social and gender analysis attempts to understand the roles of different social groups,(including women and men) in relation to what they do in the village and in relation to the resources they have. There is also a need to understand gender relations: how women and men relate to one another and who makes decisions over which resources.

Social and gender analysis identifies the roles, relations, responsibilities, access to and control over resources, decision-making and power, as well as the needs and potentials of different social groups of both women and men. Social and gender analysis is not limited only to the social sectors, but can also be used at all levels and areas of village development.

While carrying out social and gender analysis increases knowledge of social and gender roles, inequalities and different impacts, this alone will not automatically bring about change. The results of social and gender analysis should be used to bring about necessary changes in relation to planning, priorities, choice of methods, division of labour and implementation of activities.

Sex and Gender

Sex refers to the biological differences between men and women, which are universal and do not change. Gender refers to social attributes that are learned when growing up as a member of a community. Because these attributes are learned behaviours, they can and do change over time. In addition, they vary between different cultures and ethnic groups.

Gender therefore refers to the socially given attributes, roles, activities, responsibilities and needs connected to being men (masculine) and women (feminine) in a given society at a given time. Women's and men's gender identity determines how they are perceived and how they are expected to think and act as men and women. Gender is one of the variables (along with ethnicity, age and class) used in the distribution of privilege, prestige, power and a range of social and economic resources.

Changes in Gender Identity and Gender Relations

Gender roles and characteristics in almost all societies have undergone many recent adjustments and changes in response to development, technological change and globalisation, which have led to massive economic and social changes in all parts of the world. Changes in gender roles and relations often meet resistance, particularly in the form of tradition.

Social and gender analysis can demonstrate that change in certain aspects of social roles and relations between women and men can improve the quality and conditions of life for everyone.

Access and Control over Resources

When examining how resources are allocated between women and men, it is important to distinguish between access to resources (e.g. land, labour, credit, income) and control over them. Access gives a person the use of a resource, e.g. and to grow crops. Control allows a person to make decisions about who uses the resource or to dispose of the resource, for instance by selling the land.

Sexual Division of Labour

In all communities, tasks and responsibilities are typically undertaken by either women or men. This allocation of activities on the basis of sex is known as the sexual division of labour, and is learned and clearly understood by all members of that community.

1. In Community work : This work involves activities for the village usually voluntary unpaid work, such as organising festivals or ceremonies, receiving visitors, or maintaining a village resource, such as a well.
2. Reproductive work : This work involves all the tasks associated with supporting the immediate and extended family, young and old. It includes childcare, food preparation, care for the sick or old, socialisation of the young, and so on. Reproductive work is the basis of productive work. Women of all ages are mainly responsible for this work, which is usually unpaid.
3. Productive work : This is work that produces items for consumption by the household and goods and services for exchange in the market place. Both men and women contribute to family income with various forms of productive work, although men usually dominate in productive work.

Strategic gender needs and interests

Strategic gender interests relate to issues of power and control and the division of labour. They may include:

- Changes in the division of labour (women to take on work not traditionally seen as.
- women's work, men take more responsibility for child care and domestic.

- work).
- Legal rights.
- An end to domestic violence.
- Equal wages.
- Women's control over their own bodies (family planning).

They are not as easily identified as the practical needs and interests, therefore specific support and opportunities to do so may have to be provided and facilitated from outside.

Gender Equity

Gender equity is concerned with promoting personal, social, cultural, political and economic equality for all. Traditions and discriminatory practices have resulted in the systematic devaluation of attitudes, activities and abilities attributed to, and associated with, girls and women. The consequences of these discriminatory practices negatively affect men as well as women. Initially however, gender equity initiatives will place greater emphasis on improving conditions and attitudes as they affect girls and women. In the long-term, these initiatives will also improve the situation for boys and men.

Empowerment

It is about women or men developing their ability to:

- Collectively and individually take control over their own lives.
- Identify their needs and agendas.
- Demand support from their communities and the state to see that their interests are responded to.

In most cases, the empowerment of women requires change in the division of labour and transformation of society.

Modernization of Society

Modernization refers to a model of an evolutionary transition from a 'pre-modern' or 'traditional' to a 'modern' society. The teleology of modernization is described in social evolutionism theories, existing as a template that has been generally followed by societies that have achieved modernity. While it may theoretically be possible for some societies to make the transition in entirely different ways, there have been no counterexamples provided by reliable sources.

Accordingly, internal situations in societies immediately affect the processes of modernization. A state in which favourites are rewarded and governmental corruption is prevalent causes the state to suffer in terms of modernization. This can repress the state's economic development and productivity and lead money and resources to flow out to other countries with more favourable investment environments. Such mechanisms slow the process of modernization and lead to the need to sort out internal conflicts so as to aid the process of modernization.

State theory is said to be mixed with internal politics, and that each country will have its own unique pathway to development. For a country to become more developed it is said that stability both inside and outside the country is essential. The State theory essentially implies that in order for modernization to grow and for societies to become more developed the state must be tamed and power to arbitrarily seize private property curtailed. From the taming of the state, a capitalist economy can better arise, resulting in increased productivity supporting the internal modernization of society.

Impact of Modernization on Indian Society

India has the distinction of evolving one of the longest continuing civilization in the world, which is constantly adapted itself to the changing political and socio-economic contents and specific watershed events in history. Indian Society has proved to be a remarkable stable unit of society which has shown great flexibility and adaptability in the phase of rapid social changes.

Modernization is when society goes through industrialization, urbanization and other social changes that completely transform the lives of individuals. Technology is a major form of modernization which does not quite change society on its own rather than the reaction society shows towards it. The way we all communicate with each other as the outcome and how we rely on technology for certain tasks. The internet for example has helped the world including third world countries to connect with other countries and to inform everyone of what is current news. The acceptance of diversity among people is huge for modernization.

Development in Modernization Theory

Development, like modernization, has become the orienting principle of our time. Countries that are seen as modern are also seen as developed, and that means that they are generally more respected by institutions such as the United Nations and even as possible trade partners for other countries. The extent to which a country has modernized or developed dictates its power and importance on the international level.

Globalization and Modernization

Globalisation and modernisation are the buzzwords of the new millennium. They serve to sharpen the focus on the dynamic nature of political, economic and social systems and, in this book, the editor and contributors attempt to locate educational changes in a selected number of Muslim countries within the over-arching global scene.

There has been considerable debate about the legitimacy of these terms and both have inspired definitions, nuances and accompanying emotions that run the whole gambit from welcoming acceptance to murderous aggressions. Terms like ancient, medieval or modern, when describing eras in the history of Europe, with the most recent one being referred to as post-modern, have been strongly debated.

Globalization can be defined as the integration of economic, political and social cultures and is related to the spreading of modernization across borders. It theorizes the development of a global economy in the sense that the world is moving in the direction of more efficient use of resources and the means of production.

Communication is another major area that has grown due to modernization. Communication industries have enabled capitalism to spread throughout the world. Telephony, television broadcasts, news services and online service providers have played a crucial part in globalization.

With the many apparent positive attributes to globalization there are also negative consequences. Economic development can often initially highlight the disparities between a society's rich and its poor. In major cities of developing countries there exist pockets where technologies of the modernized world-computers, cell phones and satellite television-exist right alongside stark poverty. This often begets an acute awareness of those in society initially or chronically left behind by economic progress.

Globalisation has many advocates some of which are globalists, transformationalists and traditionalists. Globalists are globalisations modernisation theorists so are therefore very positive about the concept. They argue that globalisation is good for everyone as there are benefits for all including vulnerable groups such as women and children. This is done because globalisation is typically western and it's the western values which are transmitted therefore allowing women to rights they wouldn't have had before e.g. re-production rights.

Criticism in Modernization Theory

Modernization theory has been criticized, mainly because it conflated modernization with westernization. In this model, the modernization of a society required the destruction of the indigenous culture and its replacement by a more westernized one. Technically modernity simply refers to the present, and any society still in existence is therefore modern.

Proponents of modernization typically view only Western society as being truly modern arguing that others are primitive or unevolved by comparison. This view sees unmodernized societies as inferior even if they have the same standard of living as western societies. Opponents of this view argue that modernity is independent of culture and can be adapted to any society. Japan is cited as an example by both sides. Some see it as proof that a thoroughly modern way of life can exist in a non-western society.

Need of Modernization

Education improves productivity and increase in productivity leads to modernization. In the word of Indian education commission.

The link between education and productivity can be forged through the development of the following points.

(i) Making science a basic component of education and culture

(ii) Making work experience an integral part of general education

(iii) Vocationalization of education. Meet the need of industry agriculture and trade.

Modernization demands that Indian men and women should use new scientific methods of thinking understanding and decision making.They should shun the old values, superstitions and selfish ends and develop their personalities in such a way that they aim at the service of the nation and people at large. If we will not change the old values and some methods of production than we can't develop our education system and even can't reach to the modernization. Self dependence, our economy is backward, our prestige in other countries is lost and every Indian is in debt, Unemployment, corruption, favouritism and nepotism are the causes for Modernization.

Effects of Modernization on Education

Society has made a great effort to modernize the world in education, communication, travel, health, commerce, housing, and in many other ways, so as to increase the standard of living; but what has this socialization and modernization done to the family-the basic institution of society? Never before has there been greater instability. The divorce rate is higher now than at any time in history. Modernization has transferred the responsibility of education from the family to public institutions where modern thought has become paramount and moral principles have become abandoned.

The crime rate has increased alarmingly. Drug addiction, disobedience to law, increase in venereal disease, and corruption in all forms seem to be accepted. In this day of modernization, freedom of thought and action is sponsored and promoted without consideration of the responsibilities that must accompany such freedoms if society is to be stabilized. Surely we would agree that the family institution has been seriously, if not irreparably, damaged in our society.

Modernism has become the order of the day in some religious thought. Modernists advocate a restatement of traditional doctrine on the grounds that today's modern scholastic and scientific advances require a new critical interpretation of the Bible and the history of dogma. The term "modernism" is often used interchangeably with "liberalism." Its advocates claim that religious truths are subject to constant reinterpretation in the light of modern knowledge; therefore, new and more advanced concepts are required to express modern thought and progress.

In this day of increased knowledge, higher thought, and a modernization of the old, the simple has been overlooked and the profound sought after. The basic, simple, fundamental truths of the gospel are being ignored.

Today is not different. We are surrounded by frustrations and advances in thought and learning which raise questions and doubts. These seem to drag men down and destroy faith and morality. Where, then, is hope in this world of frustration and moral decay? It lies in the knowledge and understanding of the truths taught by the Master without deviation and believed in and lived by its membership. These are eternal truths and will be so in perpetuity regardless of changing circumstances in society, development of new scientific achievements, or increase of man's knowledge.

Understanding Modern India

Many people in the western world think of India as an inert and distant [grouping] of people and poverty, a combination of the exotic and tragic. This misperception, popularized through years of media stereotyping, conceals reality.

In fact, India is a vibrant society with an increasingly vigorous internal dynamic and an increasing influence, directly and indirectly, in the world. Its significance lies not only in its size -- some 930 million Indians are 15 percent of the planetary population -- but also in the questions raised by the path India has chosen in domestic and foreign policy. This nation is the largest functioning democracy, with regular and freely contested elections. Thus, it is the test of whether democracy is a suitable system of government for large numbers of relatively poor people in a world where democracy, as we understand it, is a much-endangered political species, especially in Third World countries.

Modern India is also a test of two middle-ground philosophies. As an early proponent of non-alignment in international politics, India has attempted to establish a mid-position between Western and [communist] oriented states. Over the years, its leadership in carving out a Third World posture demonstrated that there is a viable route for nations who did not want to take sides in Cold War politics, an approach which many other nations in Asia, Africa, Latin America and the Middle East have followed and hope to sustain.

India's economic policies have also broken new ground. They were the first large-scale test of the modern mixed economy: central government planning with a combination of both private and public ownership of economic enterprises. It is perhaps still too early to evaluate the results. On the one hand, poverty remains [widespread] and unemployment is high. On the other, Indian agriculture has performed much better than either Soviet or Chinese agriculture. India now feeds her population and has imported hardly any grain in the past four years.

Also, India now ranks as the ninth largest industrial economy in the world. A further significance of India today comes from the geopolitics of South Asia. Bordering the Indian Ocean into which the Persian Gulf flows, it is a key location in an era of oil logistics. Add the proximity of Russia, Afghanistan, Pakistan and China, and India's situation becomes critical to the tensions and interactions of current global politics. From this perspective alone, apart from the many human, cultural and other reasons, it behooves thoughtful people around the world to make efforts to understand this vast and vital nation.

It is possible to say almost anything about India and have it apply to some part of that subcontinent. India is a land of [poverty] and, in some ways, of plenty. It is a nation both powerful and weak, ancient and modern, climatically dramatic in its contrasts. The very term "India" implies a unity which exists more as a tentative political form than as a human and socio-cultural reality. From the intertwining of its complex history with contemporary society, one can distill five important features which will perhaps give us some aids in understanding modern India.

The first feature to remember when thinking of India is its diversity. It is a country in which there are fifteen official languages, over 300 minor languages and some 3,000 dialects. Twenty-four languages have more than one million speakers each. The largest spoken language is Hindi, but this is the mother tongue of only about 40 percent of the population. Often Indians cannot understand each other and frequently use English as a link or administrative language. But language is not the only diversity.

There are four principal social groupings, what we sometimes call castes, and several thousand sub- categories of the castes. Although predominantly Hindu, all the world's major religions are represented in India. Ethnic differences also abound. This mosaic is culturally extraordinary. It is a source of divisiveness in a nation

The fifth and final feature we must remember is that poverty, spirituality and modernity mix and coexist in India, without the paradoxical implications which a Western perspective suggests. It is the essence of Indian spirituality which enables even the most deprived to endure poverty and it is modernity which provides the prospect of improvement.

It is this spirit, a composite of many small individual visions and inspirations, which characterizes modern India and offers the best hope for the nation and its people.

Social Consequences of Economic Reforms

India's recent progress toward economic growth stems from reforms undertaken after the 1991 fiscal crisis, which lifted India from decades of slow growth under socialist rule and offered an opportunity to improve living conditions in the immense, poor country. And the recent growth has been impressive—among the highest growth rates in the world.

A great portion of the world's poor live in India, and will depend on its future growth to overcome poverty. But the recent progress is not enough. Certainly, great steps have been taken toward reform on trade, industrial policy, and the financial system; substantial progress has been made in reducing poverty; and India has a growing and thriving middle class.

However, much remains to be done: the government intrudes where it need not, in everything from coal mining to discos, and fails to manage the basic services that it should, like decent roads, a stable power distribution infrastructure, and quality primary education.

About a quarter of India's one billion-plus population, who constitute a third of the world's poor, continue to live in poverty. Over 70% of Indians live in deprived rural areas. This is the challenge of a country heralded as the home of the new Silicon Valley, where oxen and trucks share highways, and where preventable diseases like polio are rampant. In a country run largely by economists, social reform has lagged behind economic reform.

The state of Bihar seems to encapsulate all of India's woes—a poverty rate greater than 40%; utter corruption; a deeply rooted caste system which has historically limited opportunities to those born into the lower castes; and 75% of its villages without primary schools, health care, and electricity.

In contrast, the state of Kerala is India's success story of social reform, which boasts over 90% literacy; health and mortality measures comparable to developed countries; and a strong commitment to universal education and equity. Still, over 90% of its residents are unable to find employment within the state. If India is to achieve continued economic growth and define herself as a world power, social and economic reform must occur in tandem.

Poverty and Inequality

Although poverty has continued to fall with economic reform, it is evident that growth in and of itself will not eliminate poverty. Over a quarter of the country continues to live in poverty.

Wealth is generally more concentrated in urban rather than rural areas where the majority indians live. Economic growth also tends to be higher in wealthier states in the south and west such as Gujarat and Maharashtra than poorer states like Bihar, Orissa, and Uttar Pradesh in the north and east. Investment will naturally flock to the more developed regions equipped with infrastructure advantages.

Additionally, with mounting pressure from internal migration from depressed states like Bihar, investing in human development and poverty reduction in states left behind may be key to enhancing the national stability that allows liberalization and growth to proceed.

Education

India produces both world-renowned engineers and one-third of the globe's illiterate population; so, while discussing India's education system, education is perhaps the country's great unequalizer. Those graduating from India's top-notch Indian Institutes of Technology (IITs) and Indian Institutes of Management (IIMs) are poised to compete with the world's best and brightest. But the top accounts for only a tiny tip of a distorted pyramid.

In all parts of the economy, the country's human capital presents a constraint, from looming shortages of high-tech workers to labor productivity in manufacturing that is about half that of China. Even within India's celebrated higher education system, few of the 2,000 engineering schools and numerous other institutions meet international standards.

Health

About half of Indian children will forever bear the physical and mental consequences of what the World Bank calls the country's "silent emergency." That about 20% of children's deaths in the world and a quarter of all maternal childbirth mortality occur in India further indicate the depth of India's neglect of health. Even among similar-income countries, India's expenditures on health are woefully low, at less than one per cent of the country's GDP and half of China's per capita spending. And while AIDS is approaching epidemic proportions, it continues to receive relatively scant attention from the government. This utter neglect has also impeded India's ability to receive foreign assistance to combat the disease.

Still, the picture of India's health is not entirely bleak. Since Independence, the life expectancy of its population has increased astonishingly from about 32 years to almost 65 years, and its infant mortality rate has been halved. Facilities and care for the minority who can afford it have reached world-class levels. While challenges are vast in addressing the health of the poor, innovative health programs that capitalize on the resources of the local communities offer promise.

Rural Employment

If economic growth is to continue, employment opportunities must be made available to India's rural poor. The majority of people reside in rural areas. Roughly half of the poor are employed in agriculture, which makes up about a quarter of India's GDP, but its growth waxes and wanes with the monsoons. It also attracts only 7% of public and private investment, limiting its impact on overall economic and employment growth. India must strengthen labor-intensive industries like manufacturing if it is to reduce poverty and increase growth in rural areas.

Fewer workers are being employed in the agriculture sector as the use of machinery and labor-reducing cropping techniques have increased. India's surplus of rural workers could be shifted to manufacturing textiles or to the construction sector given India's enormous infrastructure needs.

Manufacturing, however, has in fact grown at an annual rate of 7%, but these gains have been due to increased productivity, not job growth. China's manufacturing market, on the other hand, has boomed with job-oriented growth. The labor-intensive textile industry could add an estimated

12million jobs over the next five years if India would reform its restrictive labor laws and regulations.

Caste

While caste is often portrayed as a feature of Indian life of fading importance, and one concentrated in rural areas, the caste system continues to assert itself through social inequalities and voting patterns. Efforts to address caste inequalities by affirmative action have been mixed and are consigned to the shrinking public sector.

Politically, while the divisions and identity politics run deep, recent elections offer a sliver of hope that India's politics is beginning to move away from a destabilizing emphasis on communities and caste and toward a focus on development and governance.

Future of Economic Reforms

India's next wave of reform must focus on improving the provision of education, health, and other social services in order to achieve higher growth rates. This will require higher levels of public investments through tax-increasing or subsidy-reducing legislation. Yet, India's governments continue to be saddled with large deficits, with funds spent largely on repaying debt. Even if more funding is allocated toward social programs, India must tackle corruption, power conflicts between central, state, and local governments, and the poor management and distribution of resources. Efforts must be made to improve delegation of authority to local levels and to increase accountability and transparency. Only then will continued growth be sustainable and the social livelihood of millions of Indians be improved.

Socio-cultural Repercussions of Globalization

Globalization has been defined as the process of rapid integration of countries and happening through greater foreign trade and foreign investment. In essence, it refers to increased possibilities for action between and among people in situations irrespective of geographical considerations as per the definition of social theorists. As a result, globalization has brought to India new technologies, new products and also the economic opportunities.

As the world gets increasingly interconnected through globalization, a sundry of changes are taking place, some of which evade our attention mainly because we are more concerned about the economic and political impacts of the phenomenon. Life as we know it is changing.

Changes enter our lives through technology, consumer products, new thoughts, lifestyles and visions of others. In this sense, globalization is a social and cultural process in which individuals of different cultural backgrounds interact with each other in all spheres of life more intensively than before. This integration is increasingly exposing people to different ways of thinking, cultural values and new forms of family life. Women are getting out of the family home; children are educated to partake in a world other than that of their parents.

Global trends such as cooperation in the same production or trade networks enable societies and individuals to know more of each other.

As human communities share their experiences through the global networks of work and information, a greater cultural understanding develops that may help improve the lives of individuals and their families. Said differently, globalization is a phenomenon created through human activity that in turn constantly changes human activity/behavior.

One of the most interesting phenomena of globalization is the shaping of online communities. This process has led to the evolution of new identities for people around the world while disregarding where they live and what their nationality is. This is a new phase of acculturation. New ideas, new methods of work and good life and governance are being shared worldwide even in the most secluded places of the globe.

All of these changes have substantial impacts on the family because the family is the strategic social unit where division of labor, social role play, collective decisions for members and their future, their movements and development are decided on. Such decisions define the identities of family members and their interaction with the larger society.

Moreover, all of these decisions may change, be debated, be renegotiated and their conflicts resolved. In other words, not only societal but intra-familial issues are affected by globalization, now more than ever.

Needless to say, the impact of globalization on families is differential, depending on many factors, but specifically depending on where the family lives and the social class it belongs to. Women may get out of the family circle to join the workforce in traditional-conservative environments. But to denote that they belong to a cultural environment that is morally different, they may dress differently and cover their heads. Hence two culturally different worlds meet to be permanently changed.

Globalization's most profound impact is changing gender roles and securing women's place in the workplace. The empowerment of women in turn changes the hierarchical role distribution that works against women both in the family and in society at large.

Cultural differences will remain and coexist with Globalization, although the criteria for cultural differentiation (criteria underlying social aggregation) will be modified due to Globalization. On the other hand, Globalization will draw strength from cultural differences to increase its scope and power of diffusion.

Cultural globalisation has increased cross-cultural contacts but may be accompanied by a decrease in the uniqueness of once-isolated communities: sushi is available in Germany as well as Japan, but Euro-Disney outdraws the city of Paris, potentially reducing demand for "authentic" French pastry. Globalisation's contribution to the alienation of individuals from their traditions may be modest compared to the impact of modernity itself, as alleged byexistentialists such as Jean-Paul Sartre and Albert Camus.

The IOM found more than 200 million migrants around the world in 2008, including illegal immigration. Remittance flows to developing countries reached $328 billion in 2008.

Non-governmental organizations influence public policy across national boundaries, including humanitarian aid and developmental efforts.

Religious movements were among the earliest cultural forces to globalize, spread by force, migration, imperialists and traders. Christianity, Islam, Buddhism and influenced endemic cultures in places far from their origins.

Social Policy in the Indian Development Process

Political theorists may be tempted to draw insights from the rather haphazard pattern of social policy implementation in India, finding in its very lack of direction and vision some association with the chaotic democratic polity within which it occurred, and the variegated demands which were sought to be fulfilled at different points of time. Most social policy provisioning has not been universal in terms of actual effects, even when it has been declared as such. Rather, it has been directed to specific (and restricted) target groups.

These groups included those with sufficient political voice, such as urban organised workers, or increasingly in the 1990s, particular caste groupings. There have also been much trumpeted attempts to include (in however limited a fashion) a small proportion of those who naturally appear to be deserving, such as households under the poverty line, women from lower income groups, and so on.

However, because such provisioning, whether in terms of protective legislation or in terms of actual resource transfers, has been extremely limited relative to the scale of requirement, it has meant that social policy has not been a basic instrument of development strategy in the manner outlined in the previous section. Rather, it has emerged essentially in the form of *ad hoc* responses to particular demands emanating from groups that (at least temporarily) have acquired some degree of political voice.

It is also true that the overall development strategy, however flawed it was in terms of low social development and lack of fulfilment of basic needs, did at least meet some of the functions of social policy mentioned above. In broad terms, the management of at least some of the social effects of modernisation was achieved in that the most destabilising effects were avoided.

Similarly, the legitimisation of and indeed the social acceptance of the suppression of current consumption on the part of workers and peasants, was also achieved; however, as pointed out above, the same was not true of the capitalist class and the elites who were unwilling to accept the economic discipline necessary for a sustained path of aggregate development. It is also true that the growing size of the public sector served as a cushion against very sharp fluctuations in aggregate economic activity. However, in a longer term sense the economic regime and associated social policy failed miserably in raising aggregate social labour productivity and reducing the employment slack in the system, or in underwriting labour costs for employers, including exporters.

The more significant forms of social policy in the Indian context have included: agrarian reform; food procurement and distribution; education; employment creation through public works; affirmative action in the form of reservation for public services employment and educational institutions; antipoverty programmes directed towards small asset creation or micro credit; changes in forms and structures of governance through decentralisation and some devolution of resources.

Conclusion of Social Policies in India

After discussing social policy in India, while achieving some limited successes in terms of management of the contradictions and instabilities emerging from the development process, has nevertheless been inadequate in terms of the basic functions defined at the start of this paper.

Furthermore, the recent changes in social policy and public intervention that have been associated in India with the globalisation phase of neo-liberal economic reform, may have actually undermined some of the gains that were achieved earlier. This is because recent macroeconomic tendencies have been associated with greater inequality and fragility of incomes, which has in turn certain important social implications.

Significance of Social Policies

Social policy has a significance that goes beyond even the valid concerns about basic equity and minimal living standards, which form part of the social and economic rights of citizens. In fact, it can play a major role in the capitalist development project, at several levels. At the most basic level, social policies of different types are crucial to the state is capacity to manage modernisation, and along with it the huge economic and social shocks that are necessarily generated.

Thus, for example, social policies of affirmative action in parts of Southeast Asia (as in Malaysia) have been essential to maintaining ethnic harmony over periods when existing income inequalities and social imbalances across groups within the aggregate population would be otherwise accentuated by economic growth patterns. Similarly, when over enthusiastic and possibly insensitive developmental projects overturn existing local communities or destroy material cultures without satisfactory replacement, social policy can become the basic instrument for rehabilitation and renewed social integration. The massive human shifts (geographic, economic, social) that most development projects entail are potentially sources of much conflict, and often social policy is the most effective means of containing such conflict or at least keeping it within levels that do not destabilise society or derail the development project itself.

The second important, and related, role of social policy is of course that of legitimisation not only of the state, but of the development project itself. This need for legitimisation arises both for the long run process and in terms of short run crisis management. Thus, over the long run, or planning horizon, it is especially important in growth trajectories that rely on high investment and savings rates, thereby suppressing current consumption in favour of high growth for larger future consumption, and which therefore imply sacrifices typically made by workers and peasants.

In such a scenario, social policy that is directed towards providing basic needs and social services to those who are otherwise deprived of the gains from economic growth in terms of increased current consumption, would be not just important but even necessary to ensuring social stability and continuity of the process itself.

Implementation of Social Policy in Society

"Policy implementation encompasses those actions by public or private individuals (or groups) that are directed at the achievement of objectives set forth in prior policy decisions." They make a clear distinction between the interrelated concepts of implementation, performance, impact and stress.

Implementation research has been too restricted in time (i.e., an emphasis on cross-sectional versus longitudinal analysis), too restricted in number (i.e., an emphasis on case study versus comparative analyses), too restricted in policy type (i.e., an emphasis on single policy type versus multiple policy types), too restricted in defining the concept of implementation (i.e., limited to a single output measure versus multiple measures), and too restricted in approach (i.e., the utilization of either "top-down" or "bottom-up" approach versus both).

Research into Implementation

Research into implementation has evolved over the last twenty years. The literature on implementation is arbitrary not necessarily in any sequence, but there are certain highlights that can be identified. Three generations of research into policy implementation exists as follows:

1. The first or classical generation of thinking on the subject began with the assumption that implementation would happen 'automatically' once the appropriate policies had been authoritatively proclaimed.
2. The second generation set out to challenge this assumption, to explain implementation 'failure' in specific cases, and to demonstrate that implementation was a political process no less complex (and often more so) than policy formulation.
3. The third or analytical generation, by contrast, has been less concerned with specific implementation failure and more with understanding how implementation works in general and how its prospects might be improved.

Economic Development in India

The Economic development in India followed a socialist-inspired policies for most of its independent history, including state-ownership of many sectors; extensive regulation and red tapeknown as "Licence Raj"; and isolation from the world economy. India's per capita income increased at only around one per cent annualized rate in the three decades after Independence. Since the mid-1980s, India has slowly opened up its markets through economic liberalization. After more fundamental reforms since 1991 and their renewal in the 2000s, India has progressed towards a free market economy.

In the late 2000s, India's growth has reached 7.5%, which will double the average income in a decade. Analysts say that if India pushed more fundamental market reforms, it could sustain the rate and even reach the government's 2011 target of 10%. States have large responsibilities over their economies. The annualized 1999-2008 growth rates for Gujarat (9.6%), Haryana (9.1%), or Delhi(8.9%) were significantly higher than for Bihar (5.1%), Uttar Pradesh (4.4%), or Madhya Pradesh(6.5%). India is the ninth-largest economy in the world and the fourth largest by purchasing power parity adjusted exchange rates (PPP). On per capita basis, it ranks 128th in the world or 118th by PPP.

Economic Growth

The economic growth has been driven by the expansion of services that have been growing consistently faster than other sectors. It is argued that the pattern of Indian development has been a specific one and that the country may be able to skip the intermediate industrialization-led phase in the transformation of its economic structure. Serious concerns have been raised about the jobless nature of the economic growth.

Favourable macroeconomic performance has been a necessary but not sufficient condition for the significant reduction of poverty among the Indian population. The rate of poverty decline has not been higher in the post-reform period since 1991. The improvements in some other non-economic dimensions of social development have been even less favourable. The most pronounced example is an exceptionally high and persistent level of child malnutrition.

9

GANDHIAN MODEL OF VILLAGE AND SOCIETY

• Mahatma Gandhi was not a development economist, yet his theory is important to development. The Gandhian theory of development is based on the ideologies of Mahatma Gandhi, who is regarded in India as the Father of the Nation. At the outset, Gandhian economics rejects the precepts and assumptions of mainstream economics. It represents an alternative to mainstream economic theories as a way to promote economic progress without emphasizing material pursuits, or compromising human development.

Gandhian Philosophy of Development

Gandhi's idea to develop the Indian society was based on his understanding of the society and hence based on the village system. Talking about the importance of village, he wrote in 1936, *Harijan* in "I would say if the village perishes, India will perish too. It will be no more India. His one mission in the world will get lost."

He was aware of the realities of the village life and knew the plight of half starved masses of India. He often acknowledged the same in his vivid descriptions of Indian villages. He wrote, "instead of having graceful hamlets dotting the lands, we have dung-heaps. The approach to many villages is not a refreshing experience. Often one would like to shut one's eyes and stuff one's nose, such is the surrounding dirt and offending smell". His understanding of the plight of the people has been extremely well brought out in his writings, identifying his emphasis on removal of poverty over aesthetics.

Economic Philosophy

Gandhi's ideas on economics are embedded in his philosophy of life. Gandhian economics differs from mainstream economics in the following manner:

1. It replaces the assumption of the perfect mobility of labour with the assumption that community and family stability should have priority.
2. It rejects the more-is-always-better principle. It replaces the axiom of non-satiation with a principle of limits, the recognition that there is such a thing as 'enough' material wealth.
3. It recognizes that consuming more than 'enough' creates more problems than it solves, and causes consumer satisfaction or utility to decline, rather than increase.
4. It aims at a better quality of life, rather than higher standards of living as propagated by other economists.

Let us have a clear idea of Gandhi's philosophy of life to understand Gandhian economics. Gandhi viewed life as a whole, and not in its isolated compartments. According to the Indian scriptures, there are four aspects of an individual's life: *Artha* (money), *Kama* (desire), *Dharma* (righteousness), and *Moksha* (liberation). These aspects are interrelated, and, therefore all of them should be harmoniously developed. Money is required to satisfy the basic requirements of life, however, it is not the end in itself. Man's aim is not to multiply worldly desires and engage his whole life in acquiring wealth to satisfy all his desires.

The goal of life is to control desire and transform it, through righteousness, into liberation. He argues for the liberation of man from the cyclical order marked by artha, kama, dharma and moksha. According to him, true happiness lies in the all round development of a human being's personality, and in living a full life. Gandhi's ideas on economics are a part of his general philosophy of life. In these ideas, he outlined principles on which he wanted to build the ideal socialist society. The principles are as follows:

(1) *Humanism*: Man is both the means, and the end of all activity. He is also the measure of performance. Everything functions with a human face. All ideas, institutions, and actions are to be judged in terms of whether they help in building a better man.

(2) *Simple Living*: Gandhi had faith in materialism without lust and passion. Material progress must be subservient to moral growth. The ultimate aim of man is not to accumulate wealth and enjoy luxuries of life, but to attain the higher values of life, and to lead a simple and full life. Simple living and high thinking should be the motto of life.

(3) *Social Justice*: Society is divided between rich and poor, between the Gandhian Development strong and the weak, between the privileged and unprivileged, and Theory between the elite and the masses. The principle of social justice requires that the former must help the latter in fulfilling their basic requirements. The ideal functioning of the society must aim at providing social justice and reducing inequalities.

(4) *Non Violence*: Social change is to be brought about through non violent methods. Ends and means are inseparable in life, and only good means yield good results. An ideal society can only be established by adopting peaceful and non violent means, and not through hatred and war. In Gandhian economics, the principle of non violence means the following things: (a) the absence of capitalistic exploitation; (b) the decentralization of production units; (c) cheaper defence organization; (d) less inequality of income; and (e) self sufficiency of communities. 5) Love and Co-operation: An ideal society should be established on the principles of love and cooperation. In such a society, the love of others and not self love; co-operation and not egocentric acts, pre-dominate. Relation between humans should be based on truth, love, and cooperation, and not on money and matter.

(6) *Harmony*: The ideal economic condition according to Gandhi is self sufficiency of the economy. For this, the following harmonies should be maintained: (a) the requirements of the people must be in harmony with the resources of the economy and,; (b) production technology should match the country's requirements.

Principle of Satyagraha

Gandhi adopted the principle of Satyagraha as a movement of civil disobedience and tax resistance. Gandhi laid down preconditions as absolutely necessary for the practice of Satyagraha. These are as follow:

First, there can be no Satyagraha for an unjust cause. Otherwise the principle of truth will be flouted. Second, Satyagraha excludes the use of violence in any form, in thought or action. Third, Satyagraha presupposes a clear distinction between a willing obedience to the laws which are good, and opposition to those which are immoral. The superiority of the law of conscience has to assert itself over other laws. Fourth, Satyagraha is an instrument available only to those who have no hatred towards their opponents. Fifth, a Satyagrahi must have the capacity and willingness to sacrifice. That is why Gandhi insisted more on a small revolutionary minority rather than a whole majority. Sixth, Satyagraha means constant engagement in constructive social work so that Satyagraha as a struggle does not become negative. Seventh, Satyagraha calls for total humility on the part-of those who practice it. And, last, Satyagraha is the expression of discipline and sincerity. It challenges the honesty and capacity for national work, and willingness to submit to discipline.

Village and Cottage Industry

Labour: The exploitation of labour is an evil of the capitalist system. It causes unrest among the workers, and, if it persists for a long time, it provokes them to revolt against the system. According to Gandhi, the exploitation of labour is easured as a difference between what the worker gets, and what he deserves. Whenever a worker is paid less than the basic wage rate, or the minimum living wage rate, he is said to be exploited.

The exploitation of labour is a normal feature of capitalism. The capitalists, in their effort to increase profits, tend to reduce wages. The extent of exploitation can be minimized by stabilizing the wage rate at a reasonable level. The ultimate solution lies in bridging the gap between the capitalists and the workers. Gandhi was totally against making a man a cog in the giant wheel of industry, His view was that people should not lose their independence, identity, and, thus, their creativity. Production:

Gandhi advocated production by the masses. He preferred the decentralization of small units of production to the concentration of large scale units in a few places. He wanted to carry the production units to the homes of the masses, particularly in villages. One advantage of the village and cottage industries is that they increase employment. Another advantage is related to the consideration of efficiency. There are many reasons to believe that it is cheaper to produce any commodity in small and cottage industries because: (a) no separate establishment charges are required (b) integration of cottage industries with agriculture (c) very few tools are needed; (d) problems of storage; (e) negligible cost of transporting goods to the consumer (f) no waste—duplication—due to competition, and (g) no problem of over production. All these factors make the production by the small units economical. Small is beautiful. This is the logic behind the Gandhian scheme of decentralization of village and cottage industries.

Capital: According to Gandhi, capital is the source of all wealth. It is required for producing commodities and paying wages to the workers. Capital is of two types: money capital and labour capital. A labourer's skill is his capital. Both money capital and labour capital are necessary for production. Gandhi observed, 'Just as the capitalist cannot make his capital fructify without the cooperation of labour, similarly the working man cannot make his labour fructify without the cooperation of capital.'

For better industrial relations, both capital and labour need to be organized. It is easy to organize capital but not labour. This weakens the workers' bargaining position and increases the possibility of exploitation of labour. An entrepreneur's power to exploit labour depends upon the extent of concentration of capital in the hands of capitalists. Gandhi suggested two methods to reduce the evil effects of the concentration of capital. According to him:

- The ownership of capital should be decentralized; and If the concentration of capital is considered essential, the state should have the full control over the use of capital.

Poverty and Inequality: Gandhi was not an economist. But he had a clear understanding of the issues of poverty and income inequality. Poverty is not created by the poor man himself. According to him, poverty and inequality are inextricably connected. Poverty is the manifestation of affluence itself. The anatomy of affluence appears to be fair. But means to gather this status is unfair and illegitimate. Thus, the poverty of many is caused by the richness of some. Man's greed has resulted in poverty, and it is the cause of persistence of poverty in the economy. Gandhi said:

- "I suggest that we are thieves in a way. If I take anything that I do not need for my own immediate use, and keep it, I steal it from somebody else. I venture to suggest that it is the fundamental law of Nature, without exception, that Nature produces enough for our wants from day to day, and if only everybody took enough for himself and nothing more, there would be no pauperism in this world, there would be no man dying of starvation in this world."

According to Gandhi, economics which disregards moral values is untrue. He introduced moral values as a factor in regulating all economic transactions and international commerce. He was not advocating socialism perse but humanistic values. He contended:

- "My ideal is equal distribution, but so far as I can see, it is not to be realized. I, therefore, work for equitable distribution."

Employment: Gandhi emphasized employment. The full employment of human resources is the primary need of a country. By full employment, Gandhi meant the employment of each and every individual. Full employment cannot be attained through the dckclopn~ent of large scale industries. These industries generally use capital intensive and labour saving technologies, and do not provide sufficient employment opportunities. Moreover, most unemployed people live in rural areas. The cause of rural underemployment is the seasonal nature of agriculture.

The agricultural workers work on land for six months and for the other six months they remain idle. It will be disadvantageous for the mechanized industries to employ such underemployed casual labour. Again, the underemployed agricultural workers have religious, cultural and social attachments with rural life, and, therefore, cannot be expected to leave their homes easily for employment in the urban industries. Thus, mechanization and large scale production provides no solution to the problem of unemployment in the agriculture-based, over-populated economies.

As Gandhi pointed out:

- "Mechanization is good when the hands are too few for the work intended to be accomplished. It is an evil when there are more hands than required for the work, as is the case in India."

The problem of unemployment, according to Gandhi, can be tackled only by developing village and cottage industries. These industries are capital-saving and labour- using. They take employment opportunities to the doors of the unemployed and ideally fit in with the rural conditions.

Technology: It is erroneous to think that Gandhi was against technology. The essence of science is acquiring knowledge through experimentation. Gandhi offered, on behalf of the Spinners' Association, a prize of a lakh of rupees for the invention of a charkha, a spinning wheel, which could be made and repaired in the villages, and would produce four times the yarn spun on the traditional charkha. He had no objection to the use of machinery to increase production and improve the condition of the workers. But he did not approve of machinery that, in his view, produced goods along with starvation. He was against the indiscriminate multiplication of machinery. Gandhi said,

- "What I object to is the craze for machinery, not machinery as such. The craze is for what they call labour saving machinery. Men go on 'saving labour' till thousands are without work, and thrown on the open streets to die of starvation."

For Gandhi, human consideration was supreme, and that of science and technology was secondary.

Profits: In the Gandhian view, the term profit is used in the residuary sense. Profit is equal to total receipt minus production costs. Capital depreciation and distribution costs are negligible in this scheme of production. Thus, the main costs of production are expenditure on raw materials, and payments to the workers. Profit is the excess of total receipts over these costs.

Technological improvements are beneficial to the entrepreneurs and harmful to the workers. With the introduction of machinery, the entrepreneur's profit increases, while the workers face unemployment, and reductions in wages. Gandhi did not consider profit to be essential for the survival of a firm.

Gandhi's Views & Work for Village Development

India does not need to be industrialized in the modern sense of the term . It has 7,50,000 villages scattered over the vast area 1900 miles long 1500 broad. The people are rooted to the soil and the vast majority are living a hand to mouth life. What ever may be said to the contrary, having traveled throughout the length and breath of the land with the eyes open and having mixed with millions are living in enforced idleness for the last four month in a year. Agriculture does not need revolutionary changes.

The Indians peasant requires a supplementary industry. The most natural is the introduction of the spinning wheel not the handloom The latter cannot be included introduced in every home, whereas the farmer can, and it used to be so even a century ago. It was driven out not by economic pressure but by force deliberately used as can be proved from authentic records. The restoration therefore of the spinning wheel solves the economic problem of India at a stroke.

Gandhi's Panchayat Raj

Independence must begin at the bottom. Thus, every village will be a republic or Panchayat having full powers. It follows, therefore, that every village has to be self-sustained and capable of managing its affairs even to the extent of defending itself against the whole world. It will be trained and prepared to perish in the attempt to defend itself against any onslaught from without. Thus, ultimately, it is the individual who is the unit.

This does not exclude dependence on and willing help from neighbours or from the world. It will be free and voluntary play of mutual forces. Such a society is necessarily highly cultured in which every man and woman knows what he or she wants and, what is more, knows that no one should want anything that others cannot have with equal labour.

This society must naturally be based on truth and non-violence which, in my opinion, are not possible without a living belief in God, meaning a self-existent, All-knowing living Force which inheres every other force known to the world and which depends on none and which will live when all other forces may conceivably perish or cease to act. I (Gandhi) am unable to account for my life without belief in this all-embracing living light.

Village Swaraj

Gandhi's idea of village Swaraj is that it is a complete republic, independent of its neighbours for its own wants and yet interdependent for many others in which dependence is necessary. Thus, every village's first concern will be to grow its own food crops, and cotton for its cloth. It should have a reserve for its cattle, recreation and playground for adults and children. Then, if there is more land available, it will grow useful money crops, thus excluding Ganja, tobacco, opium and the like. The village will maintain a village theatre, school and public hall. It will have its own waterworks ensuring clean water supply. This can be done through controlled wells or tanks. Education will be compulsory up to the final basic course. As far as possible, every activity will be conducted on the co-operative basis. There will be no castes such as we have today with their graded untouchability. Non-violence with its technique of Satyagraha and non-co-operation will be the sanction pf the village community. There will be a compulsory service of village guards who will be selected by rotation from the register maintained by the village.

Function of Panchayat

It is the function of the Panchayat to revive honesty and industry.... It is the function of the Panchayats to teach the villagers to avoid disputes, if they have to settle them. This will ensure speedy justice without any expenditure. You will need neither the police nor the military... Then the Panchayat should see to cattle improvement. They should show steady increase in the mild yield..... the Panchayat should also see to an increase in the quantity of foodstuff grown in their village. This is to be accomplished by properly maturing the soil. You have your indigenous games. You should banish intoxicating drinks and drugs from your midst.

- I hope you will eradicate untouchability if there is any trace of it still in you village. The Hindus, the Muslims, the Sikhs, the Parsees and the Christians should all live as brothers and sisters. If you achieve all I have mentioned, you will demonstrate real independence, and people from all over India will come to see your model village and take inspiration from it.

Gandhi's Views on Education

Character cannot be built with mortar and stone. It cannot be built by hands other than your own. An education which does not teach us to discriminate between good and bad, to assimilate the one and eschew the other, is a misnomer. Education should be so revolutionized as to answer the wants of the poorest villager, instead of answering those of an imperial exploiter. Education in the understanding of citizenship is a short-term affair if we are honest and earnest. Basic education links the children, whether of cities or the villages, to all that is best and lasting in India. Is not education the art of drawing out full manhood of the children under training? Literacy in itself is no education.

Literacy is not the end of education nor even the beginning. Literacy education should follow the education of the hand-the one gift that visibly distinguishes man from beast. Real education has to draw out the best from the boys and girls to be educated. True education must correspond to the surrounding circumstances or it is not a healthy growth. What is really needed to make democracy function is not knowledge of facts, but right education. National education to be truly national must reflect the national condition for the time being.

Nayee-Talim

The function of Nayee-Talim is not to teach an occupation, but through it to develop the whole man. I (Gandhi) believe that religious education must be the sole concern of religious associations. By education I mean an all-round drawing out of the best in the child and man-body, mind and spirit. By spiritual training I mean education of the heart. Experience gained in two schools under my control has taught me that punishment does not purify, if anything, it hardens children. I consider writing as a fine art. We kill it by imposing the alphabet on little children and making it the beginning of learning. I do regard spinning and weaving as the necessary part of any national system of education. The aim of university education should be to turn out true servants of the people who will live and die for the country's freedom. A balanced intellect presupposes a harmonious growth of body, mind and soul. Love requires that true education should be easily accessible to all and should be of use to every villager in this daily life.

The notion of education through handicrafts rises from the contemplation of truth and love permeating life's activities. The fees that you pay do not cover even a fraction of the amount that is spent on your education from the public exchanger. Persistent questioning and healthy inquisitiveness are the first requisite for acquiring learning of any kind. If we want to impart education best suited to the needs of the villagers, we should take the Vidyapith to the villages. In a democratic scheme, money invested in the promotion of learning gives a tenfold return to the people even as a seed sown in good soil returns a luxuriant crop. All education in a country has got to be demonstrably in promotion of the progress of the country in which it is given. The schools and colleges are really a factory for turning out clerks for Government. The canker has so eaten into the society that in many cases the only meaning of education is a knowledge of English. The emphasis laid on the principle of spending every minute of one's life usefully is the best education for citizenship .

Gandhian Sarvodaya Plan

Gandhi was a practical idealist. He said that true economics stands for social justice and moral values. He never spoke in terms of economics logic or jargon. He advocated the dignity of man and the dignity of labour to redress the sufferings of the people. He advocated moral growth, not material development. He said we must replace apathy with sympathy, exploitation with benevolence, profit with welfare and materialistic development with human development. He demonstrated the bankruptcy of modem civilization based on materialistic parameters as a solution for social problems. He said that cities are plague spots. He said that previously, the British were ruling, but now their philosophy, their technology, and lifestyle rule us.

Gandhi was convinced that the salvation of the Indian economy depends on rural development. Rural development depends on agricultural development, which is the integration of both, the farm and nonfarm activities of the village economy. He never accepted the inherent contradiction between economic development and human development. So he thought of integrating and establishing harmony between both the two, through sarvodaya. Having set the goal, he also worked out schemes for achieving it. For achieving the goal of non violent socialism, Gandhi presented the sarvodaya plan.

The sawodaya plan provides the foundations, on which the economic organization of a nation striving for the ideals of socialism is to be built. Sarvodaya means all round wellbeing of all. He argues for the combination of purity of ends and nobility of means. The objective of the sarvodaya plan is the establishment of sarvodaya social order on the principles of non violence, truth, love, and cooperation. *The sarvodaya plan includes following*:

(a) economic equality and communal harmony.
(b) full attention to the cultivators and the labourers.
(c) all cultivators organizing their own committees.
(d) all labourers forming their own unions.
(e) education for all (technical or basic).
(f) hand-spinning in every family.

Gandhi's sarvodaya is essentially a programme for the regeneration of the Indian Village. In his Khadi scheme, Gandhi proposed the following measures to develop the khadi industry

- compulsory introduction of spinning in all primary and secondary schools;
- the cultivation of cotton in areas where it is not grown;
- the organization of weaving by multipurpose cooperative societies;
- All employees in the education and co-operative departments, municipal, district boards, and grampanchayats would be required to pass a test in spinning, in order to qualify;
- control of prices of handloom cloth woven of mill yarn;
- the imposition of a ban on the use of mill cloth in areas where the hand woven cloth was in abundance;
- the use of hand spun cloth in all government, and textile and weaving departments;
- the old cloth mills would not be allowed to expand, and new ones would not be opened; and
- the import of foreign yarn, or cloth to be banned.

The revitalization of the village economy, among other things, includes measures such as the development of village and cottage industries, the improvement of village sanitation, protection from robbers and wild animals, the development of agriculture, conducting ail activities on co-operative basis, the constitution of village panchayats, self-sufficiency in basic requirements, the removal of illiteracy, and the abolition of the caste system. Special attention would be provided to the development of village industries, sanitation, and hygiene. In short, the basic objective would be to develop the village into a complete, self-sufficient republic.

This is a long range programme. The immediate task is to establish sarvodaya at the village level. To start with, social order should change according to sarvodaya principles in each village. Therefore, Gandhi evolved schemes for the regeneration of villages and revitalization of village economy. Gandhi's struggle against poverty and unemployment, and his work of national reconstruction starts from the village. The purpose is to bring all-round development of the village and make it a self-sufficient economic unit.

Gandhian Philiosophy of Sustainable Development

Gandhi's ideas are relevant for protecting the environment and to preserve the carrying capacity of Earth. Gandhi emphasizes three aspects: economy, society and environment. He says, the present materialistic lifestyle has to be changed for sustainable development. Gandhian economics guides us towards a sustainable lifestyle. According to Gandhian philosophy, the following steps are given to attaining a sustainable lifestyle:

1. Sustainable agriculture: We should give up chemical fertilizers and pesticides and substitute them with bio-manures and bio-pesticides. Vermi culture and vermi compost is a must for restoring the health of the soil.
2. Khadi and village industries are eco friendly. They create employment and alleviate poverty. So we should promote khadi and products of village industries.
3. Appropriate technologies: We should adopt technologies which are simple, and which our villagers are able to comprehend and operate themselves. The use of electricity should be avoided, or kept to the minimum.
4. Renewable energy sources: Coal and petroleum are non-renewable energy sources and are getting exhausted very fast. Solar energy is limitless and inexhaustible. We can harness solar energy for heating and lighting. Water and wind energies can also be harnessed for producing electricity.
5. Sylviculture (or tree plantation): Cutting trees for fuel and for the construction of houses is inevitable. Our policy should be to plant two trees for every tree we cut. Trees as a source of energy are non-renewable if we only cut them and do not grow them.

Gandhi's advocacy of democratic trusteeship was supported by Schumacher's concept, 'Small is Beautiful'. According to Gandhi, Democratic Trusteeship should have the "responsibility for a bundle of assets instead of ownership of them". This is a neat description of how we all have to learn to live in this planet. The trustees should be responsible for the bundle of assets—the air, sea, and land—through which nature and our life evolved, and is sustained. These assets should not to be selfishly fought over, bought, sold, and pillaged.

According to Gandhian thought, under democratic common ownership, "man's spirit can be freer so that he can become more creative, productive and responsible". The Gandhian focus is on the simplicity of life based on minimum human needs. According to Gandhi, "the earth has enough resources for our needs - not for our greed".

If we follow Gandhi's advice, especially following the economy of cooperation of the honey bees and birds, keeping Gandhiji's ideals in mind we can surely achieve a sustainable lifestyle. A sustainable life style automatically ensures sustainable development.

Role of State in Economic Development

Economic development, achieved largely through productivity growth, is very important to both developed and developing nations. However, even though we know that higher productivity leads to improved economic outcomes (for example, higher income, more choices to the consumers, better quality products, etc.), there has been no consensus among researchers about either the desired path of development or the role of state in economic development.

The role of the state in economic development began to change dramatically with the advent of the Industrial Revolution. In the West, the resulting industrialization and economic development were based on the establishment of individual property rights that encouraged the growth of private capital. Competition and individual enterprise thrive in this environment because individuals pursue their self-interest of survival and wealth accumulation. The instinct to survive under competitive pressures yields innovation and productivity increases, which eventually lead to both increased profits for business and lower prices to consumers.

However, the rise and spread of capitalism led a number of thinkers to examine the consequences of the market-based approach to development. Socialists argued that capitalism (or private ownership of capital) can lead to greater inequalities of income and wealth, while developmental economists argued that private decisions may not always lead to socially desirable outcomes (particularly in the case of market imperfections). Indeed, many policymakers at the time saw market failures as quite common and therefore assumed that only appropriate government interventions could guide an economy to a path of sustained economic development.

In the early 20th century, the former Soviet Union attempted a bold experiment of improving individual well-being without sacrificing the objective of greater equality of income and wealth through total ownership of capital by the government.

Unfortunately, during their time as colonies to the Western nations, these countries, for the most part, had been deprived of the industrialization that had engulfed those same Western nations. Based on the successful experience of the former Soviet Union, many economists and policymakers concluded that, particularly in a poor country, planning was essential for the efficient allocation of an economy's resources. The governments in these newly independent nations assumed a significant role in economic development. They sought to quickly and substantially raise the standard of living through directed and controlled economic development.

Apart from everything else, these developing countries invested heavily in education to promote literacy and to ensure an adequate supply of technical manpower to meet their growing needs. Further, these previously colonized nations did not want to subject their poor and weak economies to international economic fluctuations and thus sought to industrialize through import substituting industrialization, where imports were expected to be increasingly replaced by domestic production.

Role of Market in Economic Development

In earlier thinking about development, it was assumed that the market mechanisms of developed economies were so unreliable in developing economies that governments had to assume central responsibility for economic activity. This was to be done through economic planning for the entire economy, which in turn would be implemented by active government participation in the economy and pervasive controls over all private-sector economic activity.

Government participation took many forms: Public-sector enterprises were established to manufacture many commodities, including steel, machine tools, fertilizers, heavy chemicals, and even textiles and clothing; government marketing boards assumed monopoly power over the purchase and sale of many agricultural commodities; and government agencies became the sole importers of a variety of goods, and they often became exporters as well.

Controls over private-sector activity were even more extensive: Price controls were established for many commodities; import licensing procedures eliminated the importing of commodities not given priority in official plans; investment licenses were required before factories could be expanded; capacity licenses regulated maximum permissible outputs; and comprehensive regulations governed the conditions of employment of workers.

The consequence, frequently, was that indigenous entrepreneurs often found it more financially rewarding to devote their energies and ingenuity to the task of procuring the necessary government import licenses and other permits and exploiting the loopholes in government regulations than to the problem of raising the efficiency and productivity of resources.

For public-sector enterprises, political pressures often resulted in the employment of many more persons than could be productively used and in other practices conducive to extremely high-cost and inefficient operations. The consequent fiscal burden diverted resources that might otherwise have been used for investment, while the inefficient use of resources dampened growth rates.

Related to the belief in market failure and in the necessity for government intervention was the view that the efficiency of the price mechanism in developing countries was very small. This was reflected in the view of foreign-exchange shortage, already discussed, in which it was thought that there are fixed relationships between imported capital and domestic expansion. It was also reflected in the view that farmers are relatively insensitive to relative prices and in the belief that there are few entrepreneurs in developing countries.

Development of Domestic Industry

The positive case for the expansion of the manufacturing sector may now be considered. It is based on the general assumption that the manufacturing sector will in due course become the leading sector, drawing in workers (in part, siphoning off a portion of the increase in the labour force that would otherwise tend to drive down labour productivity in agriculture) from the traditional agricultural sector and providing them with higher-productivity jobs than could be obtained in agriculture. Agricultural productivity would necessarily be rising simultaneously, as investments in that sector permitted increasing output.

Whereas it was earlier thought that this process would follow the historical experience of countries such as England and Japan, the lesson from the successful developing countries is that by providing incentives and infrastructural support to encourage exports, there are significant opportunities for expansion of manufacturing of labour-intensive commodities, opportunities that can promote rapid growth.

Thus, given the much greater size of the international economy, and the much lower transport and communications costs that confront contemporary developing countries as contrasted with conditions in the 19th century, the potential for rapid growth is much greater now. Countries such as South Korea and Taiwan have experienced in a decade proportionate increases in per capita incomes that it took England and Japan a century to achieve. Whether other developing countries can follow this lead depends on a number of factors, including their economic policies and the continued growth of the international economy.

Non-Governmental Organizations

A non-governmental organization (NGO) is any non-profit, voluntary citizens' group which is organized on a local, national or international level. Task-oriented and driven by people with a common interest, NGOs perform a variety of service and humanitarian functions, bring citizen concerns to Governments, advocate and monitor policies and encourage political participation through provision of information.

Some are organized around specific issues, such as human rights, environment or health. They provide analysis and expertise, serve as early warning mechanisms and help monitor and implement international agreements. Their relationship with offices and agencies of the United Nations system differs depending on their goals, their venue and the mandate of a particular institution.

Formation of NGOs require innovative thinking, creativity, conceptualization of vision, ability to assess an existing gap in the provision of a service(s) or goods which calls for the skills to analyze what is and what ought to be- the real and the ideal. NGOs are difficult to define and classify due to the term's inconsistent use. NGO, non-profit organizations within defined boundaries excludes NGOs that fall outside each specific boundary. Additionally, it is beneficial for NGO networks to create a classification that allows similar organizations to exchange information more easily. To attempt a classification of NGOs requires a framework, that includes the orientation and the organization's level of operation.

An NGO's orientation refers to the type of activities an organization takes on. These activities might include environmental, development, or advocacy work. An NGO's level of operation indicates the scale at which an organization works on, like the difference in work between an international NGO and community or national NGO.

Function of NGOs

The function of NGOs can vary widely, from service organizations to human-rights advocacy and relief groups. The designation came into popular use after the founding of the United Nations to differentiate between governmental and non-governmental bodies. The NGO was deemed "any international organization that is not founded by an international treaty." NGOs not only serve as checks-and-balances for government, and governmental watchdogs, but are crucial cogs in wider governmental initiatives, such as relief response to a natural disaster.

The International Standards Organization (ISO) is a non-governmental organization. As such, its standards are voluntary, but many of its member institutes are part of the governmental structures of their countries, and ISO standards have found their way into many laws. Information technology professionals, for example, are probably familiar with the ISO/IEC 27000 series of standards for IT security management.

A non-governmental organization (NGO) is not part of a government and is therefore typically independent of governments. Although the definition can technically include for-profit corporations under certain circumstances, the term is generally restricted to social, cultural, legal, and environmental advocacy groups having goals that are primarily non-commercial. NGOs are usually non-profit organizations that gain at least a portion of their funding from private sources.

They can however, and sometimes do, go in for commercial activities to raise resources and sustain themselves but the profits of these activities cannot he distributed to members as dividend and has instead to be retained in the organisations to further the interest and objects of the beneficiaries. Because the label "NGO" is considered too broad by some, as it might cover anything that is non-governmental, many NGOs now prefer the term private voluntary organization (PVO).

Though voluntary associations of citizens have existed throughout history, NGOs along the lines seen today, especially on the international level, have developed in the past two centuries. One of the first such organizations, the International Committee of the Red Cross, was founded in 1863. The International Red Cross and Red Crescent Movement is today the world's largest group of humanitarian NGO's.

Role of NGO's in Development

Development is a progress of positive change quantitatively and qualitatively. Many people define it in their own context according to their surroundings and immediate needs. The definition by the South may not be the same as in the North but there are key components of the definitions that are similar everywhere. Therefore, some define it as a process by which members of a society inspire themselves and their institutions in ways that enhance their ability to mobilize and manage resources sustainably to produce sustainable and justify distributed improvements in their quality of life consistent with their aims and aspirations.

It is a process involving community participation in critically identifying and analyzing their needs and problems, setting goals and making their won decisions on sustainable use of available resources to improve their quality of life. This implies that it is a struggle against oppression and all that make life less human. It is a process of building new communities and alternative structures, which empower the poor and enable all people to become subjects of their own destiny.

It involves a movement from unequal relationships to the democratization of all aspects of life and true self-reliance. In essence, development is about people and the way they live and every society/ community must initiate its own development process and the government should mainly facilitate the process through good/democratic policies.

The task of development became overwhelmingly challenging on the part of governments. Citizens grew poor and poorer especially in the third World Countries with alarming scarcity of goods and lack of sufficient provision of services. This led to the rise of NGOs to become partners in the Development work and at the same time NGOs are being accused of trying to `crowd out' government process. The inability of governments to deliver sufficiently the promised goods and services eroded their legitimacy.

Researches undertaken so far suggest that most governments in the south are not only backing away from the traditional responsibilities, but also have completely failed. People started to loose faith in some of their governments policies aimed at improving welfare.

Governments themselves began to doubt their own development strategies and thus realized the need for radical change involving private organizations voluntarily formed by the people themselves. NGOs therefore increasingly have to take on all development work and at the same time NGOs are being accused of trying to 'crowd out' government.

Another reason for the existence of NGOs is that people come together in independent groups to promote some type of activity that is not being undertaken by governments. Alternatively, governments may already be involved in an activity but groups are formed in order to challenge the way government is handling it.

10

SOCIAL EVILS IN INDIAN SOCIETY

No society in the world is free from social evils and the Indian society is no exception. There are plethora of social evils in our society, but here we have discussed only selected few.

Dowry System in India

Dowry is derived from the ancient Hindu customs of "kanyadan" and "stridhan". In "kanyadan", the father of the bride offers the father of the groom money or property, etc. whereas for "stridhan", the bride herself gets jewelry and clothes at the time of her marriage, usually from her relatives or friends. In "varadakshina", the father of the bride presents the groom cash or kind. All of these could be done voluntarily and out of affection and love.

The dowry custom continues to rule society. In majority of Indian families the boy has inheritance rights while the girl is given a hefty sum at the time of her marriage in lieu of the Government regulated equal rights for girls in parental property. The evil of thc dowry system has spread its tentacles in almost all parts of the country and sections of society. There are several reasons for the prevalence of the dowry system, but the main one is that it is a necessary precondition for marriage. "No dowry, no marriage," is a widespread fear. There has also been an emergence of a feudal mindset with a materialistic attitude in a new globalized economy.

The price tag for the groom is now bigger and bolder. The emergence of an affluent middle class, the torchbearer of social change in modern India, is the main factor for the perpetuation of the dowry system. Families arrange most marriages, and a man who does not marry for love learns he can marry for possessions. For this man, and his family, a woman becomes the ticket to shortcut riches through the system of dowry. There are a number of things people desire to have in their own houses but cannot afford; they use the opportunity of a son's marriage to get them. The girl's parents do not protest against the blatant extravaganza, as they regard the alliance as a stepping-stone towards higher social status and better matches for the remaining children. Dowry as a phenomenon has gone beyond the ritual of marriage. Pregnancy, childbirth and all kinds of religious and family functions are occasions when such demands are made. A more sophisticated public image of an extended gifting session has replaced the old system.

Now there is demand for receptions in marriage palaces. The trousseau includes designer wear for the bride and groom's family. Chefs are flown in for multi-cuisine wedding dinners. The bride's family usually pays for all this. The rich revel in the exchange of their black money, but this in turn exerts pressure on the other classes to ape them with serious social consequences. The women have become a kind of commodity. It is them who are the worst sufferers because dowry is most often a monetary agreement between two men - the bride's father and the groom. Caste-based practices have only added fuel to the fire.

Marriages in political families are arranged to consolidate the caste base for support in electoral politics, so they do not challenge the dowry system. Dowry rituals have now spread even to communities where they were unknown. It has gone to different castes, crossed the boundaries of provinces and education and religion. Muslims and Christians, such as the Syrian Christians of Kerala and the Roman Catholics of Mangalore have started demanding dowry.

Rise in Dowry Crimes

Official statistics show a steady rise in dowry crimes. More than 9, 5000 women are killed every year in India over dowry. Bihar and Uttar Pradesh still record the maximum number of dowry crimes, but Bangalore, India's fastest growing city also shows an alarming rise - four women reportedly die every day because of dowry harassment and domestic violence. The cases of dowry torture are the highest accounting for 32.4% of crimes against women in the country.

Dowry Prohibition Act

The Dowry Prohibition Act, in force since 1st July 1961, was passed with the purpose of prohibiting the demanding, giving and taking of dowry. In 1980 the Government set up a committee which recommended amendments in the Dowry Prohibition Act and also suggested expanding the definition of dowry and instituting family courts and National Commission for women. Many parliamentary debates led to some amendments in 1983,1984 and 1986. To stop the offences of cruelty by husband or his relatives on the wife, Section 498-A was added in the Indian Penal Code and Section 198-A in the Criminal Procedure Code in the year 1983.

The Dowry Prohibition Act clearly stipulates that a person who gives or takes or helps in the giving or taking of dowry can be sentenced to jail for 5 years and fined Rs.15, 000/- or the amount of the value of dowry, whichever is more. The Act also prohibits the giving and taking directly or indirectly any property or valuable security, any amount either in cash of kind, jewelry, articles, properties, etc. in respect of a marriage.

The control is provided by stating a limit and names of gifters and their relationship to the married couple to be signed by both sides of parents. In 1986, the Act was amended again, empowering State governments to appoint Dowry Prohibition Officers, who not only had a preventive role but also had powers to collect evidence against people who took dowry.

Despite protest by women's organizations, serious activism, legal amendments, special police cells for women, media support and heightened awareness of dowry being a crime, the practice continues unabated on a massive scale. Despite every stigma, dowry continues to be the signature of marriage. Women need real social, political, financial and moral support in their fight against the system. They have to be empowered so that they can take their decisions about their own life by refusing the dowry system.

Drug Abuse in India

Every year, June 26 is celebrated as International Day against Drug Abuse and Illicit Trafficking every year. It is an exercise undertaken by the world community to sensitize the people in general and the youth in particular, to the menace of drugs. The picture is grim if the world statistics on the drugs scenario is taken into account. With a turnover of around

$500 billions, it is the third largest business in the world, next to petroleum and arms trade. About 190 million people all over the world consume one drug or the other. Drug addiction causes immense human distress and the illegal production and distribution of drugs have spawned crime and violence worldwide. Today, there is no part of the world that is free from the curse of drug trafficking and drug addiction. Millions of drug addicts, all over the world, are leading miserable lives, between life and death.

India too is caught in this vicious circle of drug abuse, and the numbers of drug addicts are increasing day by day. According to a UN report, One million heroin addicts are registered in India, and unofficially there are as many as five million. What started off as casual use among a minuscule population of high-income group youth in the metro has permeated to all sections of society. Inhalation of heroin alone has given way to intravenous drug use, that too in combination with other sedatives and pain-killers. This has increased the intensity of the effect, hastened the process of addiction and complicated the process of recovery. Cannabis, heroin, and Indian-produced pharmaceutical drugs are the most frequently abused drugs in India. Cannabis products, often called charas, bhang, or ganja, are abused throughout the country because it has attained some amount of religious sanctity because of its association with some Hindu deities.

The International Narcotics Control Board in its 2002 report released in Vienna pointed out that in India persons addicted to opiates are shifting their drug of choice from opium to heroin. The pharmaceutical products containing narcotic drugs are also increasingly being abused. The intravenous injections of analgesics like dextropropoxphene etc are also reported from many states, as it is easily available at one-tenth the cost of heroin. The codeine-based cough syrups continue to be diverted from the domestic market for abuse

Drug abuse is a complex phenomenon, which has various social, cultural, biological, geographical, historical and economic aspects. The disintegration of the old joint family system, absence of parental love and care in modern families where both parents are working, decline of old religious and moral values etc lead to a rise in the number of drug addicts who take drugs to escape hard realities of life. Drug use, misuse or abuse is also primarily due to the nature of the drug abused, the personality of the individual and the addict's immediate environment.

The processes of industrialization, urbanization and migration have led to loosening of the traditional methods of social control rendering an individual vulnerable to the stresses and strains of modern life. The fast changing social milieu, among other factors, is mainly contributing to the proliferation of drug abuse, both of traditional and of new psychoactive substances. The introduction of synthetic drugs and intravenous drug use leading to HIV/AIDS has added a new dimension to the problem, especially in the Northeast states of the country.

Impact on Society

Drug abuse has led to a detrimental impact on the society. It has led to increase in the crime rate. Addicts resort to crime to pay for their drugs. Drugs remove inhibition and impair judgment egging one on to commit offences. Incidence of eve- teasing, group clashes, assault and impulsive murders increase with drug abuse. Apart from affecting the financial stability, addiction increases conflicts and causes untold emotional pain for every member of the family. With most drug users being in the productive age group of 18-35 years, the loss in terms of human potential is incalculable. The damage to the physical, psychological, moral and intellectual growth of the youth is very high.

Adolescent drug abuse is one of the major areas of concern in adolescent and young people's behavior. It is estimated that, in India, by the time most boys reach the ninth grade, about 50 percent of them have tried at least one of the gateway drugs.

However, there is a wide regional variation across states in term of the incidence of the substance abuse. For example, a larger proportion of teens in West Bengal and Andhra Pradesh use gateway drugs (about 60 percent in both the states) than Uttar Pradesh or Haryana (around 35 percent). Increase in incidences of HIV, hepatitis B and C and tuberculosis due to addiction adds the reservoir of infection in the community burdening the health care system further. Women in India face greater problems from drug abuse. The consequences include domestic violence and infection with HIV, as well as the financial burden.

Eighty seven per cent of addicts being treated in a de-addiction center run by the Delhi police acknowledged being violent with family members. Most of the domestic violence is directed against women and occurs in the context of demands for money to buy drugs. At the national level, drug abuse is intrinsically linked with racketeering, conspiracy, corruption, illegal money transfers, terrorism and violence threatening the very stability of governments.

India has braced itself to face the menace of drug trafficking both at the national and international levels. Several measures involving innovative changes in enforcement, legal and judicial systems have been brought into effect. The introduction of death penalty for drug-related offences has been a major deterrent. The Narcotic Drugs and Psychotropic Substances Act, 1985, were enacted with stringent provisions to curb this menace. The Act envisages a minimum term of 10 years imprisonment extendable to 20 years and fine of Rs. 1 lakh extendable up to Rs. 2 lakhs for the offenders. The Act has been further amended by making provisions for the forfeiture of properties derived from illicit drugs trafficking. Comprehensive strategy involving specific programmes to bring about an overall reduction in use of drugs has been evolved by the various government agencies and NGOs and is further supplemented by measures like education, counseling, treatment and rehabilitation programmes.

India has bilateral agreements on drug trafficking with 13 countries, including Pakistan and Burma. Prior to 1999, extradition between India and the United States occurred under the auspices of a 1931 treaty signed by the United States and the United Kingdom, which was made applicable to India in 1942.

However, a new extradition treaty between India and the United States entered into force in July 1999. A Mutual Legal Assistance Treaty was signed by India and the United States in October 2001. India also is signatory to the following treaties and conventions:

- 1961 U.N. Convention on Narcotic Drugs.
- 1971 U.N. Convention on Psychotropic Substances.
- 1988 U.N. Convention Against Illicit Traffic in Narcotic Drugs and Psychotropic Substances.
- 2000 Transnational Crime Convention.

The spread and entrenchment of drug abuse needs to be prevented, as the cost to the people, environment and economy will be colossal. The unseemly spectacle of unkempt drug abusers dotting lanes and by lanes, cinema halls and other public places should be enough to goad the authorities to act fast to remove the scourge of this social evil.

Moreover, the spread of such reprehensible habits among the relatively young segment of society ought to be arrested at all cost. There is a need for the government enforcement agencies, the non-governmental philanthropic agencies, and others to collaborate and supplement each other's efforts for a solution to the problem of drug addiction through education and legal actions.

Illiteracy in India

When illiteracy begins to impinge upon livelihoods issues it becomes critical. Illiteracy often results in missed opportunities. Women usually receive lower wages than men. In Kishanganj district of Bihar women and girls work in the tea gardens and brickklins but as they are illiterate they often get exploited and do not get proper wages. Both men and women often earn less than the minimum wage but they are often unaware of the Minimum Wages Act. Illiteracy and lack of information can adversely affect human rights.

In an era when technology has shrunk the world into a global village and when information has been brought to the fingertips of a small section of society, it would be unfortunate if the masses were denied access to basic information due to the inability to read and write.

During the first Five Year Plan, the program of Social Education, inclusive of literacy, was introduced as part of the Community Development Program 1952. The National Policy on Education in 1968 not only endorsed the recommendations of the Education Commission but also reiterated thc significance of universal literacy and developing adult and continuing education as matters of priority. While the formal elementary education program was supplemented by a Non-formal Education system, it was also decided to undertake Adult Literacy programs culminating in the Total Literacy mission approach.

(a) A multi-pronged approach of universalization of elementary education and universal adult literacy has been adopted for achieving total literacy.

(b) A systematic program of non-formal education in the educationally backward states.

(c) The National Literacy Mission that aims at making 100 million adults literate.

The major thrust of these programs is on promotion of literacy among women, Scheduled Castes and Scheduled Tribes particularly in the rural areas. The Adult Education Program consists of three components: basic literacy (including numeracy), functionality and civic awareness. The third component is obviously literacy. The National Adult Education Program (NAEP) was inaugurated on October 2, 1978. Then came the National Literacy Mission (NLM). In 1989, the district-based Total Literacy Campaigns (TLC) emerged as a program strategy for the National Literacy Mission against this background.

In the budget of 1999-2000, the total allocation of resources (both Plan and non-plan) for the four programs of Elementary Education, Operation Black board, Non-formal education and Adult Education was 3037, 400, 350 and 113.4 crores respectively. The Total Literacy campaign districts had been set the optimistic goal of achieving 80% literacy amongst the target age-group of 15-35 years. Now Sarva Shikha Abiyan is doing rounds in all the districts in most of the states for which there is huge fund allocation under 9th and 10th Five year plans.

In spite of the enormous expansion of adult education, nonformal and elementary education in India, the problem of illiteracy has been lingering on. It is both colossal and complex given the size of the country, its huge population, wide regional and gender disparities, economic and other cultural factors such as poverty, communalism, casteism etc. It needs action from people, communities Government agencies, NGOs and international organizations such as UN bodies to totally eradicate illiteracy from India.

Poverty in India

According to a recent Indian government committee constituted to estimate poverty, nearly 38% of India's population (380 million) is poor. This report is based on new methodology and the figure is 10% higher than the present poverty estimate of 28.5%.

The committee was headed by SD Tendulkar has used a different methodology to reach at the current figure. It has taken into consideration indicators for heath, education, sanitation, nutrition and income as per National Sample Survey Organization survey of 2004-05. This new methodology is a complex scientific basis aimed at addressing the concern raised over the current poverty estimation.

Since 1972 poverty has been defined on basis of the money required to buy food worth 2100 calories in urban areas and 2400 calories in rural areas. In June this year a government committee headed by NC Saxena committee estimated 50% Indians were poor as against Planning Commission's 2006 figure of 28.5%.

Poverty is one of the main problems which have attracted attention of sociologists and economists. It indicates a condition in which a person fails to maintain a living standard adequate for his physical and mental efficiency. It is a situation people want to escape. It gives rise to a feeling of a discrepancy between what one has and what one should have. The term poverty is a relative concept. It is very difficult to draw a demarcation line between affluence and poverty. According to Adam Smith, Man is rich or poor according to the degree in which he can afford to enjoy the necessaries, the conveniences and the amusements of human life.

Even after more than 50 years of Independence India still has the world's largest number of poor people in a single country. Of its nearly one billion inhabitants, an estimated 260.3 million are below the poverty line, of which 193.2 million are in the rural areas and 67.1 million are in urban areas. More than 75% of poor people reside in villages. Poverty level is not uniform across India. The poverty level is below 10% in states like Delhi, Goa, and Punjab etc whereas it is below 50% in Bihar (43) and Orissa (47). It is between 30-40% in Northeastern states of Assam, Tripura, and Mehgalaya and in Southern states of TamilNadu and Uttar Pradesh.

Poverty has many dimensions changing from place to place and across time. There are two inter-related aspects of poverty - Urban and rural poverty. The main causes of urban poverty are predominantly due to impoverishment of rural peasantry that forces them to move out of villages to seek some subsistence living in the towns and cities. In this process, they even lose the open space or habitat they had in villages albeit without food and other basic amenities. When they come to the cities, they get access to some food though other sanitary facilities including clean water supply still elude them. And they have to stay in the habitats that place them under sub-human conditions. While a select few have standards of living comparable to the richest in the world, the majority fails to get two meals a day. The causes of rural poverty are manifold including inadequate and ineffective implementation of anti-poverty programmes.The overdependence on monsoon with non-availability of irrigational facilities often result in crop-failure and low agricultural productivity forcing farmers in the debt-traps. The rural communities tend to spend large percentage of annual earnings on social ceremonies like marriage; feast etc.Our economic development since Independence has been lopsided.

There has been increase in unemployment creating poverty like situations for many. Population is growing at an alarming rate. The size of the Indian family is relatively bigger averaging at 4.2.The other causes include dominance of caste system which forces the individual to stick to the traditional and hereditary occupations.

Since the 1970s the Indian government has made poverty reduction a priority in its development planning. Policies have focused on improving the poor standard of living by ensuring food security, promoting self-employment through greater access to assets, increasing wage employment and improving access to basic social services. Launched in 1965, India's Public Distribution System has helped meet people's basic food needs by providing rations at subsidized prices. Although it has affected less than 20% of the Poor's food purchases, the system has been important in sustaining people's consumption of cereals, especially in periods of drought. It has provided women and girls with better access to food and helped overcome the widespread discrimination against female consumption within households. It has also reduced the burden of women, who are responsible for providing food for the household.

The largest credit-based government poverty reduction programme in the world, the Integrated Rural Development Programme provides rural households below the poverty line with credit to purchase income-generating assets. Launched in 1979, the programme has supplied subsidized credit to such groups as small and marginalized farmers, agricultural laborers, rural artisans, the physically handicapped, scheduled castes and scheduled tribes. Within this target population, 40% of the beneficiaries are supposed to be women. Although the programme has reached 51 million families, only 27% of the borrowers have been women. The programme has significantly increased the income of 57% of assisted families.

Rural Poverty

Rural poverty is largely a result of low productivity and unemployment. The Jawahar Rozgar Yojana, a national public works scheme launched in 1989 with financing from the central and state governments, provides more than 700 million person days of work a year about 1% of total employment for people with few opportunities for employment. The scheme has two components: a programme to provide low-cost housing and one to supply free irrigation wells to poor and marginalized farmers. The public works scheme is self-targeting.

Since it offers employment at the statutory minimum wage for unskilled manual labor, only those willing to accept very low wages the poor are likely to enroll in the scheme. By providing regular employment and thereby increasing the bargaining power of all rural workers, the public works scheme has had a significant effect in reducing poverty.

It has also contributed to the construction of rural infrastructure (irrigation works, a soil conservation project, drinking water supply). Evaluations show that 82% of available funds have been channeled to community development projects. Targeting was improved in 1996 when the housing and irrigation well components were delinked and focused exclusively on people below the poverty line.

Poverty Reducttion Efforts

The participation of civil society organizations in poverty reduction efforts, especially those directed to women, has increased social awareness and encouraged governments to provide better services. Cooperatives such as the Self-Employed Women's Association provide credit to women at market rates of interest but do not require collateral; they also allow flexibility in the use of loans and the timing of repayments. These civil society organizations have not only contributed to women's material well being; they have also helped empower them socially and politically. Such credit initiatives, by bringing women out of the confines of the household, are changing their status within the family and within village hierarchies.

The demands of civil society organizations for better social services have spurred the government to launch campaigns to increase literacy and improve public infrastructure. And their calls for greater accountability and real devolution of power are increasing the likelihood that expenditures for poverty reduction will reach the needy, especially women.

The Indian state has undoubtedly failed in its responsibilities towards its citizens over the last 50 odd years. There is a need for the state to move out of many areas and the process has been started with economic liberalization. The process of decentralization should devolute lot more powers, both functional and financial, to panchayats.

The lack of transparency and accountability has hampered our economic development at all levels. The problem of poverty persists because of a number of leakages in the system. New laws have to be evolved to ensure more accountability. Bodies like the Planning Commission should be modified into new constitutional bodies that can hold governments accountable for their failure to implement development programmes. A strong system of incentives and disincentives also needs to be introduced. The encouragement of non-governmental organizations and private sector individuals in tackling poverty is imperative, as the state cannot do everything.

Child Labour in India

India has the dubious distinction of being the nation with the largest number of child laborers in the world. The child labors endure miserable and difficult lives. They earn little and struggle to make enough to feed themselves and their families. They do not go to school; more than half of them are unable to learn the barest skills of literacy. Poverty is one of the main reasons behind this phenomenon. The unrelenting poverty forces the parents to push their young children in all forms of hazardous occupations. Child labor is a source of income for poor families. They provide help in household enterprises or of household chores in order to free adult household members for economic activity elsewhere. In some cases, the study found that a child's income accounted for between 34 and 37 percent of the total household income.

In India, the emergence of child labor is also because of unsustainable systems of landholding in agricultural areas and caste system in the rural areas. Bonded labour refers to the phenomenon of children working in conditions of servitude in order to pay their debts. The debt that binds them to their employer is incurred not by the children themselves but by their parent. The creditors-cum-employers offer these loans to destitute parents in an effort to secure the labor of these children. The arrangements between the parents and contracting agents are usually informal and unwritten. The number of years required to pay off such a loan is indeterminate. The lower castes such as dalits and tribal make them vulnerable groups for exploitation.

The environmental degradation and lack of employment avenues in the rural areas also cause people to migrate to big cities. On arrival in overcrowded cities the disintegration of family units takes place through alcoholism, unemployment or disillusionment of better life etc. This in turn leads to emergence of street children and child workers who are forced by their circumstances to work from the early age. The girls are forced to work as sex -workers or beggars. A large number of girls end up working as domestic workers on low wages and unhealthy living conditions.

Some times children are abandoned by their parents or sold to factory owners. The last two decades have seen tremendous growth of export based industries and mass production factories utilizing low technologies. They try to maintain competitive positions through low wages and low labor standards. The child laborers exactly suit their requirements.

They use all means to lure the parents into giving their children on pretext of providing education and good life. In India majority of children work in industries, such as cracker making, diamond polishing, glass, brass-ware, carpet weaving, bangle making, lock making and mica cutting to name a few. 15% of the 100,000 children work in the carpet industry of Uttar Pradesh. 70-80% of the 8,000 to 50,000 children work in the glass industry in Ferozabad. In the unorganized sector child labor is paid by piece-by-piece rates that result in even longer hours for very low pay.

Inadequate schools, a lack of schools, or even the expense of schooling leaves some children with little else to do but work. The attitudes of parents also contribute to child labor; some parents feel that children should work in order to develop skills useful in the job market, instead of taking advantage of a formal education. From the time of its independence, India has committed itself to be against child labor.

Article 24 of the Indian constitution clearly states that "No child below the age of fourteen years shall be employed to work in any factory or mine or employed in any hazardous employment" The Bonded Labour System Act of 1976 fulfills the Indian Constitution's directive of ending forced labour A Plethora of additional protective legislation has been put in place.

There are distinct laws governing child labour in factories in commercial establishments, on plantations and in apprenticeships. There are laws governing the use of migrant labour and contract labour. A recent law The Child Labour (Prohibition and Regulation law) of 1986 designates a child as a person who has not completed their 14th year of age. It purports to regulate the hours and the conditions of child workers and to prohibit child workers in certain enumerated hazardous industries.

However there is neither blanket prohibition on the use of child labour, nor any universal minimum age set for child workers. All of the policies that the Indian government has in place are in accordance with the Constitution of India, and all support the eradication of Child Labor. The problem of child labor still remains even though all of these policies are existent. Enforcement is the key aspect that is lacking in the government's efforts.

Child labor is a global problem. If child labour is to be eradicated, the governments and agencies and those responsible for enforcement need to start doing their jobs. The most important thing is to increase awareness and keep discussing ways and means to check this problem. We have to decide whether we are going to take up the problem head-on and fight it any way we can or leave it to the adults who might not be there when things go out of hand.

Unemployment in India

India as a nation is faced with massive problem of unemployment. Unemployment can be defined as a state of worklessness for a man fit and willing to work. It is a condition of involuntary and not voluntary idleness. Some features of unemployment have been identified as follows:

1. The incidence of unemployment is much higher in urban areas than in rural areas.
2. Unemployment rates for women are higher than those for men.
3. The incidence of unemployment among the educated is much higher than the overall unemployment.
4. There is greater unemployment in agricultural sector than in industrial and other major sectors.

Economists and social thinkers have classified unemployment into various types. Generally unemployment can be classified in two types:

(1) Voluntary unemployment : In this type of unemployment a person is out of job of his own desire doesn't work on the prevalent or prescribed wages. Either he wants higher wages or doesn't want to work at all. It is in fact social problem leading to social disorganization.

Social problems and forces such as a revolution, a social upheaval, a class struggle, a financial or economic crisis a war between nations, mental illness, political corruption mounting unemployment and crime etc. threaten the smooth working of society. Social values are often regarded as the sustaining forces of society. They contribute to the strength and stability of social order.

But due to rapid social change new values come up and some of the old values decline. At the same time, people are not is a position to reject the old completely and accept the new altogether. Here, conflict between the old and the new is the inevitable result which leads to the social disorganization in imposed situation. In economic terminology this situation is voluntary unemployment.

(2) In voluntary unemployment : In this type of situation the person who is unemployed has no say in the matter. It means that a person is separated from remunerative work and devoid of wages although he is capable of earning his wages and is also anxious to earn them. Forms and types of unemployment according to Hock are.

(a) Cyclical unemployment - This is the result of the trade cycle which is a part of the capitalist system. In such a system, there is greater unemployment and when there is depression a large number of people are rendered unemployed. Since such an economic crisis is the result of trade cycle, the unemployment is a part of it.

(b) Sudden unemployment - When at the place where workers have been employed there is some change, a large number of persons are unemployed. It all happens in the industries, trades and business where people are employed for a job and suddenly when the job has ended they are asked to go.

(c) Unemployment caused by failure of Industries - In many cases, a business a factory or an industry has to close down. There may be various factors responsible for it there may be dispute amongst the partners, the business may give huge loss or the business may not turn out to be useful and so on.

(d) Unemployment caused by deterioration in Industry and business - In various industries, trades or business, sometimes, there is deterioration. This deterioration may be due to various factors. In efficiency of the employers, keen competitions less profit etc. are some of the factors responsible for deterioration in the industry and the business.

(e) Seasonal unemployment - Certain industries and traders engage workers for a particular season. When the season has ended the workers are rendered unemployed. Sugar industry is an example of this type of seasonal unemployment.

The problem of unemployment has becoming a colossal. Various problems have caused this problem. There are individual factors like age, vocational unfitness and physical disabilities which restrict the people. External factors include technological and economic factors. There is enormous increase in the population. Every year India adds to her population afresh. More than this every year about 5 million people become eligible for securing jobs. Business field is subject to ups and downs of trade cycle and globalization. Economic depression or sick industries are often close down compelling their employees to become unemployed. Technological advancement contributes to economic development .But unplanned and uncontrolled growth of technology is causing havoc on job opportunities. The computerization and automation has led to technological unemployment. Strikes and lockouts have become inseparable aspect of the industrial world today. Due to these industries often face economic loses and production comes down. Since workers do not get any salary or wages during the strike period they suffer from economic hardships.

They, become permanently or temporarily unemployed. Today young people are not ready to take jobs which are considered to be socially degrading or lowly. Our educational system has its own irreparable defects and its contribution to the unemployment is an open truth.Our education does not prepare the minds of young generation to become self-employed on the contrary it makes them dependent on government vacancies which are hard to come. Our State right from the beginning of Five year plans has introduced several employment generating schemes and programmes over the years but in the absence of proper implementation and monitoring have failed to achieve the required targets.

The UPA Government had come up with Rural Employment Guarantee program which aims to provide minimum days of employment to people living in the villages. This is a laudable programme if implemented sincerely because it will provide employment to people during natural calamities like drought, floods etc.

The remedial measures for reducing unemployment may lay greater emphasis on creation of opportunities for self-employment, augmentation of productivity and income levels of the working poor, shift in emphasis from creation of relief type of employment to the building up of durable productive assets in the rural areas and instead of attempting to revert somewhat to protectionist policies the pace of privatization may be accelerated.

Crime against Children

According to National Crime Records Bureau and NHRC

- Crime against children increased by 3.8% nationally (14,975 cases in 2005 from 14,423 in 2004).
- Child rape increased by 13.7% (4,026 cases from 3,542 in 2004); Madhya Pradesh reported the highest number (870) followed by Maharashtra (634).Together they accounted for 37.3% of rape cases.
- Delhi tops a list of 35 Indian cities on crime against children (852 cases of violence against children in 2005, 27% of all cases) followed by Indore (448), Pune (314) and Mumbai (303).
- 1,327 children were reported murdered in 2005 up from 1,304 in 2004 (an increase of 1.8%).Uttar Pradesh reported the highest number (390) accounting for 29.4% of cases.
- Nearly 45,000 children go missing every year; more than 11,000 are never traced.
- 3,518 children were kidnapped in 2005 (301 from Delhi, 3,196 in 2004, 2,571 in 2003).
- Children who form 42% of the India's population are at risk on the streets, at their workplace and even inside their own homes. The recent Nithari case has highlighted the plight of children of migrant workers. There has been a 40% increase in intra-state migration in the last 10 years. While migrant do get employment there is no safety net for their children; they get neither education nor healthcare. Single migrant children or children of migrant workers are often not counted anywhere-census or any government scheme.
- According to the study conducted by NGO Shakti Vahini in 2006, 378 of the 593 districts in India are affected by human trafficking the children being the most affected. They are easy

prey for traffickers who lure them from villages with the promise of employment. The street children are perceived as vagrants by the police and with no legal safeguards to protect them violence and exploitation are daily routine for them. India has the largest number of street children in the world. In 2001 it was estimated that there are 100,000 to 125,000 street children each in Mumbai, Kolkata and Delhi with 45,000 in Bangalore.

- In terms of budget allocation 4.91% of Union Budget 2006-07 has been allocated for health, education, development and protection of children.The share of resources for child protection is minuscule-0.034%.Child protection has never figured in any planning document so far.
- There arc several laws but the problem is with the implementation. The Central Monitoring Commission which is supposed to monitor crime against children under the Juvenile Justice Act was amended in 2000.This committee has not met even once since the amendment. The Act stated that every police station should have a juvenile police unit but this is still not being followed. The offences against children bill which provides protection against sexual abuse also awaits cabinet nod.
- According to child rights activitists to avoid crimes against children it is important to have community level child protection mechanisms like community watch dogs and committees for child protection, child welfare and anti-trafficking. These will create an interface between communities and state/district mechanisms. These can also monitor vulnerable children in communities and provide a base where people can report and address issues like abuse, exploitation and neglect. Creating spaces within communities and schools so that children can report offences against them can be also done. To overcome lack of awareness about child protection laws the information dissemination is important.

Problem of Child Abuse

Child abuse is usually classified into three major types: physical, sexual and emotional. Each has recognizable characteristics. The indicators of physical abuse in the child are bruises, burns, fractures, lacerations and abrasions, abdominal injuries and human bite marks. The behavioral indicators of physical abuse are the abused child is wary of contact with adults, he/she becomes apprehensive when other children cry, show aggressiveness in behaviour, seem frightened of parents or caretakers and afraid to go home or cries when it is time to go home. Child sexual abuse has been defined as the involvement of dependent and immature children in sexual activities they don't fully comprehend to which they are unable to give informed consent.

The Juvenile Justice Act 1986 defines child sexual abuse as interaction between a child and an adult in which the child is being used for the sexual stimulation of the perpetrator or another person. Sexual abuse is not often identified through physical indictors alone. A child can confide in a trusted person that she /he has been sexually assaulted. There are some physical signs of sexual abuse like difficulty in walking or sitting, pain or itching, bruises or bleeding, venereal disease and pregnancy in early adolescence.

The sexually abuse child may appear withdrawn or retarded, may have poor peer relationships, may be unwilling to participate in activities, may indulge in delinquent behaviour.Emotional abuse is the neglect or maltreatment of children. It may involve a disregard of the physical, emotional, moral or social needs of the children. Besides these there are social abuses of children like kidnapping and forcing them to beg in streets.

The major causes of child abuse are adaptational failure or environmental maladjustment mostly on the part of the adult perpetrators but to some extent on the part of adults responsible for family socialization as well. The dominant causes of battering children found in a study were children disobeying parents, quarrels between the parents and the child beaten as scapegoat, child not taking interest in studies, child spending time away from home, child refusing to hand over his total earnings to his parents/guardians and child indulging in deviant behavior like theft and smoking etc.

The main causes for sexual abuse given are adjustment problems of the perpetrators, family disorganization, victim's characteristics and the psychological disorders of the abusers. Four important causes of emotional abuse can be identified are poverty, deficient parental control and non cordial relations within family, maltreatment faced by parents in their own childhood or intergenerational transmission of child maltreatment and alcoholism of parents.

There can be multiple effects of abuse on children like self-devaluation, dependency, mistrust, and revictimization, withdrawal from people, emotional trauma, deviant behavior and interpersonal problems.

Gender Gap in India

In the latest gender gap index report released by the World Economic Forum (WEF) India keeps company with the worst in the world. Among the 128 countries that have been evaluated by the WEF India ranked 114 followed among others by Yemen, Chad, Pakistan and Saudi Arabia. Even China, Philippines, Sri Lanka and Botswana fare much better than us.

The survey considers the proportion of resources and opportunities made available to women on educational, economic, political and health parities. It is only in the realm of political empowerment India has done some what alright ranking 21st. That is also thanks to a long spell of prime minister ship by Mrs. Indira Gandhi. It raises question as why women are at receiving end if they are politically empowered.

India is still largely a feudal and patriarchal society. In many parts of our country especially in UP, Bihar, Rajasthan, Haryana and Punjab women are often treated as if they were a piece of property. In these parts the sex-ratio is most skewed because families often snuff out the lives of girl children before or immediately after they are born. In many parts of India women are viewed as an economic liability despite contributing in several ways to our society and economy.

India's policies and projects for women are woefully inadequate. For instance the literacy rate for females is merely 48% against 73% for males. Public health is another area of failure. Hundreds of women in rural India die every year during child birth for want of medical attention. There are thousands more who do not even have access to a primary health centre. Importantly reforming property laws more vigorously so that gender parity becomes a reality must rank among the government's priorities.

While these changes are necessary they will amount to nothing if we as a society continue to deny our women the dignity, liberty and opportunities that are rightfully theirs. No society will ever prosper as a whole as long as half of it is constantly treated as somehow less than the other half.

Domestic Violence against Women

Domestic violence can be described as when one adult in a relationship misuses power to control another. It is the establishment of control and fear in the relationship through violence and other forms of abuse. It is basically an abuse of power. The abuser tortures and controls the victim by calculated threats, intimidation and physical violence.

Although men, women and children can all be abused, in most cases the victims are women. In every country where reliable, large-scale studies have been conducted, results indicate that between 16 and 52% of women have been assaulted by their husbands\partners. These studies also indicate widespread violence against women as an important cause of morbidity and mortality.

These physical attacks may also include rape and sexual violence. Psychological violence includes verbal abuse, harassment, confinement and deprivation of physical, financial and personal resources. For some women emotional abuse may be more painful than the physical attacks because they effectively undermine women's security and self-confidence.

Violence within the home is universal across culture, religion, class and ethnicity. The abuse is generally condoned by social custom and considered part and parcel of marital life .An example of this can be seen through the gist of a popular Spanish riddle: Question: What do mules and women have in common? Answer: A good beating makes them both better."

In India the records of National Crimes Bureau, Ministry of Home Affairs government of India revealed a shocking 71.5% Increase in cases of torture and dowry deaths during the period from 1991 to 1995 .In 1995, torture of women constituted 29.2%of all reported crimes against women.

The question arises why women put up with the abuse in the home? The answer lies in their unequal status in society. They are often caught in a vicious circle of economic dependence, fear for their children's lives as well as their own, ignorance of their rights before the law, lack of confidence in themselves and social pressures. These factors effectively force women to a life of recurrent mistreatment from which they often do not have the means to escape. The sanctity of privacy within the family also makes authorities reluctant to intervene, often leads women to deny they are being abused. This is equally common in the higher as well as in the lower segments of a society. A woman who files a charge of abuse is often forced to drop it by her husband's family if she wants an uncontested divorce.

Social prejudices reinforce domestic violence against women. They are treated as their spouses' property; husbands assume that this subordinate role gives them right to abuse their wives in order to keep them in their place. Against this background is the tradition of dowry, an expectation of gifts and cash from the bride's family, one can imagine the anxiety these expectations may cause to a woman and the consequences she has to face if it is inadequate. Women's physical and mental health is often permanently damaged or impaired and in some cases violence can have fatal consequences as in the case of dowry deaths in India. Physical torture as well as mental torture usually occurs on a regular basis causing suffering and inflicting deep scars on the psyche of the victims and their families. Many assault incidents result in injuries ranging from bruises and fractures to chronic disabilities. Domestic violence has devastating repercussions on the family. Mothers are unable to care for their children properly.

Often they transmit to them their own feelings of low self-esteem, helplessness and inadequacy. Violence against women is the most pervasive human rights violation in world today. We need to think and ponder as how this form of degradation of women can be stopped. It needs support from all quarters be it government, NGOs and women themselves.

There is also a need to improve women's economic capacities that include access to and control of income and assets and also share in the family's property. The government should strengthen and expand training and sensitization programs.

Gender Inequality

Sociologically the word gender refers to the socio-cultural definition of man and woman, the way societies distinguish men and women and assign them social roles. The distinction between sex and gender was introduced to deal with the general tendency to attribute women's subordination to their anatomy. For ages it was believed that the different characteristics, roles and status accorded to women and men in society are determined by sex, that they are natural and therefore not changeable. Gender is seen closely related to the roles and behavior assigned to women and men based on their sexual differences.

As soon as a child is born families and society begin the process of gendering. The birth of the son is celebrated, the birth of a daughter filled with pain; sons are showered with love, respect, better food and proper health care. Boys are encouraged to be tough and outgoing; girls are encouraged to be homebound and shy. All these differences are gender differences and they are created by society. Gender inequality is therefore a form of inequality which is distinct from other forms of economic and social inequalities. It dwells not only outside the household but also centrally within it. It stems not only from pre-existing differences in economic endowments between women and men but also from pre-existing gendered social norms and social perceptions.

Gender inequality has adverse impact on development goals as reduces economic growth. It hampers the overall well being because blocking women from participation in social, political and economic activities can adversely affect the whole society. Many developing countries including India have displayed gender inequality in education, employment and health. It is common to find girls and women suffering from high mortality rates. There are vast differences in education level of two sexes. India has witnessed gender inequality from its early history due to its socio-economic and religious practices that resulted in a wide gap between the position of men and women in the society.

The origin of the Indian idea of appropriate female behavior can be traced to the rules laid down by Manu in 200 B.C.: "by a young girl, by a young woman, or even by an aged one, nothing must be done independently, even in her own house". "In childhood a female must be subject to her father, in youth to her husband, when her lord is dead to her sons; a woman must never be independent." Women's lives are shaped by customs that are centuries old. "May you be the mother of a hundred sons" is a common Hindu wedding blessing. Statistics reveal that in India males significantly outnumber females and this imbalance has increased over time. The sex ratio according to 2001 census report stands at 933 per 1000 males. Out of the total population, 120 million are women who live in abject poverty. The maternal mortality rate in rural areas is among the world's highest. From a global perspective India accounts for 19% of all live births and 27% of all maternal deaths. The deaths of young girls in India exceed those of young boys by over 300,000 each year and every 6th infant death is specifically due to gender discrimination.

Women face discrimination right from the childhood. Gender disparities in nutrition are evident from infancy to adulthood. In fact, gender has been the most statistically significant determinant of malnutrition among young children and malnutrition is a frequent, direct or underlying, cause of death among girls below age five. Girls are breast-fed less frequently and for a shorter duration in infancy. In childhood and adulthood, males are fed first and better. Adult women consume approximately 1,000 fewer calories per day than men according to one estimate. Nutritional deprivation has two major consequences for women: they never reach their full growth potential, and suffer from anemia, which are risk factors in pregnancy. This condition complicates childbearing and results in women and infant deaths, and low birth weight infants. The tradition also requires that women eat last and least throughout their lives even when pregnant and lactating. Malnourished women give birth to malnourished children, perpetuating the cycle.

BIBLIOGRAPHY

- Agarwalla, S.S., Religion and Caste Politics (Jaipur: Rawat Publications, 1998)
- Avasthi, Abha, Dimensions of Violence and Terrorism (Lucknow: Bharat Book Centre, 1998).
- Azim, S., Muslim Women: Emerging Identity (Jaipur: Rawat Publications, 19970
- Bahl, Maj. Gen. Y., Kargil Blunder: Pakistan's Plight, India's Victory (New Delhi: Manas Publications, 2000)
- Bose, Sumantra, The Challenge in Kashmir: Democracy, Self Determination and a Just Peace (New Delhi: Sage Publications, 1997)
- Chari, P.R., ed., India Towards Millennium (New Delhi: Manohar Publishers & Distributors, 1998)
- Das, Veena, Critical Events: An Anthropological Perspective on Contemporary India (Delhi: Oxford University Press, 1995)
- Dutta, N.C., ed., Politics of Identity and Nation Building in North-East India (New Delhi: South Asian Press, 1997)
- Ghosh, Partha S., BJP and the Evolution of Hindu Nationalism: From Periphery to Centre (New Delhi: Manohar Publishers & Distributors, 1999)

- Hansen, Thomas Blom, and Jafferlot, Christophe, eds., The BJP and the Compulsions of Politics in India (Delhi: Oxford University Press, 1998)
- Hardin, Russel, One for All: The Logic of Groups Conflict (Princeton: Princeton University Press, 1995)
- Indradeva, Society and Culture in India: Dynamics through the Ages (Jaipur: Rawat Publications, 1999)
- Jha, P.S., Kashmir 1947: Revival Versions of History (Delhi: Oxford University Press, 1996)
- Jhunjhunwala, B., Varna Vyavastha: Governance through Caste System (Jaipur: Rawat Publications, 1999)
- Kakar, Sudhir, The Colors of Violence: Cultural Identities, Religion and Conflict (Chicago: Chicago University Press, 1996)
- Kumar, B.B., Tensions and Conflict in Northeast India (New Delhi: Cosmo Publications, 1995)
- Larson, Gerald James, India's Agony over Religion (Albany: State University of New York Press, 1995)
- Mahajan, Sucheta, Independence and Partition: The Erosion of Colonial Power in India (New Delhi: Sage Publications, 1999)
- Mishra, H.B., Terrorism: Threat to Peace and Harmony (New Delhi: Authors Press, 1999).
- Nag, Sajal, Nationalism, Separatism and Secessionism (Jaipur: Rawat Publications, 1999)
- Omprakash, S., Terrorism in India (New Delhi: Ess Ess Publisher, 1997)
- Pantham, Thomas, Political Theories and Social Reconstruction: A Critical Survey of the Literature on India (New Delhi: Sage Publications, 1995)
- Rajan, Nalini, Secularism, Democracy, Justice: Implications of Rawlsian Principles in India (New Delhi: Sage Publications, 1998)
- Saberwal, Satish, Roots of Crisis: Interpreting Contemporary Indian Society (New Delhi: Sage Publications, 1996)
- Sachdeva, Gulshan, Economy of the North-East: Policy, Present Conditions and Future Possibilities (Delhi: Konark Publishers, 2000)

- Saha, B.P., Trans-border Terrorism: Internationalisaton of Kashmir Tangle (New Delhi: Har-Anand, 1996)
- Sahadevan, P., India and Overseas Indians: The Case of Sri Lanka (New Delhi: Kalinga Publications, 1995).
- Saiyad, A.R., Religion and Ethnicity among Muslims (Jaipur: Rawat Publications, 1995)
- Sajal, B., Ethnicity, Communalism and State Politics (Jaipur: Rawat Publications, 2000)
- Saksena, H.S., Perspective on Tribal Development (Jaipur: Rawat Publications, 1999)
- Samaddar, Ranabir, The Marginal Nation: Transborder Migration from Bangladesh to West Bengal (New Delhi: Sage Publications, 1998)
- Samanta, Amiya K., Gorkhaland: A Study in Ethnic Separatism (New Delhi: Khanna Publishers, 1996).
- Sanajoba, N., Human Rights in the New Millennium (New Delhi: Manas Publications, 2000)
- Saraswathi, Government, Politics and People (Jaipur: Rawat Publications, 1995)
- Sarkar, Bhaskar, Tackling Insurgency and Terrorism: Blueprint for Action (New Delhi: Vision Books, 1998)
- Sarkar, Col. Bhaskar, Kargil War: Past, Present and Future (New Delhi: Lancer Publisher & Distributors, 1999)
- Sarkar, Tanika, and Butalia, Urvashi, eds., Women and the Hindu Right (New Delhi: Kali for Women, 1995)
- Sathyamurthy, T.V., ed., Region, Religion, Caste, Gender and Culture in Contemporary India (Delhi: Oxford University Press, 1996)
- Savur and Munshi, Contradictions in Indian Society (Jaipur: Rawat Publications, 1995)
- Schofield, Victoria, Kashmir in the Crossfire (London: I.B. Tauris Publishers, 1996)
- Sekher, T.V., Migration and Social Change (Jaipur: Rawat Publications, 1997)
- Seshadri, K., Stagnancy and Change in Indian Society and Politics (Jaipur: Rawat Publications, 1999)

- Shabbir, M., ed., B.R. Ambedkar: Study in Law and Society (Jaipur: Rawat Publications, 1997)
- Shah, G., ed., Social Transformation in India (Jaipur: Rawat Publications, 1998)
- Sharma, Brig. B.N., India Betrayed: The Role of Nehru (New Delhi: Manas Publications, 1997)
- Sharma, D.P., The Punjab Story: Decade of Turmoil (New Delhi: APH Publishing Corporation, 1996)
- Sharma, R., Power Elite in Indian Society (Jaipur: Rawat Publications, 1999)
- Sharma, S., Indian Elite and Nationalism (Jaipur: Rawat Publications, 1997)
- Sharma, S.L., Ethnicity and Stratification among Tribals in Urban Setting (Jaipur: Rawat Publications, 1996)
- Tanwar, Raghuvendra, Politics of Sharing Power: The Punjab Unionist Party 1923-1947 (New Delhi: Manohar Publishers & Distributors, 1999)
- Vanaik, Achin, India in a Changing World (New Delhi: Orient Longman, 1995)
- Verrna, S., Women's Struggle for Political Space (Jaipur: Rawat Publications, 1997)
- Vijapur, Abdulrahim P., Perspective on Human Rights (Jaipur: Rawat Publications, 1999)
- Wankhede, G.G., Social Mobility and Scheduled Castes (Jaipur: Rawat Publications, 1999)
- Webster, JCB, Religion, and Dalit Liberation (Jaipur: Rawat Publications, 1999)
- Yadav, K.C., ed., From Periphery to Centrestage: Ambedkar, Ambedkarism and Dalit Future (New Delhi: Manohar Publishers & Distributors, 1999)
- Yinger, J.M., Ethnicity: Source of Strength-Source of Conflict (Jaipur: Rawat Publications, 1998)
- Zelliot, Eleanor, From Untouchable to Dalit: Essays on the Ambedkar Movement (New Delhi: Manohar Publishers & Distributors, 1998).

INDEX